OBAMA'S RACE

CHICAGO STUDIES IN AMERICAN POLITICS

A series edited by Benjamin I. Page, Susan Herbst,
Lawrence R. Jacobs, and James Druckman

ALSO IN THE SERIES

OBAMA'S RACE

The 2008 Election
and the
Dream of a
Post-Racial America

MICHAEL TESLER
AND
DAVID O. SEARS

THE UNIVERSITY OF CHICAGO PRESS

CHICAGO AND LONDON

MICHAEL TESLER is a doctoral student in political science at the University of California, Los Angeles. This is his first book.

DAVID O. SEARS is distinguished professor of psychology and political science at the University of California, Los Angeles, and has served on the board of overseers for both the American National Election Studies and the General Social Survey. He is the coauthor or coeditor of numerous books, most recently *Racialized Politics: The Debate about Racism in America*, *Oxford Handbook of Political Psychology*, and *The Diversity Challenge: Social Identity and Intergroup Relations on the Multiethnic Campus*. He is recipient of the 2002 Warren E. Miller Prize for lifetime intellectual accomplishment given by the Elections, Public Opinion, and Voting Behavior section of the American Political Science Association.

The University of Chicago Press, Chicago 60637
The University of Chicago Press, Ltd., London
© 2010 by The University of Chicago
All rights reserved. Published 2010
Printed in the United States of America

19 18 17 16 15 14 13 12 11 10   1 2 3 4 5

ISBN-13: 978-0-226-79382-5 (cloth)
ISBN-13: 978-0-226-79383-2 (paper)
ISBN-10: 0-226-79382-6 (cloth)
ISBN-10: 0-226-79383-4 (paper)

Library of Congress Cataloging-in-Publication Data

Tesler, Michael.
Obama's race : the 2008 election and the dream of a post-racial America /
Michael Tesler and David O. Sears.
    p. cm. — (Chicago studies in American politics)
Includes bibliographical references and index.
ISBN-13: 978-0-226-79382-5 (cloth : alk. paper)
ISBN-10: 0-226-79382-6 (cloth : alk. paper)
ISBN-13: 978-0-226-79383-2 (pbk. : alk. paper)
ISBN-10: 0-226-79383-4 (pbk. : alk. paper)   1. Obama, Barack.
2. Presidents—United States—Election—2008.   3. Post-racialism—United
States.   4. United States—Race relations—Political aspects.   5. United
States—Politics and government—2009–   I. Sears, David O.   II. Title.
III. Series: Chicago studies in American politics.
    E907.T47 2010
    324.973′0931—dc22

                                              2010016319

CONTENTS

ACKNOWLEDGMENTS

This book is the culmination of several fortuitous events and circumstances. Our first, and perhaps most important, stroke of good luck came during Tesler's second quarter of graduate school when he sought out Sears for a directed study about racial attitudes and their impact on politics. The work in that class set the foundation for all of our future collaborations, with this book being one of the results.

A year after that independent study course, our good fortunes continued when Tesler approached Lynn Vavreck for guidance in a study of public opinion and voting behavior. Knowing his affinity for data analysis, Lynn asked if he would be willing to do some work for her on incoming survey data from the campaign study she was conducting. Thanks to Lynn, he had the extraordinary opportunity of applying everything he had learned about racial attitudes to unparalleled data about the first African American with a realistic chance of winning the presidency. Even more graciously, and crucial for this project, she then allowed us to use these findings in our ongoing collaboration. Lynn simply cares about her students above all else. For this, and for her tremendous advice and encouragement throughout the project, we wish to express our sincerest gratitude first and foremost to Lynn Vavreck.

We incurred many other debts along the way. We benefited greatly from the feedback of our colleagues here at UCLA. Our nascent ideas about racial attitudes and Obama were routinely bounced off the regulars of the 2008 Election Lunch Group at our weekly meetings throughout the campaign year. We thank them all, especially Ryan Enos, Seth Hill, Brian Law, Jeff Lewis, Barbara Sinclair, and Lynn Vavreck. Several other members of the UCLA family have also helped us develop our ideas. We thank Matt Atkinson, Jim DeNardo, Mary McThomas, John Zaller, the Sears Political Psychology Lab, and the students in Tesler's Spring 2009 undergraduate racial attitudes seminar for their insights. We also thank the UCLA Graduate Division for their generous fellowships in support of the project.

We have received excellent feedback on various parts of the book presented at conferences and invited talks at the Midwest Political Science

Association, the International Society of Political Psychology, Ohio State University, Princeton University, Stanford University, Stony Brook University, University of California, Irvine, and UCLA. Specifically, we thank Paul Beck, Thomas Craemer, Stanley Feldman, Zoltan Hajnal, Leonie Huddy, Simon Jackman, Phillip Klinkner, Tali Mendelberg, Paul Sniderman, and Nick Valentino. Our series editor for the University of Chicago Press, Benjamin Page, provided similarly thoughtful comments on our book prospectus. Chapter 3 especially owes a lot to his advice.

We believe the book's strength resides in its ability to leverage both cross-sectional time-series data and an election-year panel study. We are, therefore, especially appreciative of Simon Jackman, Doug Rivers, and Lynn Vavreck's work in carrying out the Cooperative Campaign Analysis Project (CCAP), a six-wave panel study of registered voters.

Like so many other students of American political behavior, we also owe a profound debt to the Center for Political Studies at the University of Michigan for conducting—and the National Science Foundation for funding—the American National Election Studies. In particular, we are thankful to the late Warren E. Miller for overseeing the time-series design for so many years and to Donald R. Kinder's work in developing our study's focal explanatory variable—racial resentment—and shepherding it into the survey's standard core questionnaire. This book simply could not have been done without either of these surveys working, as will be seen, in complementary ways.

Nor could our final chapter have been written without new cross-sectional time-series and panel data collected during Obama's first year in office. We sincerely thank the National Science Foundation for their generous financial support of our effort to reinterview over 3,000 CCAP panelists in November 2009 (SES-0968830). Special thanks also go to Michael Dimmock, Scott Keeter, and the Pew Research Center for providing us early access to their 2009 update of the longstanding Pew Values Study. Our first insights into how racialized evaluations of President Obama compared to his immediate White House predecessors were entirely dependent on this outstanding resource.

Finally, it has been a true pleasure to work with the University of Chicago Press. We thank John Tryneski, our editor, along with Rodney Powell and everyone else at the Press who helped us navigate through the publication process.

Introduction

Obama as Post-Racial?

He is interesting for not fitting into old racial conventions. Not only does he stand
in stark contrast to a black leadership with which Americans of all races have
grown exhausted—the likes of Al Sharpton, Jesse Jackson, and Julian Bond—he
embodies something that no other presidential candidate possibly can: the ideal-
ism that race is but a negligible human difference. Here is the radicalism, innate
to his pedigree, that automatically casts him as the perfect antidote to America's
corrosive racial politics.

SHELBY STEELE, *A Bound Man*

From the moment Barack Obama entered the national spotlight he has indeed been cast "as the perfect antidote to America's corrosive racial politics."
The Illinois legislator, who was campaigning at the time to become the lone
African American in the U.S. Senate, burst upon the American political
landscape as the keynote speaker at the 2004 Democratic National Convention. His was an almost universally acclaimed speech that immediately cata-
pulted him from a little-known state politician to America's newest hope for
a post-racial political future. Obama famously proclaimed in the address,
"There's not a black America and white America and Latino America and
Asian America; there's the United States of America." The speech also prominently affirmed his hope in the country's ideals—"The hope of a skinny kid
with a funny name who believes that America has a place for him, too. The
audacity of hope!" Such powerful appeals to racial unity and hope had some
political commentators believing that we were potentially witnessing the
first black president.[1]

Obama remained faithful to these unifying campaign messages throughout his first two years in the U.S. Senate. His self-imposed role as a racial
bridge builder was clearly on display in the racially charged aftermath of
Hurricane Katrina.[2] A large majority of African Americans believed that
the federal response to the Katrina-induced suffering in New Orleans would
have been faster if most of the victims had been white.[3] Similar charges
were made by high-profile black political figures like Jesse Jackson and Al

1

Sharpton. Obama's critique of the federal response, however, was couched in race-neutral language. He described the Bush administration's "incompetence" as "color-blind" but believed it revealed a lack of empathy for poor inner-city residents who happen to be disproportionately African American (Mendell 2007, 317). Senator Obama struck a similar class-based tone in another September 2005 interview, stating, "It is way too simplistic to just say this administration doesn't care about black people. I think it is entirely accurate to say that this administration's policies don't take into account the plight of poor communities and this is a tragic reflection of that indifference" (quoted in Zeleny 2005, 1). That universalistic race-neutral criticism was classic Obama. Notably conservative commentators compared his measured assessment of the tragedy favorably with Jesse Jackson's more racially charged remarks.[4] Yet he still recognized the role of race in helping to create the economic conditions that underlay the Bush administration's apparent apathy toward the victims in New Orleans.

Aside from his Katrina comments, Barack Obama remained relatively quiet during his first year in the U.S. Senate. Much of that time was spent writing his second book, *The Audacity of Hope: Thoughts on Reclaiming the American Dream*, which was published in the fall of 2006. The memoir's chapter titled "Race" reiterated his 2004 convention speech's hope in "a vision of America finally freed from the past of Jim Crow and slavery, Japanese internment camps and Mexican braceros, workplace tensions and cultural conflict" (Obama 2006, 231). *The Audacity of Hope*, however, also cautioned those who interpreted his keynote address as the watershed to a post-racial America not to lose sight of the country's glaring racial inequities. He similarly defended the limited use of affirmative action for African Americans, while emphasizing universal, as opposed to race-specific, governmental programs because they are both "good policy" and "good politics" (247). Race is an unparalleled minefield in American politics. Barack Obama's convention speech, his critiques of the federal government's response to Hurricane Katrina, and his chapter on race relations in *Audacity* all navigated this rough terrain, though in an adroit manner that was not particularly alienating to any one side of the country's most polarizing issue.

On the heels of *The Audacity of Hope*'s popularity, Senator Obama hit the campaign trail to stump for Democrats running in the 2006 midterm congressional elections. Enormous crowds of all races and ethnicities attended these events to witness the growing phenomenon that was Barack Obama. His widespread appeal had political pundits abuzz with speculation about a potential presidential run less than two years into his first senatorial term. Obama's picture even graced the cover of *Time* magazine in October 2006 with the caption, "Why Barack Obama Could be the Next President." The cover story detailed how his transcendence of racial stereotypes had captured the American public's imagination and how his consensus-building nature had him well positioned for a potential 2008 presidential bid (Klein 2006). Similar accounts began to spread like wildfire in the national media.

These stories often contrasted Obama's 2008 prospects with Jesse Jackson's 1984 and 1988 campaigns for the Democratic nomination. Despite Jackson's remarkable support among African American voters in the party's 1984 and 1988 primaries (74 percent and 92 percent, respectively), his overall vote share topped out at only 29 percent in 1988. Reverend Jackson's attempts to broaden his base of support that year had earned him a larger proportion of the white vote than he received in 1984, but his rootedness in the American civil rights struggle and his campaign's unabashed advocacy for black rights still left the vast majority of whites staunchly opposed to his candidacy.

Unlike Jackson, though, political handicappers near the end of 2006 were giving Senator Obama a realistic (albeit small) chance of winning the Democratic nomination in 2008 because they believed his appeal transcended race. Indeed, Barack Obama had told an almost all-black audience early into his senatorial campaign, "I am not running a race-based campaign. I am rooted in the African American community, but not limited by it" (quoted in Mendell 2007, 188). There was no doubt whatsoever that if Senator Obama sought the presidency he would run a similarly race-neutral campaign.[5] His unique ability to reach beyond race had political commentators instantly anointing him as the first truly viable black candidate for a major party's nomination.

Senator Obama's reluctance to make race a major issue in his presidential campaign was already on display the day he announced his intention to seek the Democratic nomination. The Senator's pastor, Jeremiah Wright, was initially scheduled to give the invocation preceding Obama's February 10, 2007, presidential campaign announcement at the Illinois State Capitol. *Rolling Stone* magazine, however, was working on a story at the time titled "Obama's Radical Roots,"[6] which detailed some of the controversial racial comments Reverend Wright had made before the Trinity United Church of Christ—where the Obamas were longtime members. Trinity United's black liberation theology eventually took center stage during the campaign in March 2008. Obama staffers, though, were already well aware of the problems Wright could cause them. The campaign's chief strategist, David Axelrod, had previously orchestrated the victories of several black candidates. In doing so, he had earned a niche reputation for making African Americans seeking elected office acceptable to white voters (Hayes 2007). Not only had Axelrod's tactics helped Obama become the third African American popularly elected to the U.S. Senate, but he also ran Deval Patrick's (D-MA) successful 2006 campaign to become only the second black governor in America since Reconstruction. Patrick's racially unifying campaign was anchored with the Obama-like slogan, "together we can." Axelrod knew that Obama's connection to Wright's considerably more divisive sermons threatened his candidate's well-cultivated post-racial image. It is certainly no surprise, then, that Reverend Wright was scratched from appearing at his congregant's first official presidential campaign event.

The Obama campaign's concerted effort to steer clear of racial controversy seemed to be working quite well in 2007. Despite the historic nature of his candidacy, the campaign atmosphere leading up to the first primaries was relatively free of racial acrimony. Perhaps the year's only significant controversy surrounding Obama's race came when fellow Democratic hopeful Joe Biden said the following about his future running mate: "I mean, you got the first mainstream African American who is articulate and bright and clean and a nice-looking guy." Biden's remarks drew criticism for implying that other African Americans did not possess these qualities. His insensitive comments, however, further emphasized the differences between Obama and the more stereotypically black candidates who had previously sought the Democratic nomination, Jesse Jackson and Al Sharpton.[7] Moreover, Obama once again used a potentially racially divisive moment to showcase his renowned reconciliatory appeal. He forcefully defended Biden during a December 2007 debate in Iowa, highlighting the Senator's long record of support for racial equality.

If anything, the most pressing racial issue of 2007 seemed to be whether Barack Obama was actually "black enough." Senator Obama, as the son of a white mother and a Kenyan father, lacked African *American* ancestry. That factor, combined with his upbringing outside of the continental United States, his generational distance from the civil rights movement, and his distinctly nonracial campaign messages had some in the black community doubting his authenticity (see Walters 2007 and Hendon 2009 for detailed discussions of this subject). Obama was also criticized by some prominent African Americans for canceling a scheduled appearance at the annual State of Black America town hall meeting in 2007. Jesse Jackson even reportedly described him as "acting white" in September of that year for not attending a march in Jena, Louisiana, to protest the suspect imprisonment of six black teenagers (Ifill 2009, 25). Obama responded to this question about whether he is "authentically black enough" in a July 2007 debate by jokingly saying, "You know, when I'm catching a cab in Manhattan—in the past, I think I've given my credentials." His modest support from African Americans in 2007 was no laughing matter for the Obama campaign, though. It seems hard to believe in retrospect, but opinion polls repeatedly showed Hillary Clinton with sizable leads over Barack Obama among black voters throughout most of that year.[8]

His strategists, nonetheless, resisted any temptation to run a more race-conscious campaign. Most of Obama's top staffers viewed his ambiguity on matters of race as an asset; they decided, therefore, to soldier on with the racial balancing act that Obama had been engaged in since the 2004 Democratic Convention.[9] Or, as *Newsweek*'s Evan Thomas (2009) wrote about the campaign's racial strategy, "If black voters want to claim him as the black candidate, fine. If voters wanted to see him as biracial or post-racial, that was fine, too" (71).

The results of this plan of action were obviously hard to argue with. The campaign's race-neutral approach helped Obama win the all-important (and almost all-white) Iowa caucuses on January 3, 2008. He not only won the first presidential contest of the year, but he racked up resounding 8-point victories against both the formidable Democratic frontrunner, Hillary Clinton, and John Edwards—a candidate who had parlayed his strong second-place showing in Iowa four years earlier into the 2004 vice presidential nomination. That caucus night seemed to possibly signal a new post-racial political era: Barack Obama had won the lily-white Iowa caucuses with his distinctly nonracial messages of hope and change.

Summary of Key Findings

Obama's campaign for the presidency in 2008, however, was anything but post-racial. Instead, the racial hopes and fears evoked by his potential to become the country's first black president sharply divided racial conservatives from racial liberals. Public opinion and voting behavior, in fact, were considerably more polarized by racial attitudes than at any other time on record. This phenomenon whereby racial predispositions are brought more heavily to bear on political evaluations is often described as *racialization*. For example, opinions about policies like affirmative action and welfare have been described as highly racialized because they are strongly determined by racial attitudes (Kinder and Sanders 1996; Sears, Van Laar, Carillo, and Kosterman 1997; Gilens 1999; Winter 2008).

Our central psychological argument is that race was more chronically accessible to voters in 2008 than it had been in any previous campaign. *Accessibility* refers to the associative link between a particular attitude object and a particular political evaluation. Attitudes about the Vietnam War were perhaps most accessible in voters' minds in 1968, even though the candidates differed on numerous other, lower-profile, issues. Similarly, attitudes toward the Iranian hostage crisis in 1980, and toward terrorism in 2004, were surely accessible to voters in those years. *Chronic accessibility* means that a particular predisposition is almost inevitably and ubiquitously activated among voters because there is an especially strong connection between that attitude and the political evaluation in question. The historic racial significance that was unmistakably associated with Barack Obama's candidacy meant that voters' racial predispositions were in most cases highly accessible to them—or at least so is our argument—allowing racial attitudes to play a major role in forming their evaluations of him. That leads us to expect that vote choice was inevitably highly racialized, despite Obama's (and to a large extent John McCain's) best efforts to minimize attention to race throughout the campaign.

Earlier research on racialization primarily focused on racially resentful opposition to policies that are both quite unpopular with white Americans and disproportionately associated with African Americans, such as affirmative action and welfare. From a logical point of view, however, racialization could just as easily be the product of support for policies that benefit African Americans or for black candidates. We describe such racially liberal support as "the other side" of the *two sides of racialization* because this aspect of racial attitudes' impact on political evaluations has been largely overlooked in the past. One of our principal findings, in fact, is that these two sides of racialization—that is, racially resentful opposition to *and* racially liberal support for Barack Obama—resulted in a considerably larger influence of racial attitudes on the presidential vote in 2008 than in any other campaign in modern history.

A number of results presented throughout the book unambiguously inform this conclusion that the 2008 campaign was more racialized from start to finish than any other recent campaigns. Beginning in chapter 2, we show that evaluations of Barack Obama by the entire electorate were highly racialized even in 2007 when he was consistently portrayed as the racially transcendent candidate. Yet, while racial attitudes had a bigger impact on evaluations of Barack Obama than they had on his Democratic rivals, much of that difference was produced by Obama's strong support from racial liberals. Obama's activation of racially liberal support, especially among white racial liberals, will be a recurrent theme throughout the book. Primary vote choice between Hillary Clinton and Barack Obama was similarly polarized by racial attitudes from the campaign's onset. No other factor, in fact, came close to dividing the Democratic primary electorate as powerfully as their feelings about African Americans. The impact of racial attitudes on individual vote decisions in the 2008 Democratic primary was so strong that it appears to have even outstripped the substantive impact of racial attitudes on Jesse Jackson's more racially charged campaign for the nomination in 1988.

Chapter 3 shows that racial attitudes were also a much more important determinant of general election vote choice in 2008 than they were in any of the presidential contests of the recent past, despite the absence of explicit references to race during the campaign. We also demonstrate that a matchup between Hillary Clinton and John McCain would not have evoked racial predispositions nearly as powerfully as the McCain-Obama choice did. Moreover, despite the Obama campaign's best effort to neutralize the intrusion of aversive feelings toward African Americans into presidential choices (Ambinder 2009), their effect on McCain-Obama preferences was unaltered throughout the course of the campaign. That continuity suggests racial predispositions may have been, and continue to be, chronically psychologically accessible in response to Obama, thereby making it difficult for new information and events to dampen the effects of race. Although racial attitudes mattered much more this election year in a country that tends to be rather racially conservative, we show that Obama overcame that obstacle by garnering unprecedented support from racial liberals early on and activating Democratic partisanship and performance evaluations of a deeply unpopular incumbent president in the late stages of the campaign.

Not only did Obama racialize presidential vote preferences more powerfully than any other previous candidate did, but chapter 4 shows he produced a "spillover of racialization." In other words, public responses to people and policies strongly associated with Obama, whether situated in opposition or accordance with him, were also more polarized by racial attitudes than they had been before the election year. For example, racial conservatism became an increasingly important ingredient of Democrats' favorability ratings of Hillary Clinton, Obama's main opponent during the primary season. During the fall campaign, racial attitudes similarly became increasingly important in assessments of John McCain, as well as in opposition to tax increases after "Joe the Plumber" called attention to Obama's position on this issue in October 2008.

After Obama's poor showing among Latinos in the California and Texas primaries, much media speculation suggested that racial prejudices might pose a particular obstacle to Obama's prospects in that growing minority population. However, chapter 5 shows that Obama polarized whites and Latinos alike along the lines of racial conservatism. That is, racial attitudes substantially influenced both groups' voting behavior in the Democratic primaries and in the general election. But we found little evidence that race actually played a *stronger* role in Latinos' primary voting compared to whites', contrary to that earlier media speculation. Racial attitudes were also perhaps the most important determinant of African Americans' primary vote choices. Blacks who possessed strong feelings of racial solidarity were about 50 percentage points more likely to support Obama against Hillary Clinton than were blacks with the lowest levels of group consciousness.

Chapter 6 shows that racial attitudes were such a strong determinant of vote choice in the Democratic primary that they helped produced one of the great ironies in American political history: Hillary Clinton, the longstanding poster child of the antifeminist backlash, won a significantly greater percentage of the primary vote from gender *conservatives* than she did from gender *egalitarians*. Indeed, three different surveys show that Hillary Clinton performed about 15 percentage points better against Barack Obama with strong gender traditionalists than she did with Americans possessing the most liberal beliefs about gender roles. The paradox is easily resolved when we take into account the fact that gender conservatives tend also to be conservative about racial issues and gender liberals are similarly liberal in their outlooks on race. In other words, we demonstrate that racial attitudes were so powerful that they actually made Hillary Clinton the preferred choice of modern day *sexists* in the Democratic primaries.

We shift our focus in chapter 7 from antiblack to anti-Muslim attitudes. These feelings had a substantial impact on opposition to Obama in both the primaries and the general election. Moreover, general election vote choice in 2008 was more heavily influenced by feelings about Muslims than either 2004 voting or preferences in McCain-Clinton trial heats. Opinions about Muslims had similarly large effects even for individuals who knew Obama was not an adherent of Islam. They also hold up after controlling for the significant relationship between anti-Muslim and antiblack attitudes. We conclude from these results that Obama is not just evaluated as an African

American but as someone who exemplifies the more primitively frightening out-group status of "otherness."

The results presented in these chapters suggest that the hopes of some for a post-racial Obama era were far from a sure thing and probably even a long shot. Rather, if anything, American partisan politics could easily become increasingly organized by racial attitudes during the Obama presidency. That implication, however, is primarily dependent on whether *President* Obama continues to evoke racial predispositions as strongly as *Candidate* Obama did in 2007 and 2008. Chapter 8, in fact, details several factors that could potentially make President Obama a less racialized figure than he was in 2008. Yet we also present substantial new evidence from the first year of his presidency showing that the American public was as divided by racial attitudes as ever in their assessments of him.

In sum, our results clearly indicate that Barack Obama's candidacy polarized the electorate by racial attitudes more strongly than had any previous presidential candidate in recent times. Whether that polarization continues throughout his presidency remains to be seen. Rather than marking the onset of a new post-racial politics, however, the election of Barack Obama may well have been the watershed to another of America's periodic hyperracial political eras.

1

Background

Race in Presidential Elections

Most working- and middle-class white Americans don't feel that they have been particularly privileged by their race. . . . So when they are told to bus their children to a school across town; when they hear that an African American is getting an advantage in landing a good job or a spot in a good college because of an injustice that they themselves have never committed; when they're told that their fears about crime in urban neighborhoods are somehow prejudiced, resentment builds over time. Like the anger within the black community, these resentments aren't always expressed in polite company. But they have helped shape the political landscape for at least a generation. Anger over welfare and affirmative action helped forge the Reagan Coalition.

BARACK OBAMA, "A More Perfect Union," campaign speech,
Philadelphia, March 18, 2008

The above analysis from Barack Obama of how racial resentments helped shape the American political landscape of the preceding decades was quite astute. Our results showing that similar attitudes profoundly affected people's opinions about him in 2008 are, in fact, situated within a long line of social science research detailing the centrality of race in contemporary partisan politics (see Hutchings and Valentino 2004 for a review). Much of that research is based upon the theory of symbolic racism, which has become the focal construct for explaining the role of racial attitudes in American politics. This chapter briefly reviews the existing literature on the role of racial attitudes in American presidential elections, then details the meaning and measurement of symbolic racism, and finally describes both the statistical methods and the sources of evidence used in our study to discern the impact of racial attitudes on Barack Obama's campaigns for the Democratic nomination and the White House.

Racial Issues in American Presidential Elections

Racial issues have had quite a variable history in American presidential elections. That history can be briefly characterized in terms of four eras. Perhaps their strongest influence came in the elections of 1860, when they triggered the Civil War, and in 1864, when military successes barely counteracted racial antagonism, overcoming widespread Northern sentiment for a negotiated settlement with the Confederacy and so allowing Lincoln's reelection. Lincoln's actions to end chattel slavery made him known over the years as "the Great Emancipator" and the Republican Party became known as "the party of Lincoln." The efforts of the Radical Republicans of Reconstruction to help freed slaves further cemented the political party's pro-black legacy.

A second era began with the Compromise of 1877. Put simply, that agreement traded an end to the post–Civil War Reconstruction and the military occupation of the South for Republican control of the White House. The compromise also resulted in a general withdrawal of the Republican Party from Southern politics. Both political parties, and both sections of the country, had been exhausted by the violent confrontations of markedly different racial cultures during the Civil War and Reconstruction. Thereafter, racial issues had little visibility in presidential elections until after World War II. Even Franklin D. Roosevelt's generally liberal New Deal, with its electoral base in Northern industrial states, was so dependent on Southern Democratic congressional support that it was unable to promote civil rights. He accomplished little even on issues that today seem inarguable, such as antilynching legislation or the extension of Social Security benefits to such disproportionately black groups as poor farm workers and household help.

Some early foreshadowing of renewed attention to racial issues began with disputes in the Democratic convention of 1948 over President Harry S Truman's executive order to racially integrate the armed forces. The resulting walkout of conservative Southerners led to the Dixiecrat candidacy of Governor Strom Thurmond of South Carolina, which captured nearly enough Southern votes to take victory from the incumbent Democrat. Truman's successors as Democratic nominees, Adlai Stevenson and John F. Kennedy, like FDR, were unwilling to risk further schisms within the party, and both selected Southern running mates. In that era, the American public generally perceived little difference between the national parties or their presidential candidates in support for civil rights.

A third and radically different era began in 1963. Northern Democrats, in some cases eagerly and in other cases unwillingly, asserted leadership in promoting civil rights. The turning point came in June 1963 with the Kennedy administration's confrontation with Governor George Wallace over the desegregation of the University of Alabama, and then Kennedy's widely heralded proposal of major civil rights legislation. Within the next year, this was followed by Kennedy's assassination; a nearly total regional split within the Democratic party over the Civil Rights Act of 1964, marked by the longest but ultimately unsuccessful filibuster in American history, mounted by all but one of the Southern Democratic senators; the beginnings of Southern Democratic defection to the Republican party; and finally the selection of a staunch opponent of the Civil Rights Act, Senator Barry Goldwater, as the Republican presidential nominee against its most visible supporter, President Lyndon B. Johnson. Johnson won in a landslide. But the Democratic party had become deeply split internally over race, and the repolarization of the two parties over racial issues had begun anew, after nearly a century of quiescence.

In the years to come, the Democratic Party splintered further over racial issues, with Southern and working class whites especially likely to defect. In 1968, George Wallace's third-party candidacy rode white racial backlash to victory in five Southern states. Thereafter, Richard Nixon and his Republican successors began to successfully deploy "the Southern strategy" to attract disaffected white Southern Democrats by appealing to racial conservatism. Following Nixon's election in 1968, the Republicans were not seriously challenged from the Right on racial issues. Meanwhile, Democratic candidates ran on explicitly pro–civil rights platforms. Even the Southern Democrat Jimmy Carter's brief administration promoted further civil rights liberalism. As a result, most scholars of voting behavior agree that a gradual party realignment occurred following 1968, centrally on the basis of racial issues, with many racially conservative whites permanently defecting from the Democrats to the Republicans.

The fourth and more complex contemporary era began with the election of 1980. Ronald Reagan, a long-time opponent of civil rights and supporter of "states' rights," appealed to racially conservative Southern whites even more explicitly than Nixon had. He gave his first major campaign speech as the GOP nominee in Philadelphia, Mississippi, near the site of the 1964 murders of three civil rights workers, and invoked the historically racially loaded phrase of "states' rights." But he also drew support from Southern conservatives over tax cuts, a strong national defense, and his alliances with increasingly politicized religious conservatives.

Later campaigns perpetuated the prominence of racial issues. Jesse Jackson's first presidential campaign in 1984 accelerated the departure of Southern whites from the Democratic Party (Sears, Citrin, and Kosterman 1987). In 1988, Reagan's successor, George H. W. Bush, employed racially provocative materials about the case of a violent black criminal, Willie Horton, to attack liberal Democratic crime policies (Mendelberg 2001). In the 1990s, the Southern Democrat, Bill Clinton, although quite popular among African Americans, began to distance himself from traditional black leaders, such as Jesse Jackson and Al Sharpton, and from liberal policies with implicitly racial implications in the areas of welfare and crime.

In short, elections in the pre-Obama contemporary era, stretching from 1980 through 2004, maintained the party polarization over racial issues that had begun in the 1960s. However, the parties were polarized over a series of other issues described below, complicating the specification of the exact role of race in this era.[1]

Voters' Choices in the Contemporary Era

There have been several explanations posited by voting behavior researchers for the Republican Party's electoral successes in the period from Reagan's first election to Obama's presidential victory. Perhaps the most common is that the Democratic Party had become too ideologically liberal for the center of the electorate by the end of the 1970s. The federal government in the following decade became viewed increasingly vocally by Republicans as an inefficient manager of societal issues relative to market solutions. As such, "big government" and "tax and spend liberals" became shibboleths that Reagan and his followers wielded with great success (Kaufmann and Petrocik 1999; Petrocik 1987).

Nonracial social and cultural issues such as abortion, women's rights, and the sexual revolution have also increasingly divided the two parties in the contemporary era (Adams 1997; Edsall 2006). Cultural conservatism in all those forms became increasingly entwined with religion too. In recent years, religiosity has become one of the most powerful predictors of presidential voting choices. The most devout and observant of all faiths support Republicans, and the less devout or secular, Democrats (Brewer and Stonecash 2007; Fiorina 2006; Green and Dionne 2008; Gelman 2010; Leege et al. 2002).

Still, several other careful studies have focused on socioeconomic status, documenting an increased polarization of the parties by income, with affluent voters more Republican (Bartels 2008; Gelman 2010; McCarty et al. 2006). Bartels (2008), for example, convincingly shows that traditional class-based voting remains alive and well in the contemporary era despite the emergence of highly visible social issues that have the potential to divide culturally conservative low-income voters from their presumed economic interests (Lipset 1960; Frank 2004). Indeed, low-income voters' presidential preferences in 2004 were considerably more influenced by economic than cultural issues, while high-income voters showed no such differentiation.

The nonracial factors of general ideological conservatism, cultural issues, and social class were all surely important determinants of voters' choices in the 2008 election. Our study's main goal, however, is to explain the role of racial attitudes in the election of America's first black president. That primary goal naturally steers our analysis away from such nonracial matters and toward the role of race in partisan politics during the years leading up to Obama's election. So how exactly did racial attitudes help shape the national political landscape that Barack Obama entered as the keynote speaker for the 2004 Democratic National Convention?

There is little dispute about the close link of racial attitudes to candidate evaluations and partisan political choices in the 1960s and 1970s. For example, Carmines and Stimson (1989) made a strong case that the parties realigned around racial issues in the era from the early 1960s to 1980. More contested are interpretations of voters' presidential choices in the contemporary era. Some argue that Americans had largely moved "beyond race" by the late 1980s. Dinesh d'Souza (1995) wrote *The End of Racism*, and Paul Sniderman and his colleagues (1993, 1997) concluded that by the early 1990s, racial prejudice had become a minor political force. Others, however, viewed racial conservatism as a continuing source of partisan cleavage in the United States, not just between blacks and whites but among whites as well. Mayer (2002) finds a consistent partisan division about race in presidential campaign appeals from 1964 to 2000 (also see Gerstle 2002; O'Reilly 1995; and Schaller 2006), and the Edsalls (1992) articulated the common view among liberals that conservatism of all kinds had become little more than a mask for protecting racial inequality.

Kinder and Sanders (1996) then developed the most in-depth empirical examination of the role of racial animosity in contemporary partisan political decision making. They found that resentment of African Americans was a key factor in promoting whites' opposition to both racially targeted policies and Democratic presidential candidates in the 1988 election. Mendelberg (2001) further showed that George H. W. Bush introduced racial antagonism into the 1988 campaign and that his racial appeals successfully attracted racially conservative voters. Elsewhere we have presented evidence that race continued to be centrally implicated in the realignment of white Southerners' partisanship and their growing support for Republican presidential candidates through the end of the twentieth century and into the early years of the twenty-first century (Valentino and Sears 2005, 2008).

This previous research indicates that racial predispositions occupied a focal place in modern-day partisan politics before Barack Obama rose to national prominence. Yet we will argue that during the 2008 campaign the electorate was *even more* divided by their attitudes about African Americans than they had been at any other time in the contemporary era—and a great deal more politically polarized as well. Our central hypothesis is that Barack Obama's identity as an African American made his race chronically accessible to the vast majority of Americans throughout the 2008 campaign. That is, the simple perceptual salience of his race insured that racial predispositions would be unusually central to voters' evaluations of him. In later chapters we will show this close link of racial predispositions to Obama evaluations in 2008. But part of our argument is also historical—that this link of a presidential candidate to racial attitudes was of unprecedented strength compared to previous presidential elections, quite the opposite of signaling a "post-racial" era.

Types of Prejudice

How, then, did we test our racial accessibility theory? This was the most crucial challenge that faced us. We started by considering the conceptualization and measurement of racial prejudice.

White Supremacy: Old-Fashioned Racism

In the 1840s, the abolitionist challenge to slavery had rattled the Southern slave-owning class. Both in England and in the United States, public sentiment was slowly turning against the institution of slavery. According to Frederickson (1971), the challenge inspired the development of an ideology of white supremacy, based on pseudoscientific notions about the inherent inequality of the races. This was later reinforced by the social Darwinist movement of the late nineteenth century and then by a paternalistic racism common among Progressives in the early twentieth century.

In the 1930s and 1940s, the ideas of inherent, genetically based inequality and its links to segregationist policy were firmly established. Nationally representative surveys found that a substantial majority of whites throughout the country subscribed to the ideology of white supremacy, including social distance between the races, beliefs in the biological inferiority of blacks, and approval of public policies insuring racial segregation and formalized discrimination (Schuman et al. 1997). In later research, this racist ideology has variously been called "old-fashioned racism," "Jim Crow racism," or "redneck racism" (Bobo and Kluegel 1997; McConahay et al. 1981; McConahay and Hough 1976; McConahay 1986). For simplicity, we will use just the first of these terms.

Gunnar Myrdal's pivotal book, *An American Dilemma* (1944), emphasized the roots of such old-fashioned racism in the lethal combination of irrational racial prejudice and whites' self-interest in maintaining their own superior privileges. But Myrdal stressed the contradiction of old-fashioned racism with the egalitarian norms that were presumably the legacy of the founders of the nation. He felt that contradiction was ultimately unstable (as had Alexis de Tocqueville [1835/1969], writing on the eve of the eruption of the abolitionist movement). After World War II, old-fashioned racism did indeed decline, accompanied by a growing acceptance of principles of racial equality, at least in the abstract. By the 1990s, any indications of widespread old-fashioned racism had almost disappeared (Schuman et al. 1997).

The New Racisms

Although the passage of civil rights legislation beginning in the mid-1960s gradually eliminated formal segregation and discrimination, racial inequality remained. Substantial white opposition to government action attacking it also remained. The most intense political disputes focused especially on three areas in which racial issues became prominent: busing to produce racial integration (Sears, Hensler, and Speer 1979), black candidates running for mayor in large cities (Hajnal 2007; Vanneman and Pettigrew 1972; Sears and Kinder 1971), and affirmative action (Schuman et al. 1997).

As a result, new theories arose to explain the combination of massive white support for racial equality in opportunity and treatment in the abstract, on the one hand, with continued white opposition to government action to produce racial equality on the ground, on the other. Some of these theories proposed a "new racism," postulating changes both in the content of contemporary racial conservatism and in its presumed determinants.

The Theory of Symbolic Racism

The concept of symbolic racism was the first of these new racisms. The original theory embodied three essential propositions (Kinder and Sears 1981; McConahay and Hough 1976; Sears and Kinder 1971; Sears and McConahay 1973). One was that a new form of racism, "symbolic racism," was in the process of replacing the old-fashioned racism of Jim Crow days in three senses. First, old-fashioned racism was no longer very widely accepted outside the South and consequently could no longer be very influential in conventional politics.[2] Second, opposition to black candidates and liberal racially targeted policies was more influenced by symbolic racism than by self-interest, as reflected in real or perceived racial threats to whites' own personal lives, contrary to the traditional Southern society Myrdal had described. Consequently, the label *symbolic* was used to highlight the roots of these beliefs in abstract moral values rather than in concrete self-interest or personal experience. Third, the origins of symbolic racism lay in a blend of early socialized negative feelings about blacks with traditional conservative values, such as individualism or moral traditionalism.[3] The label *racism* was used because the construct was thought in part to reflect racial antipathy, so its political influence could not be reduced to race-neutral forms of conservatism.

Symbolic racism has been described as a coherent belief system reflecting four specific themes: (1) blacks no longer face much discrimination, (2) their disadvantage mainly reflects their poor work ethic, (3) they are demanding too much too fast, and (4) they have gotten more than they deserve (Henry and Sears 2002; Sears and Henry 2005). Subsequent new racism theories, using the terms "modern racism" and "racial resentment," are virtually identical to the theory of symbolic racism, reflecting most of these same themes and using many of the same survey items in their measurements (McConahay 1986; Kinder and Sanders 1996).[4] We, therefore, use symbolic racism and racial resentment more or less interchangeably in this volume to describe the central racial attitude used in our analyses.[5]

Operationalizing Symbolic Racism with Racial Resentment Questions

A number of survey items have been utilized over the years to measure symbolic racism. In fact, an early critique was that symbolic racism was not measured consistently. Kinder and Sanders (1996), however, effectively standardized the operationalization of symbolic racism with their racial resentment scale. Racial resentment taps into the aforementioned components of the symbolic racism belief system with a battery of four questions asked in American National Election Studies (ANES) surveys from 1986 to 2008. The racial resentment items are presented as assertions, asking respondents to indicate whether they agreed or disagreed with the statement and how strongly they did so. The assertions are as follows:

Irish, Italian, Jewish, and many other minorities overcame prejudice and
worked their way up. Blacks should do the same without any special
favors.

Generations of slavery and discrimination have created conditions that
make it difficult for blacks to work their way out of the lower class.

Over the past few years, blacks have gotten less than they deserve.

It's really a matter of some people not trying hard enough; if blacks would
only try harder they could be just as well off as whites.

The racial resentment scale is constructed from these four statements by
coding the five potential responses to each assertion from 0 to 1 in intervals
of .25, with 0 being the most racially liberal response and 1 being the most
racially conservative. Answers are then summed and divided by the number
of items to provide an easily interpretable 0 to 1 scale.[6] Table 1.1 displays the
summary statistics of the racial resentment scale, our study's focal explanatory variable, for all of the surveys we used. Kinder and Sanders (1996) designed the scale to distinguish between racially sympathetic and racially resentful Americans. By this standard, a score of .50 marks the neutral point.
So individuals scoring below .50 are thought to be more racially sympathetic
(i.e., racial liberals), and individuals with scores above that rather arbitrary
midpoint are classified as more racially resentful (i.e., racial conservatives).[7]
Table 1.1 shows that America is on average a rather racially conservative
country, according to this measure. All survey years produced mean resentment scores on the racially conservative side of the spectrum. Since we are
interested in the impact of racial resentment in both the Democratic primaries and the general election, it is also important to note that the average
resentment levels for Democrats are considerably lower than these overall
national statistics. Yet even Democrats in 2008 did not, on average, fall on
the racially liberal side of the spectrum. The two 2008 surveys utilized in
this study yielded mean resentment scores of .53 and .51 for Democrats.

As can also be seen in table 1.1, the population's racial resentment scores
were remarkably stable at the aggregate level from 1986 to 2008. Every survey since 1988 yielded a sample mean falling within a small 5-point interval
between .58 and .63. Moreover, the country's overall racial resentment levels
did not change very much in response to Barack Obama and the 2008 campaign. There was little aggregate movement from prior survey years to 2008,
or from March to October 2008.

Earlier studies of survey respondents interviewed at multiple times show
that racial resentment is also highly stable at the individual level (Henry

Table 1.1. Summary statistics for racial resentment

Survey Year	Mean	Median	SD	Cronbach's α
1986	.560	.563	.240	.742
1988	.597	.625	.233	.734
1992	.581	.625	.243	.752
1994	.610	.625	.225	.703
2000	.611	.625	.237	.713
2004	.597	.625	.244	.769
2008 (ANES)	.616	.625	.236	.743
2008 (March CCAP)	.625	.625	.272	.842
2008 (October CCAP)	.629	.625	.273	.853

Source: 1986, 1988, 1992, 1994, 2000, 2004, and 2008 ANES; March and October 2008 CCAP.

and Sears 2009; Kinder and Sanders 1996). Likewise, in the Cooperative Campaign Analysis Project (CCAP, described in greater detail below), the correlation between the same panel respondents' racial resentment scores in March and October 2008 was a robust .82. The stability of racial resentment at both the aggregate and individual levels has an important practical benefit for our study. It allows us to test the impact of racial resentment, as measured in the March CCAP, on our panel respondents' vote choices later in the campaign without much danger that their levels of resentment will have changed substantially over time.

The high scale reliability of these items shown in table 1.1 ($\alpha \approx .75$ across all surveys) also suggests that symbolic racism, as measured with Kinder and Sanders's racial resentment battery, reflects an internally consistent construct rather than the four multiple and diverse themes with which it is operationalized.[8] Simply put, the seemingly diverse sentiments expressed in the racial resentment questions are answered by survey respondents as if they had one thing primarily in mind. Presumably the reason for this consistency is that racial resentment is a substantively meaningful package of beliefs about blacks to most Americans, wherever they stand on it.

Symbolic Racism's Political Impact

Many studies have shown that symbolic racism and racial resentment are strongly associated with white Americans' opposition to race-targeted policies. Their explanatory power typically outweighs that of other important political attitudes, such as ideology, party identification, and attitudes toward the size of the federal government, or older and more traditional racial attitudes, such as old-fashioned racism, negative stereotypes, or antiblack affect (Bobo 2000; Kinder and Sanders 1996; Sears, Van Laar, Carrillo, and Kosterman 1997; Sidanius, et al. 1999; see Sears and Henry 2005 for a review).[9] Symbolic racism similarly strongly predicts white Americans' opposition to black candidates and support for racially conservative white candidates (Howell 1994; Kinder and Sanders 1996; Kinder and Sears 1981; Mendelberg 2001; Sears, Van Laar, Carillo, and Kosterman 1997), and it has been shown to be an important factor in shifting white Southerners from the Democratic to the Republican Party over the past several decades (Valentino and Sears 2005). These large effects of symbolic racism are thought to be an expression of racial animosity.

Some political scientists, however, have argued that symbolic racism confounds racial animus with ordinary political conservatism, so that its effects may only reflect relatively unprejudiced aversion to liberal big government (Hurwitz and Peffley, 1998; Sniderman, Crosby, and Howell 2000; Sniderman and Tetlock, 1986a, 1986b). This issue has been addressed comprehensively elsewhere (Tarman and Sears 2005; Sears and Henry 2005) with new empirical evidence contrary to the earlier critiques.[10] More importantly, though, the evidence presented in this volume regarding racial resentment's impact on 2008 voting cannot easily be attributed to general political conservatism. The contest between Hillary Clinton and Barack Obama for the Democratic nomination, for example, basically held political ideology constant. The two candidates had ideologically identical roll-call voting records in the U.S. Senate (Carroll et al. 2008) and were perceived by the American public as equally liberal during the primary season.[11]

Ascertaining Symbolic Racism's Impact in 2008

The race between Obama and John McCain, however, clearly differed along both racial and standard partisan/ideological fault lines. It therefore raises the possibility that any effects of racial resentment on vote choices between the two are simply responses to their broader ideological differences. One approach to separating the effects of racial attitudes from those nonracial factors actually takes advantage of this unique historical circumstance. In brief, we will compare the effect of racial resentment on 2008 Obama-McCain vote intentions, matching a black liberal with a white conservative, with its effects in previous all-white liberal-conservative choices: previous presidential elections featuring only white candidates (e.g., Gore-Bush) and hypothetical Hillary Clinton versus McCain trial heats in 2008. These comparisons vary race but hold nonracial factors mostly constant because of all such Democratic candidates' ideological similarity.

We also use statistical techniques to separate the effects of racial attitudes in 2008 from other nonracial factors, such as ideology and party identification. The methods used in our analyses are standard procedures in political science. So this section is meant for, and we hope especially helpful to, readers without strong statistical backgrounds.

Our study's primary objective is to determine how racial attitudes influenced support for and opposition to Barack Obama throughout the election year. Why not just compare the differences in Obama's vote share between racial liberals and racial conservatives, then? The problem here is that symbolic racism is related to several other important factors that profoundly influence Americans' voting behavior. Party identification, for instance, is just one of the many variables that are correlated with *both* racial resentment and vote choice. Merely examining the raw vote differences between voters who are high and low in racial resentment, therefore, provides little insight into whether the electorate was polarized by racial attitudes because Obama was a candidate to become the first black president or if it was polarized because racial liberals tend to be Democrats and racial conservatives are more likely to be Republicans. In other words, that approach offers no way of ascertaining the *independent* effects of racial resentment.

Our statistical methods, however, do allow us to isolate the independent impact of racial resentment. The following example, if a little oversimplified, will hopefully help nontechnical readers understand how this method works. Suppose we wanted to estimate how racial resentment affected evaluations of Barack Obama before the election. The ANES's preelection survey asked respondents to rate several political figures on a so-called thermometer scale, ranging from 0 (coldest) to 100 (warmest). We can estimate Obama's thermometer rating as a simple straight line function of racial resentment, using a technique called linear regression. The first panel of figure 1.1 displays the relationship between Obama's thermometer ratings and racial resentment across the entire resentment spectrum. The best-fitting estimated line is the one that minimizes its distance from all the points representing each respondent's unique conjunction of thermometer rating and racial resentment. The lines in the figure are called *predicted* thermometer ratings because they predict how, according to this equation, an individual would rate Obama given his or her levels of racial resentment. Note that "prediction" here does not mean predicting the future; it just means where the individual *would* come out according to the equation that best describes the relationship found in the whole survey. In practice, the straight line that best simplifies the relationship between racial resentment and thermometer

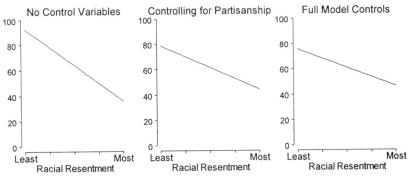

Figure 1.1. Thermometer ratings of Barack Obama as a function of racial resentment. Thermometer ratings were based on the OLS coefficients in table A1.1 of the online appendix (http://www.press.uchicago.edu/books/tesler/). Predicted thermometer ratings were calculated by setting all other variables to their sample means. *Source*: 2008 ANES.

ratings of Obama is expressed as the following equation (you had this in high school algebra):

$$Obama's\ Thermometer\ Rating = 92 - 56 \times Racial\ Resentment$$

As you can see in the first panel of figure 1.1, when racial resentment is *lowest* (scored as 0), the line reaches a thermometer rating of 92. When racial resentment is *highest* (scored as 1), the line sinks to a thermometer rating of 36. The difference between those endpoints reflects how much support Obama loses over the full range of racial resentment: 56 points.

Given the above-mentioned relationship between party identification and racial attitudes, it is not surprising that Obama was much more popular with the most racially liberal Americans than he was with the most racially resentful. Democrats tend to be more racially liberal, and both variables are associated with liking Obama. But we want to know the *relative* contribution of party identification and racial resentment to Obama's ratings. So we control for that strong correlation between the two factors. Instead of predicting an individual's thermometer rating of Obama from his or her levels of racial resentment, a multiple regression model can estimate these values while holding party identification constant. That is, it can estimate what the relationship between Obama's thermometer ratings and racial resentment *would be* if racial liberals were not more likely to be Democrats and if racial conservatives were not more likely to be Republicans. Our statistical models' ability to hold other variables constant—or control for them—allows us to determine the impact of racial resentment *independent* of those other factors. Including partisanship in our regression model with racial resentment, for example, now yields the following equation:

$$Obama's\ Thermometer\ Rating = 98.8 - (34.6 \times Racial\ Resentment) - (43.8 \times Partisanship)$$

When comparing the coefficient on racial resentment in this equation to the one just presented above, we find the negative effect of moving from least to most racially resentful on Obama's thermometer ratings was reduced substantially (from –56.6 to –34.6 thermometer degrees) after controlling for party identification. The second panel of figure 1.1 graphically displays this effect of racial resentment while setting partisanship to its sample average. We set partisanship to its mean value to get an approximation of what the relationship between racial resentment and Obama's thermometer ratings looked liked for the average American. Comparing the first two panels of the display makes it easy to see just how the relationship between Obama's thermometer ratings and racial resentment changed after we controlled for partisanship.

The third panel in figure 1.1 shows the impact of racial resentment on Barack Obama's thermometer ratings after controlling for both partisanship and several other variables, which we subsequently set to their sample averages in order to estimate the relationship shown in the display.[12] As can be seen, controlling for factors like ideological self-placement and basic demographics further reduced the negative effect of moving from least to most racially resentful on Obama's thermometer ratings down to –29.1. In other words, nearly half of the original –56.6 thermometer degree impact shown in the first panel of figure 1.1 was spuriously produced by racial resentment's correlation with other important predictors of support for Obama that were not accounted for in the original model. Controlling for all of these variables is absolutely essential if we want to make assertions about the relationship between racial resentment and voting behavior *independent* of other related factors.[13]

Base Vote Choice Model

So which factors did we control for in our regression models of vote choice? Our base vote choice model consists of only symbolic predispositions and standard demographic variables to predict vote choices. We rely upon it most heavily in our analyses. However, at various points in the book, we employ different model specifications when other variables are relevant. As you will see, the effects of racial resentment are remarkably robust even when controlling for factors like issue positions, presidential approval, economic evaluations, gender conservatism, and anti-Muslim attitudes.

Symbolic Predispositions

We employ this base model because it fosters comparisons across survey years. Symbolic predispositions such as party identification, ideological self-placement, and racial resentment tend to be among Americans' most stable political attitudes (Sears 1993). They are usually acquired during individuals' early formative years and typically persist quite stably through life (see Sears and Levy 2003 for a review). That stability makes it much easier to compare effects over time. For example, racial resentment is highly stable over time at both the individual and aggregate level. We can be confident, then, that the greater impact of racial resentment in 2008 compared to earlier election years was not caused by changes in its underlying distribution, such as greater racial liberalism or greater racial conservatism. We can be similarly confident in the results over time from our two other symbolic predispositions, party identification and ideological self-placement.[14] The same cannot be said of attitudes about most more-specific political issues. Americans as a whole do not have well-developed political belief systems (Converse 1964; Zaller 1992; Kinder 1998). Indeed, their positions on most issues are often unstable from year to year and can vary depending on the context in which they are assessed. So we could not be so confident in depending on comparisons from year to year using them.

Demographics: Controlling for African Americans Rather than Excluding Them

The model also includes five demographic variables. These include age, education, gender, race, and Southern residence.[15] Most previous symbolic racism studies have included only whites in the analyses. Our base model, though, includes a variable indicating whether an individual is black rather than excluding African Americans from the analysis. There are distinct pros and cons in this approach. Including African Americans in the analysis has important practical benefits. Chapters 2 and 3 address three main questions: (1) How did racial resentment influence vote choice in the primaries and general election? (2) How did these effects compare to the past? and (3) How did Obama manage to win? With whites now making up only about three-quarters of the national electorate and two-thirds of Democratic primary voters, the only way to fully answer the third question is to include all Americans in our analyses. For the purposes of explaining both how Obama won and the potential implications our findings have for American politics in the future, we included the black control variable in our base model of vote choice.

There are cons, however. Controlling for being black is problematic because symbolic racism was originally conceptualized as a measure of white prejudice toward African Americans. It is uncertain what racial resentment among African Americans means. Perhaps most important, we find, as will be seen, that Obama drew unusually high levels of support from racial liberals. It is crucial for us to distinguish between his unusually strong support among blacks from his equally unusually high levels of support among white racial liberals. Including blacks in the analysis makes it more difficult to determine Obama's support among white racial liberals, specifically.

As a result, we also directly address, empirically, concerns that our conclusions could simply be an artifact of including African Americans in our analyses throughout the book. As will be shown in numerous contexts, the substantive implications of our results are not altered in analyses limited to whites. Since little is known about the nature and origins of racial resentment for nonwhites, chapter 5 also contains brief exploratory analyses of symbolic racism's ingredients for Latinos and African Americans before moving on to how their placements on this construct affected both groups' 2008 voting behavior. The results suggest that symbolic racism has similar origins in antiblack affect and conservative values for whites and Latinos but that high resentment scores primarily measure weak feelings of racial solidarity among African Americans.

Sources of Evidence

Cross-Sectional Time-Series Surveys

Much of the power in our analyses resides in our ability to test the effects of racial resentment in these vote choice models with two different survey designs. One of the designs is called a *cross-sectional time series*. A cross-sectional time-series design interviews *different* survey respondents over a prolonged period of time (in our case, over several election years). This design allows us to make much stronger causal inferences than we could if we relied only on a single cross-sectional survey, such as data from only one election year (Kenski 2006). Take, for example, the book's central claim that the 2008 campaign evoked racial predispositions more strongly, both pro-Obama and anti-Obama, than any other election in recent history. The only way to reach this conclusion is to compare the effects of racial attitudes in 2008 to those in previous election years. Our utilization of cross-sectional time-series survey data allow us to do just that.

The cross-sectional time-series data in this study come from the American National Election Studies (ANES), which has been carried out by the Center for Political Studies of the University of Michigan's Institute for Social Research going back to 1948. Ever since then, the ANES has interviewed carefully drawn probability samples of Americans before and/or after every presidential and midterm election except 2006. The ANES has unusually high quality control standards and response rates. Aside from these desirable properties, they have regularly assessed respondents' levels of racial resentment since 1986. That continuous assessment allows us to compare the effects of racial resentment on public opinion and voting behavior in 2008 with previous election years.

Election Year Panel Surveys

Cross-sectional time-series designs, however, are also limited by interviewing different samples of people in each repeated survey. In contrast, a *panel study* interviews the same respondents two or more times. The panel design has a number of virtues (see Bartels 2006a and Kenski and Romer 2006 for detailed discussions). Most important for our purposes, it allows us to make much stronger claims about changes in the effects of factors like racial attitudes over the course of the 2008 campaign. One cannot be nearly as assertive about the changing impact of variables in cross-sectional surveys taken at two different times during the campaign because of reciprocal causality concerns.

A brief example from chapter 3 clearly illustrates this point. One of the chapter's key findings is that John McCain's lead over Barack Obama in late March 2008 turned into a sizable deficit on the eve of the general election, in part because Obama succeeded in making the unpopular incumbent President Bush a more important determinant of individual vote choice. We could not be very confident in this conclusion by just comparing the impact of Bush approval ratings on vote intention in cross-sectional surveys on different samples of respondents interviewed in late March and in late October 2008. We would not know from that design whether opinions about Bush caused vote choice, or if vote choice caused people to change their opinions of the president in an effort to rationalize their votes. Americans, in fact, often change their issue positions and candidate evaluations to rationalize their vote decisions (Lenz 2009; Rahn, Krosnick, and Breuning 1994; Sears and Lau 1983). The panel design, however, allows us to test the effects of Bush's approval ratings, as measured in March 2008, on the same individuals' vote intentions measured later on, in October. In fact, Bush's March approval ratings had a much larger impact on McCain-Obama vote intention in late October than they did in late March. So we can confidently conclude that the *influence* of Bush evaluations on vote choice increased over time. Only a panel design can provide that level of certainty.

Our election-year panel data come from the common content module of the Cooperative Campaign Analysis Project (CCAP) 2007–2008 six-wave panel study of registered voters.[16] The CCAP's panel surveys were conducted by YouGov Polimetrix in December (2007), January, March, September, October, and immediately after the election in November.[17] A total of 18,250 individuals were interviewed in the study, 7,025 of whom completed all six surveys. This large sample size makes our CCAP estimates more reliable than the ANES surveys, which are typically carried out on about 2,000 respondents.[18]

Like other Polimetrix surveys, the CCAP utilizes a matching algorithm to produce an Internet sample closely approximating the demographic makeup of the high-quality random sample carried out by the U.S. Census Bureau in the American Community Study (Rivers 2006; Vavreck and Rivers 2008; also see the appendix for more information about their sampling methodology). Previous Polimetrix surveys have performed well in determining public opinion and vote choice (Vavreck and Rivers 2008). Early analyses of the CCAP reveal that its demographic composition closely resembles that of registered voters in the general population (Jackman and Vavreck 2009). Our results are also weighted to general population demographic characteristics to aid comparability between different sampling techniques.[19] Most importantly, however, we repeat our CCAP results whenever possible with findings from the ANES. In fact, all of our data analytical chapters on the campaign include results from both surveys. The central effects of racial resentment turned out to be comparable. So, replicating the results in two different surveys is quite reassuring.[20]

In sum, augmenting cross-sectional time-series data with an election-year panel study allows us to compare the effects of racial attitudes in 2008 to previous election years *and* confidently discern how these effects changed throughout the course of the campaign. Our ANES and CCAP findings are also supplemented with data from several other surveys throughout the book. That data will be described in greater detail upon presentation. Our main conclusions, however, are primarily derived from leveraging the respective cross-sectional time-series and election-year panel designs of the ANES and the CCAP.

2

Racialized Momentum

The Two Sides of Racialization in the Primaries

> I think early on it may spark some curiosity or a sense of novelty, but I think very
> quickly people will be judging me on the merits. Do I have a message that resonates
> with people's concerns about health care and education, jobs and terrorism? And if
> they do, then I think race won't be a major factor.

BARACK OBAMA, campaign speech, Iowa Falls, Iowa, February 11, 2007[1]

Barack Obama seemed to be succeeding in getting voters to judge him on factors besides his race. As touched upon in the introduction, the campaign atmosphere was remarkably race neutral throughout 2007. Prior to the first presidential primary contests of 2008, the media had predominantly portrayed Obama as the post-racial candidate who transcended the divisive identity politics of the post–civil rights era. It was perhaps inevitable, though, in a country with such a long history of pernicious race relations, that Obama's racial background would not remain dormant forever.

Race, in fact, immediately crept into the discussion after the nation's first presidential primary. Only one month earlier, Hillary Clinton had been leading him by roughly 20 points in polling averages from New Hampshire, but then came his stunning victories in the Iowa caucuses. Barack Obama appeared to be unstoppable after that. Indeed he pulled ahead of her in virtually every New Hampshire poll right after his big victory in Iowa. Final polling averages from New Hampshire showed him with an apparently unassailable 38 to 30 lead over Clinton.[2] But, of course, he *lost* the state to Hillary Clinton by 2.6 points. How could that have happened?

There were several explanations posited for the gap between the New Hampshire polls and the actual vote. These variously focused on the usual difficulties in primary polling, especially in states like New Hampshire where Independents can vote, including flaws in the models pollsters used to estimate likely voters and possible movement toward Clinton among undecided women on election day in response to perceived sexist treatment toward her candidacy following the Iowa caucus.

But the one explanation on everyone's mind was that Obama underper-

formed the polls because of his race. As a result of such widespread speculation, the so-called Bradley Effect immediately became part of the popular
political vernacular. This term describes the phenomenon whereby black
candidates in the 1980s and 1990s—most notably Tom Bradley, Douglas
Wilder, and David Dinkins—often performed significantly worse at the ballot box than they had in their preelection poll numbers. The gap is thought
to result from white voters telling pollsters, especially African American
interviewers (Finkel, Guterbock, and Borg 1991), that they are willing to
vote for black candidates but then voting their racial prejudices behind the
curtain. When Barack Obama lost the Granite State in spite of his large
leads in all the polls, political commentators assumed this process had once
again reared its ugly head. In retrospect, the empirical evidence showed that
Obama did not systematically underperform his statewide poll numbers
during the primaries (Hopkins 2009) and that the Bradley Effect was not
responsible for the polling disparities in New Hampshire (AAPOR 2009).
Nevertheless, the prevalent perception at the time was that race had shown
its first signs of affecting the outcome.

Race would soon become even more salient in the primary campaign.
The demographic composition of the electorate in the second official Democratic primary state, South Carolina, virtually assured its larger role.[3] African Americans comprised over half of the primary voters in this Democratic
contest. With Obama's poll numbers rapidly improving among African
Americans,[4] there was almost no chance of him losing the state. It was,
therefore, suspected that the Clintons stepped up their racial rhetoric in an
effort to diminish the significance of an African American candidate winning the majority black electorate primary. Hillary Clinton, for instance,
compared Obama to Martin Luther King and herself to Lyndon Johnson,
saying, "Dr. King's dream began to be realized when President Lyndon Johnson passed the Civil Rights Act of 1964, . . . but it took a president to get it
done."[5] Many, including Senator Edward Kennedy, thought that this statement was intended to increase the salience of Obama's race (Balz and Johnson 2009). Bill Clinton's South Carolina racial comparison was much more
transparent. The former president responded to a question about why it took
two Clintons to try to beat Obama in South Carolina by saying, "Jesse Jackson won South Carolina twice, in '84 and '88. He ran a good campaign. And
Senator Obama ran a good campaign here." There was little doubt following
these comments that the Clintons were trying to diminish any momentum
garnered from their opponent's South Carolina victory by playing up black
candidates' historically strong support from fellow African Americans.[6]

Race was "a-burning" in South Carolina, as Teddy Kennedy told Bill
Clinton in an angry phone call while the former president campaigned for
his wife in the state (quoted in Balz and Johnson 2009, 175). But Obama
was not getting burned. He beat Clinton by 28 points in South Carolina
and performed better than expected among the state's white voters.[7] Much
more importantly, Balz and Johnson (2009, 173) report that Kennedy's decision to endorse Obama after that primary occurred in large part because
he "worried that the Clintons were trying to turn Obama into the black
candidate—the Jesse Jackson of 2008." Kennedy's endorsement neutralized
this possibility by lending instant post-racial credibility to Obama's candidacy. The senior senator from Massachusetts was reportedly drawn to his
much more junior colleague because he thought Obama had the potential
to transcend race and become a unifying influence in American politics.
By publicly passing the Democratic leadership torch from his family to the
Obamas, Kennedy was essentially conveying this belief in his endorsed candidate's racial transcendence to the entire country.[8]

The much-publicized endorsements by Ted and Caroline Kennedy (John
F. Kennedy's daughter) after South Carolina, along with Obama's big win in
that state, helped him draw even with Clinton in both popular vote tallies
and elected delegates amassed from the twenty-three states holding primaries or caucuses on February 5, 2008. Hillary Clinton had always expected
to have the nomination locked up after these Super Tuesday contests.[9] The
fact that Obama essentially pulled off a tie was itself a major victory. Even
better for his campaign's prospects, the states holding primaries and caucuses through the remainder of February had demographics that favored
his candidacy.[10] He capitalized on this happenstance scheduling by racking
up eleven straight victories after Super Tuesday. During that run of primary
wins in mid to late February, Obama began leading Clinton in national polls
for the first time. More important perhaps, he had opened up an expansive lead over her in *elected* delegates. In only three months time, he had
increased his support in national polls by 25 points and was looking more
and more like the inevitable nominee. Barack Obama was also looking more
post-racial than ever. *U.S. News and World Report* even printed a story during
this run of good luck titled, "Does Obama's Winning Streak Prove that Race
Does Not Matter?"[11]

His fortuitous February, though, quickly gave way to both the most race-
centered and probably the most politically damaging month of 2008 for
Barack Obama. Ten days after Obama's winning streak was broken in the
March 3 Ohio and Texas primaries, ABC News aired sensational videos of

Obama's longtime pastor, Jeremiah Wright. Among these Reverend Wright clips, which seemed to run on endless cable news loops in the forthcoming days, were: "The government gives [African Americans] the drugs, builds bigger prisons, passes a three-strike law, and then wants us to sing 'God Bless America'? No. No. No. Not 'God Bless America,' 'God damn America,'"[12] and "Barack knows what it means to be a black man living in a country and a culture that is controlled by rich, white people. Hillary ain't never been called a nigger."[13]

Obama's twenty-year association with Wright as a member of his Trinity United Church of Christ immediately threatened his carefully crafted post-racial image. The Obama candidacy, after all, had been situated as the antidote to the same identity politics that Wright preached. Moreover, his link to Wright played into the prevalent stereotypes about black political radicalism that have often been hindrances to African Americans seeking elected office in the past (Hajnal 2007; Sigelman et al. 1995).

Obama began drafting a speech about American race relations to counter the potential damage done to his race-neutral appeal by the media's continual coverage of Wright's controversial racial comments. He had contemplated giving a lengthy speech about race for quite some time but had been dissuaded by his staffers who thought such a statement would hurt his "post-racial brand" (Heilemann and Halperin 2010, 236). It was clear to everyone, though, that the controversy surrounding Obama and Wright simply could not go unanswered.

Obama answered Wright in his March 18 speech on race relations by condemning him in unequivocal terms. He stated on that day in Philadelphia:

> Did I strongly disagree with many of his political views? Absolutely—just as I'm sure many of you have heard remarks from your pastors, priests, or rabbis with which you strongly disagreed. But the remarks that have caused this recent firestorm weren't simply controversial. They weren't simply a religious leader's effort to speak out against perceived injustice. Instead, they expressed a profoundly distorted view of this country—a view that sees white racism as endemic, and that elevates what is wrong with America above all that we know is right with America . . . As such, Reverend Wright's comments were not only wrong but divisive, divisive at a time when we need unity; racially charged at a time when we need to come together to solve a set of monumental problems.

Obama, however, refused to completely distance himself from Wright, stating, "I can no more disown him than I can my white grandmother . . .

who once confessed her fear of black men who passed by her on the street, and who on more than one occasion has uttered racial or ethnic stereotypes that made me cringe." This was the familiar racial formula that served Obama so well in the past. He presented himself as a racially unifying figure while still trying to understand, rather than just gloss over, the underlying resentments that Americans on both sides of the color line have toward one another. More importantly, the speech seemed to serve its purpose of dampening the Reverend Wright issue. It also established Barack Obama as perhaps the one figure in American public life who could present a candid portrait of the nation's race relations in a way that would not be dismissed outright by either side of the polarizing racial divide.

Obama might not have been able to recover if the Wright story had broken in January. By mid-March, though, he had already pulled ahead of Clinton in the national polls and established an insurmountable lead in elected delegate tallies. With the vast majority of Americans casting their primary ballots before they had any idea who Reverend Wight was, much of the issue's ability to influence votes was simply attenuated by timing. Nevertheless, race had still taken center stage in a campaign in which Obama did everything in his power to prevent it from becoming a major issue. He would later say that it was naïve to think that issues of race would not come up in his historic quest to become the first African American president (Ifill 2009, 61). The Reverend Wright controversy of March 2008 definitely proved this point.

Expectations about the Impact of Racial Attitudes

Long before the first primary votes were cast, there was no shortage of evidence available to support theoretical expectations that racial predispositions either would, or would *not*, be a significant factor in determining whether Obama became his party's nominee for president. Several dynamic characteristics thought to defuse racialized voting patterns, for instance, appeared to be present in the pre-Iowa caucus electoral climate. Previous studies suggest that black candidates fare better among white voters when African Americans are clearly in the minority of the electorate and when these candidates offer assurances that they will not favor blacks over whites (Hacker 1995; Hajnal 2007). With African Americans an unmistakable minority of Democratic primary voters, and Obama's campaign messages of hope and change universal ones open to all races and ethnicities, it was possible that the impact of racial attitudes in the campaign would be negli-

gible. Citrin et al. (1990) concluded that a similar concerted effort by Tom
Bradley to appear racially impartial in the 1982 California gubernatorial
contest mitigated the impact of racial attitudes in voting behavior. It could
be, therefore, that in the more race-neutral informational atmosphere prior
to the start of the primaries, Obama's biracial lineage was not much of a factor in how he was evaluated by the American public.

On the other hand, there were also multiple reasons to believe that racial
attitudes might adversely affect his chances of winning the nomination. The
earliest research on symbolic racism showed that such antiblack attitudes
were perhaps the most important determinant of opposition to Tom Bradley
in Los Angeles's 1969 and 1973 mayoral elections, in spite of his race-neutral
rhetoric and law enforcement background (Sears and Kinder 1971; Kinder
and Sears 1981). Later research further suggests that Obama's efforts to dera-
cialize his campaign message could have been futile. Moskowitz and Stoh's
(1994) experimental findings, for example, show that voters effectively "alter
reality" in order to render a black candidate's message consistent with prior
expectations and racial beliefs. Similarly disconcerting to Obama backers
should have been Hajnal's (2007) thesis that the role of racial attitudes on
white Americans' votes may diminish only after black incumbents establish
records in office that show they will not favor African Americans over whites.
Obama's meager three years of senatorial experience, therefore, might have
left some primary voters unconvinced about his intentions. Finally, Citrin
et al. (1990) note the greater impact of racial attitudes in the 1982 nonpartisan
biracial contest for California superintendent of schools than in the state's
aforementioned biracial gubernatorial election, surmising that the lack of
a partisan anchor likely allowed racial attitudes to play a larger role. The
nature of presidential primaries meant that Democrats apprehensive about
electing an African American to the highest office in the land did not have
to cross party lines to cast such a vote. That factor could have easily opened
the door to racial attitudes' serving as a significant determinant of voting in
the 2008 primary. So there were conflicting expectations from the extant
literature about whether racial attitudes would affect primary vote choice.

But it was also possible that the effects of racial conservatism would be
enhanced or diminished during the primary season. That period, after all,
saw Obama's vote share rise by 25 points in national polls from December
2007 to April 2008. Given past research on the detrimental effects race has
on white support for black candidates, Obama's momentum during this time
period may have been produced by his deactivating antiblack feelings. That

is, Obama's momentum in the early months of 2008 could have been driven by racial conservatives growing more supportive of him as they acquired new information about his candidacy.

This same time period, however, also saw Reverend Wright almost single-handedly make race a much more salient feature of the campaign. Several studies demonstrate that when campaign communications carry such racial messages, racial predispositions can be brought more heavily to bear on individuals' political decision making via a psychological mechanism known as *priming* (Kinder and Sanders 1996; Mendelberg 2001; Valentino, Hutchings, and White 2002). One might expect from this line of research that racial resentment should have become an increasingly important determinant of opposition to Obama as the campaign proceeded through the primary season.

Our main argument, however, is that racial predispositions were already highly accessible in Americans' evaluations of Obama even in the pre-Iowa days when he was largely portrayed as the post-racial candidate who transcended identity politics. Obama's position as the first African American with a realistic chance of winning the White House was sure to evoke profound racial hopes and fears alike before the first votes were ever cast. When such a strong associative link already exists between racial attitudes and perceptions of the candidate, racial predispositions should be spontaneously activated even in the absence of situational cues like race-oriented campaign communications (Sears 1993). Racial predispositions, therefore, would likely have been brought to bear on assessments of Obama regardless of how hard he tried to neutralize them.

By this accessibility account, the impact of racial resentment on presidential vote choice in 2008 should also have been less dependent on campaign contexts than it was in the natural experiment described by Kinder and Sanders (1996) and Mendelberg (2001) concerning Republicans' treatment of race in the 1988 general election, or the conventional experiment conducted by Valentino, Hutchings, and White (2002) concerning the 2000 campaign. These three studies focused on all-white presidential contests in which race was not immediately accessible without campaign-induced (1988) or experimentally assigned (2000) racial cues. However in 2008, it was simply impossible to miss the racial significance of Obama becoming the first black president. That is, the natural association between racial attitudes and Barack Obama's candidacy should make it difficult to either deactivate or prime these racial predispositions.

Early Evidence of the Two Sides of Racialization in
Evaluations of Barack Obama

To test this hypothesis that racial predispositions were implicated in evaluations of Barack Obama even back in 2007 when his post-racial image was
still untarnished, figure 2.1 displays the effects of racial resentment on favorability ratings from the December 2007 CCAP for Obama and his two
main Democratic rivals, Hillary Clinton and John Edwards. We would argue
that one of these competitors, John Edwards, was also an unusually racialized candidate at the time, even though white. His most salient issue during
the previous four years in the national spotlight was poverty—an issue that
typically evokes strong racial predispositions (Gilens 1999).

Nevertheless, figure 2.1 shows that racial resentment still had a much
larger impact on the national electorate's evaluations of Barack Obama before the primaries than it did on those of either Edwards or Clinton. Even
with partisan, ideological, and demographic controls in place, moving from
least to most resentful decreased Obama's predicted favorability rating by
40 percent of the scale's range. This substantial effect of racial resentment
was nearly twice as large as its surprisingly sizable effect on Edwards's evaluations and more than four times greater than its negative effect on Clinton's
favorability ratings.

The large impact of racial resentment on the supposedly post-racial candidate's favorability ratings back in December 2007 is not the only noteworthy pattern seen in figure 2.1. As indicated in the previous chapter, the average American falls on the racially resentful side of the Kinder and Sanders
scale. Because the distribution of racial predispositions is skewed to the conservative side, a greater impact of racial resentment should usually diminish
support for racially liberal candidates and policies. Obama, however, actually had a higher mean favorability rating than either Clinton or Edwards in
the December 2007 CCAP in spite of racial resentment's bigger effect on his
evaluations.[14]

Figure 2.1 shows that Obama managed to overcome these large resentment effects by generating tremendous support among the least racially resentful. Indeed, while he was slightly less popular than Edwards and Clinton
among the most resentful, this deficit was offset by markedly outperform-
ing them on the liberal side of the spectrum. It is also important to note
that Obama's greater popularity among racial liberals in December 2007
was not simply an artifact of including African Americans in our statistical

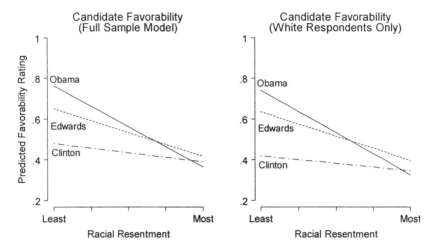

Figure 2.1. Democratic candidates' favorability ratings in December 2007 as a function of racial resentment (0=very unfavorable, 1=very favorable). Favorability ratings were based on the OLS coefficients in table A3.1 of the online appendix (http://www.press.uchicago.edu/books/tesler/). Predicted values were calculated by setting our base-model variables to their sample means. *Source*: December 2007 CCAP.

analysis—a group more likely to be both racially liberal and supportive of Barack Obama. The second panel in figure 2.1 shows, all else being equal, that white racial liberals also evaluated Obama more favorably than his two main Democratic rivals.

As mentioned in the introduction, we refer to this racially liberal *support* for Obama as the "second" or "other" side of racialization because most past research has focused primarily on racially resentful *opposition* to black candidates and race-targeted policies. Figure 2.1 clearly shows that Obama activated both sides of the symbolic racism spectrum in December 2007—meaning he drew worse evaluations from racial conservatives than his fellow, and ideologically similar, Democrats and better evaluations than Edwards and Clinton from the racial liberals. Obama continued to generate opposition from racial conservatives throughout the election year. But he drew even greater support from racial liberals. That powerful performance on the liberal side of the racial resentment scale is one of the keys to understanding how Obama won the White House despite the seemingly unfavorable twin circumstances of race being unusually salient in 2008 and the majority of Americans falling on the conservative side of the racial resentment scale.

Racialized Momentum: The Two Sides of
Racialization in Primary Vote Choice

It was one thing for Obama to activate the racially liberal side of the resentment spectrum in favorability ratings from the entire electorate, but generating parallel support from the least resentful in Democratic primary vote
choice should have been a much more difficult task. Racially liberal predispositions, for instance, were probably accessible in evaluations of Obama
back in December 2007 because his candidacy engendered great hopes for
racial equality. Yet, factors known to affect primary vote choice, like the
widespread perception before the primaries that Clinton would ultimately
win the nomination, could have prevented racial liberals from casting their
lot with him at the ballot booth (Bartels 1988; Abramowitz 1989). We might
expect, then, that Obama's momentum was produced by activating the la-
tent support among racial liberals that was clearly evident in his December
2007 favorability ratings.

Fortunately, the CCAP's panel design makes it possible to examine the relationship between racial resentment and primary vote choice in December
2007, as well as in late January and late March 2008. Testing these effects
at three separate time periods is beneficial. It allows us to assess whether
our March results were heavily influenced by the enhanced salience of race
created by that month's controversy surrounding the comments of Reverend
Wright. Was he needed to activate racial resentment in primary vote choice?
Or, consistent with our main hypothesis, were racial predispositions a major
factor even in the pre-Iowa days when Obama presented himself as the post-
racial candidate, because a large role of race was inevitable from the onset?

The monthly logistic regression coefficients displayed in the first three
columns of table 2.1 show that the effect of racial resentment increased in
each successive month. This increase appears at first glance to be highly
consistent with both the previously mentioned racial priming literature, as
well as research showing that black candidates' racial backgrounds become
increasingly salient when race is discussed more in the campaign (Reeves
1997). Despite these enhanced effects across time, though, racial resentment
was still by far the most important determinant of primary vote preference
even in the more racially neutral days leading up to the primaries. All else
being equal, moving across the resentment spectrum from least to most
resentful decreased Obama's vote share against the field of Democrats in
December by 25 percentage points and diminished his share of the Clinton-
Obama vote by almost 50 points.

Table 2.1. Predictors of support for Obama against the field of Democrats and against Hillary Clinton (logistic regression)

	Obama vs. the field of Democrats (1=Obama, 0=other Dem)			Obama and Clinton voters only (1=Obama, 0=Clinton)		
	December	January	March	December	January	March
Racial Resentment	−1.25	−1.69	−2.20	−2.16	−2.36	−2.44
	(.210)	(.186)	(.183)	(.251)	(.218)	(.201)
Partisanship	1.14	1.26	1.07	2.26	2.25	1.72
	(.269)	(.221)	(.206)	(.370)	(.299)	(.224)
Ideology	.369	.301	−.178	.064	−.041	−.437
	(.244)	(.219)	(.209)	(.296)	(.259)	(.233)
Education	.558	.477	.395	.732	.581	.458
	(.212)	(.189)	(.169)	(.249)	(.218)	(.184)
Age	−.023	−.022	−.018	−.019	−.018	−.018
	(.004)	(.003)	(.003)	(.004)	(.004)	(.003)
Black	1.34	1.24	1.25	.851	.862	1.29
	(.152)	(.147)	(.167)	(.176)	(.170)	(.185)
Male	.138	.315	.341	.459	.533	.429
	(.100)	(.091)	(.086)	(.117)	(.104)	(.092)
South	−.110	−.126	−.219	−.069	−.111	−.209
	(.111)	(.098)	(.090)	(.124)	(.112)	(.097)
Observations	3,836	4,172	4,333	2,631	3,108	3,883

Source: CCAP panelists who completed the December 2007 and January and March 2008 surveys.

Note: March measures of racial resentment, partisanship, and ideology were used in the analysis.

Moreover, just looking at coefficients and changes in probabilities across the scale obscures much of the story. Theories of racial priming have most commonly been used to explain how racially charged messages help whites bring their racial predispositions in line with candidate vote choice (Mendelberg 2001; Valentino, Hutchings, and White 2002). One might expect from this literature that racial conservatives would be less likely to support Obama in March than in the preceding primary months when race was not as big a factor in the campaign rhetoric. To test this conjecture, figure 2.2 graphs the resentment coefficients in the first three columns of table 2.1, while holding the other variables in the model constant. As can be seen, however, our vote choice model shows that racial conservatives were actually slightly *more* likely to support Obama in March 2008 than they had been earlier, despite Reverend Wright's intrusion into the campaign.

The enhanced effect of racial resentment in late March came almost entirely from the liberal end of the dimension, rather than from growing opposition among the racially resentful. All else being equal, the most racially liberal respondents in March were nearly 40 points more likely to support Obama than they had been in December. These results strongly suggest that racial liberals were quick to jump on the Obama bandwagon after he won Iowa and established himself as an attractive and viable alternative to

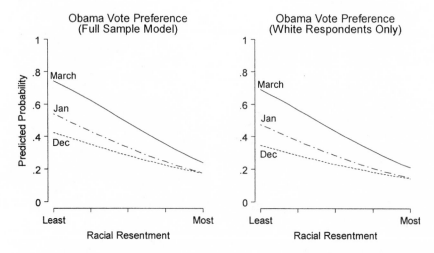

Figure 2.2. Obama vote preference against the field of Democrats as a function of racial resentment (1=Obama, 0=other Democratic candidate). Probabilities for the full-sample model were based on the logistic regression coefficients in table 2.1. Predicted probabilities were calculated by setting all other variables to the mean respondent in each separate analysis. See chapter 5 for the results by race and ethnicity. *Source*: December 2007 and January and March 2008 CCAP panelists.

Clinton—a trend that started and continued well before Reverend Wright became an issue.

This surge in support among racial liberals was by no means confined to African Americans who had been skeptical about Obama's prospects of winning before Iowa. While we defer our main treatment of racialized voting patterns by race and ethnicity to chapter 5, we need to establish early on that this enhanced support from racial liberals was not simply an artifact of including African Americans in our vote model. So the second panel of figure 2.2 shows that Obama's predicted vote share from *white* racial liberals roughly doubled from December 2007 to March 2008. Indeed, Obama's proportion of the most racially liberal white vote, as predicted by our vote choice model, increased from 35 percent in December 2007 to 70 percent in March 2008. Chapter 5 goes on to further show that Obama's growing support from the least resentful during the primary season was almost entirely produced by *white* racial liberals.

That increased monthly support from racial liberals (especially white racial liberals)—or what we describe as *racialized momentum*—is consistent with Bartels's (1988) political activation account of primaries, whereby citizens bring their predispositions more heavily to bear on candidate evaluations as they acquire more information about them. The racially resentful, however, were already strongly opposed to Obama before the primaries and thus did not need additional information or Reverend Wright to activate race-based opposition to his candidacy. The upshot of the racially resentful continuing to oppose Obama in March at nearly the same high rate they had back in December was that the well-documented wave of momentum that carried Obama all the way to the nominating convention in Denver was actually driven by an *increased* impact of racial attitudes. This enhanced effect was almost entirely brought about by Candidate Obama's activation of racially liberal support for his nomination bid.

The Obama vs. Clinton columns in table 2.1, and their graphical portrayal in figure 2.3, also help shed light on why the impact of racial resentment increased during the course of the primaries. The effect of racial resentment was considerably stronger among those choosing Clinton or Obama in December 2007 and January 2008 than when Obama opposed the entire field of Democratic candidates. Battle lines were thus clearly drawn between racial liberals and racial conservatives in their respective choices of Obama and Clinton before the primaries began. Among those selecting one of the two Democratic frontrunners as their top choice in December, nearly

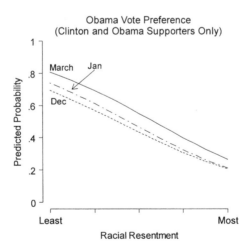

Figure 2.3. Barack Obama vote preference against Hillary Clinton as a function of racial resentment (1=Obama, 0=Clinton). Predicted probabilities were based on the logistic regression coefficients in table 2.1. Predicted probabilities were calculated by setting all other variables to the mean respondent in each separate analysis. *Source*: December 2007 and January and March 2008 CCAP panelists.

70 percent of the most racially liberal Democrats were predicted to prefer Obama, with 80 percent of the most resentful choosing Clinton.

The increased effect of racial resentment on primary vote choice from December to March might seem at first glance to reflect a growing salience of race in the campaign. But on closer examination, it was more likely a product of both Obama activating racially liberal Democrats after presenting himself as an attractive and viable alternative to Hillary Clinton and the nominating process being condensed down to the two candidates that racially liberal and conservative primary voters were most strongly behind from the beginning. In fact, the effects of racial resentment in January (pre–Reverend Wright) and in March (post–Reverend Wright) among just Clinton and Obama supporters were nearly identical.

The March CCAP's vote choice variable was phrased in the past tense for most respondents, asking them who they *voted* for in the primaries. As such, it is not ideal for assessing priming effects. After all, the vast majority of Democrats had already cast their votes before they knew who Reverend Wright was. Priming effects will be revisited in the next chapter with variables much better suited to determine how differing racialized contexts affected the impact of racial resentment throughout the election year. The important point to note for now, though, is that neither Reverend Wright in particular nor race-based campaign rhetoric in general was needed to make Americans *vote* their racial predispositions. The power of racial attitudes in a Clinton-Obama showdown was foreordained at the campaign's onset.

Explaining the Two Sides of Racialization in the Primaries

The question then turns to why race was predestined to be a factor from the beginning. The introduction alluded to pre-Iowa dynamics that had the potential of negating racialized voting patterns. Recall that it was widely believed during that stage of the campaign that Obama transcended race. Moreover, racially conservative Democrats tend to be more conservative on gender issues and they repeatedly rated Senator Clinton less favorably in the fifteen years prior to the 2008 primary than did their more racially liberal counterparts. Yet, even with these mitigating circumstances present and with controls for other predispositions and demographics in place, a large disparity existed between racial liberals and racial conservatives in their relative levels of support for Barack Obama and Hillary Clinton before the first vote was cast.

The Racially Resentful Side

Explaining why Obama was predicted to receive only about 20 percent of the most racially resentful Clinton-Obama vote share in December, all other things being equal, is rather straightforward. Previous research on symbolic racism and racial resentment leaves us well equipped to understand the motives behind racially conservative opposition to a black candidate. Symbolic racism researchers have always held that the questions used in the racial resentment battery are tapping into antiblack attitudes. A black presidential nominee should, therefore, present the quintessential opportunity for it to influence the vote. Moreover, a campaign in which there were no major substantive differences between the black and white candidates provided the perfect breeding ground for racial resentment to become the most important determinant of opposition to the African American's candidacy.

Consistent with that view, table 2.1 shows that nonracial ideology had little independent impact on primary vote choice. The more expansive models employed in table 2.2 also reveal that a wide array of issue preferences neither strongly predicted primary voting behavior nor diminished the large effect of racial resentment yielded in our base model. The minor role of issues is mostly expected given the fact that Clinton and Obama had virtually identical voting records ideologically in the U.S. Senate (Carroll et al. 2008).

Yet Obama often contrasted his staunch opposition to the Iraq War before he became a U.S. senator with Senator Clinton's 2002 vote for war authorization as a primary rationale for his candidacy. We, therefore, worried that the null relationship between respondents' Iraq positions and their primary vote choice in the March CCAP stemmed from an inability of the survey's question about when to withdraw troops from Iraq to capture the full variation in voters' opinions of the war. Fortunately, though, a sizable Gallup Poll (N = 2,021) from February 2008 included five items about Iraq—three retrospective evaluations and two prospective positions—that created a highly reliable Iraq War support scale (α = .81).[15] Even without a measure of racial resentment in this survey, the final column of table 2.2 failed to produce a statistically significant or substantively important effect of war support on vote preference in the Democratic primary. It is apparent from table 2.2 that ideological predispositions and nonracial issue positions were *not* the central cleavages in the 2008 Democratic primaries.

With ideology and issues largely neutralized, the racially resentful were free to express their attitudes toward African Americans in oppos-

Table 2.2. Predictors of primary support for Obama against the field of Democrats (logistic regression)

	Model 1	Model 2	Model 3	Model 4	Model 5	Model 6	Gallup Feb '08
Racial Resentment	−2.31	−2.30	−2.27	−2.25	−2.30	−2.30	
	(.160)	(.169)	(.168)	(.168)	(.168)	(.164)	
Partisanship	1.24	1.10	1.19	1.25	1.11	1.22	2.76
	(.179)	(.191)	(.186)	(.181)	(.198)	(.186)	(.695)
Ideology	−.124	−.233	−.130	−.060	−.190	−.099	−.780
	(.183)	(.187)	(.199)	(.186)	(.194)	(.185)	(.373)
Education	.333	.276	.300	.286	.298	.314	1.45
	(.159)	(.155)	(.157)	(.153)	(.157)	(.153)	(.271)
Age	−.018	−.019	−.018	−.018	−.021	−.019	−.025
	(.003)	(.003)	(.003)	(.003)	(.003)	(.003)	(.005)
Black	1.31	1.23	1.25	1.29	1.35	1.35	2.46
	(.138)	(.140)	(.151)	(.139)	(.152)	(.141)	(.273)
Male	.368	.383	.378	.370	.399	.363	.592
	(.075)	(.076)	(.077)	(.075)	(.077)	(.076)	(.159)
South	−.285	−.303	−.300	−.277	−.319	−.290	−.636
	(.078)	(.081)	(.081)	(.079)	(.081)	(.080)	(.173)
Economic Issues		.237					
		(.155)					
Moral Issues			−.070				
			(.146)				
Immigration				−.200			
				(.089)			
Environment					−.007		
					(.148)		
Iraq Withdrawal						−.044	
						(.118)	
Iraq Support Scale							−.275
							(.376)
Observations	5,736	5,201	5,292	5,640	5,278	5,572	838

Source: March 2008 CCAP (Columns 1–6); Feb 21–24, 2008, USA Today/Gallup Poll (Column 7).

Note: Dependent variables are coded 1 for Obama vote preference and 0 for any other Democrat. All issue positions are coded 0–1, with 1 being the most conservative response. Partisanship is a 5-category variable in the Gallup survey and the standard 7-category variable in the CCAP.

ing Obama's candidacy. From the traditional symbolic racism standpoint, these racial conservatives were voting *against* Obama, not voting *for* Hillary Clinton. Senator Clinton emerged as the top choice of racially resentful Democrats from the beginning because she was the candidate most capable of beating their least favored option. This conclusion will be strongly supported by results to be presented later on revealing that racially resentful Democrats reversed their pre-2008 unfavorable evaluations of Hillary Clinton during the primaries, and that a large proportion of racially conservative Clinton voters defected to John McCain in the general election.

The Racially Sympathetic Side

With little said in the past about the racially liberal side of the racial resentment scale, more work is required in explaining why 70 percent of the least
resentful Clinton-Obama voters were predicted by our vote model to support Obama way back in December 2007, with this percentage jumping up
to over 80 percent by late March 2008. It is first necessary to provide a brief
interpretation of what low resentment scores mean. Kinder and Sanders
(1996) assert that the questions in their resentment scale "distinguish between those whites who are generally sympathetic toward blacks and those
who are generally unsympathetic" (106). They used the term "racially sympathetic" when describing results on what we have referred to as the liberal
side of the resentment spectrum. Indeed, it would certainly seem plausible
to interpret beliefs that blacks have gotten less than they deserve, and that
racial inequality results from discrimination, as being generally sympathetic
toward African Americans.

Moreover, the evidence suggests that there is an affective element along
the lines of this "general sympathy" underlying both high and low resentment scores. The quarter of Americans scoring below the .50 midpoint on
the resentment scale in the ANES, for instance, were more than three times
more likely to say they "very often" felt feelings of "sympathy" or "admiration" toward African Americans than were the two-thirds who scored on the
conservative side of the spectrum.[16] It is also important to note that this relationship holds after controlling for nonracial ideology. Racial resentment,
in fact, is still strongly related to feelings of racial sympathy and admiration in multivariate analyses, while partisan and ideological self-placements
have quite modest effects on such attitudes. We are, therefore, confident
in building on Kinder and Sanders's assertion that individuals scoring low
on racial resentment are generally sympathetic—have a positive affective
orientation—toward African Americans.

Along with this interpretation of the left-hand side of the resentment
continuum, the closest historical comparison to Obama's 2008 primary
campaign—Jesse Jackson's 1988 nomination bid—provides an illuminating
contrast to Obama's strong support among racial liberals. The data relating
Jackson vote choice to racial resentment are not ideal, in that both measures
were collected months after the primaries during the ANES fall general
election survey. So for comparability purposes, the fall 2008 ANES retrospective assessment of primary vote choice is used here to compare patterns

of primary support for Jackson and Obama. The levels of support reported for Jackson and Obama in these surveys are quite similar to their actual vote totals, even though the surveys were conducted well after the primary season ended. The 31 percent of ANES respondents who reported voting for Jackson in the primary, for instance, was indistinguishable from his actual vote share of 29 percent; Obama's primary vote share in 2008 was also almost identical to his support in the ANES (48 and 49 percent, respectively). These similarities reassure us about the validity of survey estimates. Equally reassuring is that using the ANES measure of 2008 primary vote choice produces almost the same resentment effects as those yielded from the March CCAP, as shown by comparing figures 2.2 and 2.4.[17]

Figure 2.4 graphs the impact of racial resentment on primary vote choice for Jackson in 1988 and Obama in 2008, while holding the other variables in the model constant. The display reveals that while the effect of racial resentment on vote choice may be similarly sized for both candidates, the pattern of overall support is much different. Jackson's line looks like the typical case study of the damage symbolic racism does to black candidacies. Racial conservatives were clearly more likely to back Jackson's opponents than racial liberals were to cast their lot with him. As can also be seen, the racially resentful were similarly opposed to Obama's candidacy. Yet the most

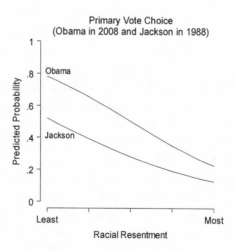

Figure 2.4 Primary vote choice for Barack Obama and Jesse Jackson as a function of racial resentment (1=Obama/Jackson, 0=other Democrats). Probabilities were based on the logistic regression coefficients in table A2.2 of the online appendix (http://www.press.uchicago.edu/books/tesler/). Predicted probabilities were calculated by setting all other variables to the mean respondent in each separate analysis. *Source*: 1988 and 2008 ANES.

intriguing question arising from this display is not why the vast majority of racial conservatives opposed these two black candidates, but why Obama outperforms Jackson among strong racial liberals by roughly 25 percentage points.[18]

The most plausible mechanism for why Barack Obama did so much better in 2008 among racial liberals than Jesse Jackson did in 1988 centers on the lack of substantive differences between himself and Senator Clinton. A vote for Jackson by racial liberals in 1988 was more than just a symbolic gesture of good will toward African Americans. Rather, it represented a fundamental break with the mainstream positions of their party. Jackson campaigned strongly on several issues that never made it into the 1988 Democratic Party's platform. Such issues include, but are not limited to, reparations for the descendants of slaves, disarmament negotiations with the Soviet Union, a Palestinian homeland, massive cuts in defense spending, and radically redistributive economic policies. Thus, there would be real policy repercussions if Jesse Jackson rather than one of the more conventional Democrats captured the nomination. Moreover, most Democratic primary voters thought Jackson had little chance of winning either the Democratic nomination or the general election if he somehow became the nominee (Abramowitz 1989). Racial liberals, therefore, not only had to reconcile any desire they had to see a black president with Jackson's controversial issue positions, but they also had to consider both the improbability of his winning and the impaired electability of the Democratic ticket in November if their party ran on such a progressive platform.

Twenty years later, racial liberals did not have to worry about any of these problems in expressing their eagerness for a black candidate. Obama established himself as a viable alternative to Hillary Clinton after winning Iowa. Furthermore, he performed slightly better than Clinton in most general election trial heats against John McCain throughout the primaries.[19] Based upon their Senate voting records, it is also hard to imagine any glaring differences in party platforms emanating from a Clinton instead of an Obama nominating convention.[20] Finally, and unlike Jesse Jackson, Barack Obama went out of his way during the campaign to appear racially impartial. One could not easily draw the inference, then, that his administration would in any way favor African American interests over whites.[21]

Purged of any major substantive differences between the top two Democratic candidates, a vote for Obama in the primaries became largely symbolic. It enabled racial liberals to express their affective orientation toward African Americans—sentiments that had already influenced 2007 favorability assessments of Obama—without any potential drawbacks. The same cannot be said about support for black candidates like Jesse Jackson. Supporting such candidates was not simply symbolic but had real issue and strategic voting consequences. We suspect that as racial liberals became increasingly aware of the lack of policy, viability, and electability risk associated with backing Obama's candidacy, they became eager to express their support for his quest to become the first African American president. That explanation goes a long way in understanding why racial liberals fueled Obama's post-Iowa momentum and why he did so much better on the liberal side of the resentment spectrum than Jackson did in 1988.

To recap, there are three central elements involved in explaining the two sides of racialization in the 2008 Democratic primaries. Consistent with previous research, racial resentment appeared to produce votes *against* the black candidate, Barack Obama, rather than *for* the white candidate, Hillary Clinton. Secondly, the less resentful racial liberals had much stronger feelings of admiration and sympathy for African Americans than their more resentful counterparts did. Finally, it was a contest with no real differences between the candidates, unlike Jesse Jackson's 1988 campaign. That factor allowed *both* racial liberals and the racially resentful to freely express their attitudes toward African Americans at the ballot booth.

Racialized Evaluations of Hillary Clinton

The large impact of racial resentment on support for Obama in the primaries is all the more remarkable because both high and low resentment Democrats had to entirely reverse their prior evaluations of Hillary Clinton to bring them about. The irony of Hillary Clinton as the preferred choice of socially conservative Democrats was not lost on some astute commentators in the media (Stein 2008; Lowery 2008). One would have expected ahead of time that the racially resentful would have no fond regard for the racially liberal former first lady.

We can do much better, though, and look directly at how warmly the racially resentful felt toward perhaps the most prominent feminist of our time before the 2008 campaign happened to pit her against Barack Obama. There are four previous ANES surveys (1992, 1994, 2000, and 2004), which contained both the full racial resentment battery and respondents' thermometer ratings of Hillary Clinton. Even when controlling for ideological self-placement, a significant and sizable negative relationship emerged

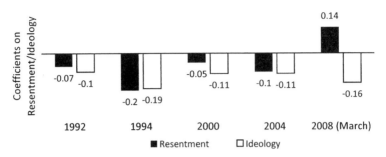

Figure 2.5. Impact of racial resentment and ideology on Hillary Clinton's ANES thermometer ratings and CCAP favorability ratings (Democrats only). Columns plot the OLS coefficients from table A3.3 of the online appendix (http://www.press.uchicago.edu/books/tesler/). Each column represents either the effect of moving from least to most resentful or extremely liberal to extremely conservative on Clinton's evaluations (coded 0–1). *Source*: 1992, 1994, 2000, and 2004 ANES; March 2008 CCAP.

between racial resentment and Clinton's thermometer ratings. Chapter 4 examines these earlier resentment effects separately for Democrats, Republicans, and Independents, but since the focus here is on the impact of racial resentment in the primaries, the analysis should necessarily be restricted to Democrats.

Figure 2.5 shows the impact of both ideological conservatism and racial resentment on Hillary Clinton's ANES thermometer ratings from 1992 to 2004 (recoded on a 0–1 scale) and her five category favorability ratings in the March 2008 CCAP (also recoded on a 0–1 scale). As expected, racially resentful Democrats felt cooler toward Hillary Clinton than did racial liberals in the earlier survey years. Three of the four years produce statistically significant negative relationships with racial resentment. Taken as a whole, moving from the most racially liberal to the most racially resentful produced an average decrease in Clinton evaluations of about 10 thermometer degrees for Democrats. In March 2008, however, the pattern is completely reversed. The most racially resentful Democrats were now considerably *more* favorable in their predicted evaluations of Hillary Clinton—the equivalent of 14 points on a 100-point scale—than their least resentful counterparts.

Most important for the present argument, this reversal is specifically *racial*. No such turnaround occurred in the impact of nonracial ideological self-placement. Figure 2.5, for instance, shows that nonracial conservatism

continued to have its familiar sizable negative effect on Democrats' evaluations of Hillary Clinton in 2008. These results are highly consistent with
those in tables 2.1 and 2.2, which indicate that racial—as opposed to nonracial ideological—predispositions were the prime determinant of primary
vote choice between Obama and Clinton.

One might be tempted to attribute the dramatic reversal in the effects
of racial resentment to racially conservative Democrats altering their prior
attitudes toward Hillary Clinton because she represented the last line of defense against a black nominee. From the earlier analysis, though, it is just as
easy to assume that a large element of the change in evaluations was brought
about by changes among racially liberal Democrats who had long admired
Clinton. They would seem likely to have grown colder to her precisely because she, in fact, represented the last major obstacle to a black nominee.
Unfortunately, the noncomparability of the ANES 101-category thermometer rating and the CCAP's five-category favorability measure prevents us
from directly determining the exact magnitude of opinion change for racial
liberals and the racially resentful.

It is still possible, however, to compare Clinton evaluations for racially
liberal (i.e., those with resentment scores of .25 or lower) and conservative
(i.e., those with resentment scores of .75 or higher) Democrats relative to
their more racially moderate fellow partisans. Racial moderates are an appropriate baseline because their evaluations should be less influenced by the
different racial dynamics occurring between 2008 and earlier survey years.
As imperfect as this comparison is, it is still quite informative. A similarly
sized movement relative to racial moderates took place from 1992–2004 averages to 2008 in both attitudinal groups' evaluations of Hillary Clinton.
Racially resentful Democrats *increased* their previous evaluations of Clinton
by 12 percentage points relative to racial moderates in March 2008, whereas
racial liberals *decreased* their relative assessments of her by 17 points.

This result again shows how the two sides of racialization were operating
simultaneously in support for and opposition to Barack Obama. As stated
earlier, racial conservatives were heavily voting their racial predispositions
in opposing Barack Obama and therefore had to alter earlier evaluations
of his main rival to make such votes congruent. In a parallel fashion, the
evidence suggests that racial liberals were also voting their attitudes toward
African Americans, but in support of Barack Obama. These individuals,
therefore, naturally grew more hostile to the only major obstacle blocking
their preferred candidate from securing the Democratic nomination.

Concluding Remarks

Obama's chief strategist, David Axelrod, said about his candidate's racial background before the primary season began, "I think we may lose some votes, but we also may gain some votes because of it. I don't think it will determine the outcome" (Quoted in Thomas 2009, 56). The results presented in the chapter on the two sides of racialization in primary vote choice strongly support Axelrod's expectation. His suggestion that the positive and negative effects of race-based voting would basically cancel each other out was certainly much more accurate than Obama's own analysis cited at the start of the chapter, which argued that he would *not* be judged by his race.

Barack Obama was unambiguously judged by his race throughout the primary season. Racial predispositions, in fact, were readily accessible when either positive or negative evaluations of Barack Obama were being expressed way back in 2007. Moreover, the racially resentful expressed these predispositions by strongly opposing his candidacy for the nomination from the campaign's onset. Yet after Obama established himself as a viable and electable candidate after Iowa, the least resentful also began to vote their racial predispositions in support for him. The upshot was a pattern of racialized momentum, whereby Obama's activation of the heretofore largely unnoticed liberal side of the racial resentment dimension won him the Democratic nomination.

3

The General Election

The Two Sides of Racialization and
Short-Term Political Dynamics

"I voted with the president over 90 percent of the time."

JOHN MCCAIN, *Your World with Neil Cavuto*, Fox News, May 22, 2003

Our central contention is that the 2008 campaign was more racialized from start to finish than any other presidential campaign in modern history. We already saw the large effects of racial resentment in the Democratic primaries. They clearly raised the specter of a greater role than usual for racial resentment in the 2008 general election. So did exit polls taken from Pennsylvania, Kentucky, and West Virginia in April and May 2008, indicating that upward of half of Hillary Clinton's supporters were hesitant about voting for Barack Obama over John McCain in November. Many media analysts immediately came to the conclusion that their hesitancy was based in race—that those Democrats who voted for Clinton in the primary but were reluctant to support Barack Obama in the general election simply did not want to vote for a black presidential candidate (Thomas 2008; Sullivan 2008). But that did not guarantee a greater role for attitudes about African Americans in 2008 than in past presidential contests. So our main questions in this chapter are: Did the general election vote show the same racialized pattern as the primaries? If so, how did Obama win the election in the face of that formidable obstacle?

A Reduced Role for Race in the General Election?

There are two major reasons for expecting that the general election might not be so racialized. First, presidential vote choices in general elections are profoundly affected by partisan attachments, which are largely neutralized in intraparty primary elections (Bartels 2000; Campbell et al. 1960). These party affiliations have themselves become unmistakably influenced by racial attitudes in recent decades. Racial issues are among the factors that have sharply polarized the two political parties at the elite level since the 1960s (Carmines and Stimson 1989; Laymen and Carsey 2002). In the mass public, racial resentment has become an increasingly important predictor of party identification (Valentino and Sears 2005, 2008).

In the primaries, the independent effects of racial resentment on vote choice were actually enhanced by this relationship between racial attitudes and party attachment. Strong Democratic identifiers are lower in racial resentment than are those choosing the other six standard categories of party identification, ranging from weak Democrats to strong Republicans. Barack Obama, however, consistently outperformed Hillary Clinton with weak Democrats and Independents but lost to her among strong Democrats. The independent effects of racial resentment on opposition to Obama in the primaries, therefore, became a little larger after controlling for the correlation between party identification and racial predispositions.

The deeply partisan nature of presidential general elections, on the other hand, necessarily implies that strong Democrats should overwhelmingly support their party's candidate irrespective of their racial attitudes. It is quite possible, then, that the well-known importance of partisanship in voting for president might have relegated racial attitudes' independent impact on the 2008 general election to a much more limited role than it had played in the primary season.

The second reason that racial resentment might have played a more limited role in the general election concerns other short-term factors in the political world. Every presidential election is to some extent a referendum on the previous administration's performance (Fiorina 1981; Miller and Shanks 1996). In 2008, President Bush's job approval evaluations from the general public were nearing record lows. The unpopular Iraq War was dragging on, seemingly inconclusively. Upcoming was the financial collapse in the fall and then the rapidly deteriorating national (and international) economy. Economic conditions threatened to overwhelm everything else that might be said or done during the campaign.

This, after all, is a standard feature of presidential elections. Short-term perceptions of national economic conditions have consistently been shown to be sizable determinants of individual-level voting behavior in national elections (Kinder and Kiewiet 1979, 1981; Fiorina 1981; Kiewiet 1983). The logic here is quite simple—the party that controls the White House benefits when voters think that the economy is strong and its candidates are punished during economic downturns. True, there is some evidence indicating that the incumbent party's candidate is not held quite as responsible for national economic conditions during open-seat presidential contests like 2008 (Holbrook 2008; Nadeau and Lewis-Beck 2001; though see Abramowitz 2008), but John McCain was still undoubtedly disadvantaged by running as a Republican in 2008. In fact, no previous ANES survey had ever come close to recording economic evaluations as dreadful as those in 2008. For example, a large majority of respondents said that the national economy had gotten "much worse" over the past year (65.9 percent) and virtually no individuals surveyed thought things were either "better" or "much better" (2.2 percent combined). This "much worse" percentage was more than 20 points greater than the proportion recorded in any prior ANES survey.[1]

When the media and/or the campaigns make the state of the national economy even more salient, its importance in voting for president has been shown to increase still further (Hetherington 1996; Johnston, Hagen, and Jamieson 2004; Vavreck 2009). In 2008, economic conditions clearly dominated both the campaigns' and the press's coverage of them. Stories about the economy for instance, comprised upward of 50 percent of campaign news in the weeks immediately after Lehman Brothers filed for bankruptcy and the stock market began its freefall in mid-September.[2] McCain even suspended his campaign in response to the seriousness of these circumstances. Likewise, the September 26, 2008, presidential debate's scheduled focus on foreign policy was altered to include questions about the economy. Such dire national economic conditions in 2008, combined with the tremendous amount of press attention given to them, naturally raised the question of whether Americans were still relying heavily on racial predispositions in formulating their general election vote decisions. With so much focus on economic issues, evaluations of the economy were likely to be particularly influential.

In short, both partisanship and economic evaluations could have consigned racial resentment to a much lesser role in the general election than the central part it had played during the primary season, as seen in the previous chapter.

Race in the General Election Campaign

Aside from the potential for party affiliation and economic conditions to reduce racial resentment's influence on presidential vote choice, both John McCain and Barack Obama were extremely reluctant to make race an issue. Senator McCain had himself been the victim of malicious race-based attacks during his 2000 run for the GOP's nomination. In the weeks before that year's make-or-break Republican primary contest in South Carolina, anonymous leaflets were circulated throughout the state suggesting that McCain had fathered his adopted daughter with a black prostitute. Some suspected that experience motivated his refusal to gain any popular advantage over Obama via similarly styled appeals to racial anxiety (Thomas 2009). The Mc-Cain campaign was also genuinely afraid that accusations of racism against them would be electorally damaging. Such fear likely prompted McCain's express admonition to his surrogates not to discuss the racially explosive Reverend Wright issue.[3]

To be sure, their campaign was not entirely free of racial content. In late July 2008, Obama had publicly warned his supporters that the opposition would attempt to scare voters by pointing out "he doesn't look like all those other presidents on those dollar bills."[4] Shortly thereafter, McCain's campaign manager, Rick Davis, issued a press release declaring, "Barack Obama has played the race card, and played it from the bottom of the deck." This gambit offered the potential to inject race into the campaign without fear of public condemnation for racial insensitivity. Moreover, the McCain campaign in general, and Sarah Palin in particular, seemed quite comfortable fueling the flames that Obama was the "other"—meaning his background was not like "the real Americans," as Palin called them.[5] Chapter 7 addresses such efforts to portray Obama as the "other"—that is, as not being like the small-town, patriotic white Americans that many thought Palin was referring to when she referenced "the real America."

Moreover, some Republican political groups working without the Mc-Cain campaign's imprimatur were far less hesitant to make race-based appeals against Obama. The National Republican Trust Political Action Committee, for instance, ran ads the final week of the campaign repeating excerpts from Wright's most sensational sermons. The spot concluded with both the written and spoken message, "Barack Obama. Too radical. Too risky," a likely appeal to prevailing stereotypes about black political radicalism (Hajnal 2007; Sigelman et al. 1995). Other independent groups similarly featured Wright in anti-Obama advertisements. Despite these few examples, though, McCain's reluctance to make race a factor meant that the informational atmosphere throughout most of the fall campaign was relatively race neutral. Given Republicans' long history of employing racial appeals for electoral advantage (Mendelberg 2001), their limited use of such messages against Obama was remarkably restrained.

As for the Democrats, Barack Obama not only tried to avoid the race issue but he also actively pursued strategies to *deactivate* the impact of racial conservatism on vote choice. The campaign's top pollster, Cornell Belcher, consistently gauged white Americans' levels of "racial aversion" using questions about African Americans similar to those in the racial resentment battery we have borrowed from Kinder and Sanders (1996; on the Obama polling, see Ambinder 2009).[6] Obama's strategists, therefore, knew that the high degree of racial aversion among the American public—reflecting the majority of the country who are racially resentful—necessitated neutralizing the effect such predispositions would have on voting behavior. Belcher, in fact, told Gwen Ifill (2009, 54) after the election, "The thing is, a *black man* can't be president of America, given the racial aversion and history that's still out there . . . However, an extraordinary, gifted, and talented young man who happens to be black can be president" (original emphasis). So the campaign flooded white working-class areas of key swing states with its moderate, race-neutral, economic message in an effort to deactivate racial aversion and hopefully get votes cast on the basis of factors that were more favorable to Obama (Ambinder 2009).

On the rare occasion when Barack Obama did directly address race during the general election campaign, as he did at the NAACP's annual conference in July 2008, he used language that actually should have been positively received by the racially resentful. A core tenet of symbolic racism is that racial inequality stems from blacks' lack of work ethic and personal responsibility. The following comments from Obama should therefore have been appreciated by Americans harboring such opinions: "Now, I know there's some who've been saying I've been too tough talking about responsibility. But here at the NAACP, I'm here to report I'm not going to stop talking about it. Because . . . no matter how many 10-point plans we propose, or how many government programs we launch—none of it will make any difference if we don't seize more responsibility in our own lives."

These remarks were certainly not well received by the longstanding poster child of the racially conservative backlash, Jesse Jackson. After similar comments by Obama about African American responsibility earlier in the year,[7] Jackson was caught on tape describing how he wanted to castrate (in more colorful language) the Democratic nominee for "talking down to black people."[8] The controversy received considerable media attention—it was the most reported-on campaign story of the week and figured prominently in the following week's campaign coverage too (Hitlin et al. 2008a, 2008b). As a result of that publicity, nearly half of the respondents surveyed by Pew in mid-July reported hearing "a lot" about Jackson's "crude comment."[9]

From the standpoint of deactivating racial resentment, the widespread media interest in Jackson's criticism could have been good for Obama. Black leaders like Jesse Jackson and Al Sharpton have long been especially likely to evoke racial resentment because their forceful advocacy for African Americans mirrors the manifest content of symbolic racism and racial resentment, as in their denunciation of continuing racial discrimination and proposals for pro-black public policies (Sears 1993; Sears, Van Laar, Carillo, and Kosterman 1997). We might expect, then, that both Obama's message of black responsibility, and the criticism of him sparked by the highly racialized Jackson, could have made him *more* popular among the racially resentful. If his support among racial conservatives increased as a result of Jackson's criticism, the upshot should have been a diminished impact of racial resentment on vote choice.

Taken together, the large potential impacts of partisanship and short-term forces unfavorable to the Republicans, such as Bush's low approval ratings and economic evaluations, as well as the McCain campaign's unwillingness to make race an issue and Obama's concerted effort to deactivate racial attitudes, raised the possibility that race would have a role in the biracial 2008 election no greater than it had had in previous contests featuring only white candidates.

A Predictable Outcome

We start our analysis of the general election with the aggregate vote division before moving on to the dynamics of individual vote choices. A substantial body of research in political science shows that the popular vote in presidential elections can usually be forecast within a few percentage points with models based upon economic and political indicators assessed months before the election. These variables are referred to as the "fundamentals." They include such nonracial factors as gross domestic product growth, presidential approval ratings, consumer satisfaction, jobs creation, terms in office, and economic expectations (see Campbell 2008a for an overview). Forecast models are based entirely upon the relationships these fundamental variables have had with presidential vote share in previous elections.

Those earlier elections, of course, had only offered white candidates, so they provided no precedents for the effect of having a black nominee. Widespread reluctance to vote for a black candidate might well have resulted in Obama performing worse than he should have based on the standard nonracial "fundamentals." Some forecasters naturally worried that Obama's race would cause his actual vote share to fall significantly below the level of support forecast from past elections. One forecast, in fact, subtracted 6.5 percentage points from Obama's expected vote share from the model to account for the detrimental effect they expected that his race would have for him (Lewis-Beck and Tien 2008).

However, Obama's share of the two-party vote in the 2008 general election was actually predicted quite accurately by most of the forecasting models that were published before the election. Five forecasts published in October 2008 produced an average predicted two-party vote share for Obama of 54.6 percent, with a median prediction of 54.3,[10] both very close to the 53.4 percent of the two-party vote share that he eventually received (Campbell 2008a).[11] At least from these aggregate vote models it appears that Obama was not too disadvantaged by his race relative to past white Democratic candidates.

Unfortunately these predictions, which were all calculated at least two months prior to the election, could not take into account the financial meltdown that occurred in mid-September of 2008. Nor could they possibly factor in Obama's big advantage in campaign resources—a factor shown to help amass votes (Shaw 2007). The financial meltdown and Obama's fund-raising should have led to his doing much better than these forecasts predicted. On the other hand, one could just as easily argue that some fundamentals unfavorable to McCain, such as economic growth and presidential approval, were not as closely linked to him as they were to past nominees. Any underperformance from what the fundamentals predicted for Obama, therefore, could also be attributed to McCain's lack of direct association with the Bush administration and to his reputation for political independence. In other words, there was good reason to think that McCain could have been judged less on retrospective evaluations than previous nominees from the incumbent party had been, and so outperform his forecasted vote share.

If we assume that the favorable campaign circumstances for Obama not accounted for by the forecasting models were mostly offset by McCain's distance from the unpopular administration in control of the White House, the 2008 general election results comport well with predictions based upon the election year's objective economic and political indicators. Perhaps the aggregate vote division turned out to be quite predictable because "the fundamentals" reduced the impact of racial resentment. If so, racial attitudes might not have had a much greater impact on voting behavior in this election than they had in the all-white contests of the past.

Racial Resentment in 2008 Compared to Previous All-White Elections

Next we test whether racial resentment did, in fact, have larger effects on individual voters' preferences in the general election than in prior all-white

Table 3.1. Predictors of GOP vote intention (logistic regression)

	1988	1992	2000	2004	McCain Trial Heats vs. Clinton	vs. Obama	2008
Racial Resentment	1.09	1.17	.646	1.52	.918	3.78	2.99
	(.379)	(.453)	(.525)	(.673)	(.163)	(.165)	(.489)
Partisanship	5.76	5.97	5.55	7.04	5.39	3.60	5.37
	(.300)	(.339)	(.514)	(.562)	(.149)	(.120)	(.416)
Ideology	2.09	2.81	3.21	1.60	2.69	2.40	2.62
	(.450)	(.373)	(.641)	(.785)	(.200)	(.183)	(.603)
Education	−.479	−.486	−1.08	−.134	.572	−.347	.772
	(.299)	(.373)	(.544)	(.153)	(.158)	(.153)	(.384)
Age	−.008	.005	−.017	.007	−.002	.009	.029
	(.005)	(.005)	(.007)	(.007)	(.003)	(.003)	(.006)
Black	−1.06	−1.03	−.922	−.602	−.434	−1.30	−3.37
	(.318)	(.425)	(.461)	(.424)	(.142)	(.200)	(.584)
Male	.130	−.122	.170	−.176	.342	−.063	.023
	(.161)	(.187)	(.238)	(.247)	(.083)	(.073)	(.210)
South	.550	.359	.160	.721	.362	.361	.669
	(.174)	(.206)	(.243)	(.279)	(.062)	(.077)	(.213)
Observations	1,466	1,448	1,134	949	12,329	12,425	1,778

Source: March CCAP for the 2008 trial heats; ANES surveys for all other years.

Note: Dependent variables are coded 1 for Republican vote intention and 0 for Democratic vote intention.

elections. Table 3.1 displays the logistic regression coefficients for racial resentment and the other variables in our standard model of GOP vote intention for five of the last six presidential election years.[12] We use the ANES's preelection measure of vote intention here instead of reported postelection vote choice to foster comparison between these results and the two trial heats pitting John McCain against Hillary Clinton and against Barack Obama in the March 2008 CCAP. The differences in racial resentment's respective impacts on vote choice and vote intention are statistically negligible in every year except 2004.[13] A detailed analysis of four other national surveys with measures of both racial resentment and 2004 vote *choice*, however, indicates that the increased resentment effect on vote choice in the 2004 ANES was anomalous. Other surveys did not show that enhanced impact.[14] We are quite confident, then, that our use of the 2004 ANES's measure of vote *intention* is an accurate reflection of racial resentment's impact on that election.

That being said, the coefficients in table 3.1 suggest that racial resentment in the McCain-Obama matchups had at least twice as strong an effect on vote intention in both the March 2008 CCAP and the fall 2008 ANES than it had in any all-white contest from 1988 to 2004, or in the all-white McCain-Clinton matchup. To aid in the interpretation of these coefficients, figure 3.1 graphs out the resentment effects, while holding the other variables in the model constant. As the display illustrates, racial resentment

Predicted Probability of GOP Vote Intention (1988-2008)

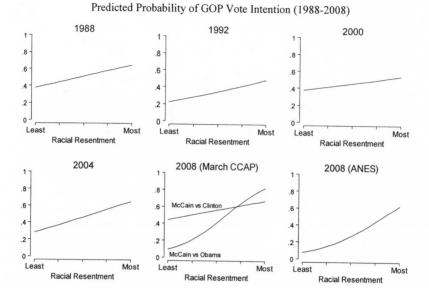

Figure 3.1. Republican vote intention as a function of racial resentment. Probabilities were based on logistic coefficients in table 3.1. Predicted probabilities were calculated by setting all other variables to the mean respondent in each separate analysis. *Source*: 1988, 1992, 2000, 2004, and 2008 ANES; March 2008 CCAP.

clearly had a much larger impact on general election votes in 2008 than it had at any earlier point in the prior two decades. This strongly supports our central claim that the 2008 election was more sharply racialized than any campaign in the prior two decades, contrary to the hopes and wishes of the Obama campaign.

Aside from the unusual importance of racial resentment in 2008 relative to prior years, other interesting patterns emerge here. The most striking is how much racial resentment was already affecting the Obama vs. McCain matchup as early as March 2008, compared to either the all-white presidential campaigns of the past or Hillary Clinton's trial heat with McCain in the same survey. With relevant factors controlled for, the elections from 1988 through 2004 yielded an average difference of roughly 25 percentage points in Republican two-party vote share between the most and the least racially resentful. As shown in the fifth panel of figure 3.1, the impact of racial resentment in the March 2008 Clinton vs. McCain CCAP matchup was almost identical to the mean effects in those earlier elections offering only white candidates. In contrast, the effects of racial resentment on Obama-McCain vote preferences in March were *almost three times greater* than in any of those earlier all-white contests. The most racially resentful were more than 70 percentage points more likely to support McCain in March 2008 than were the least racially resentful. The final panel in figure 3.1 shows that the impact of racial resentment on 2008 vote intention in the fall ANES was more than double its average impact in the ANES surveys from 1988 to 2004, though off somewhat from what it had been in the spring.

The Two Sides of Racialization in the 2008 General Election

As was the case in the primaries, understanding these large effects of racial resentment on vote preference in the general election requires a separate examination of the racially liberal side of the spectrum. It was suggested in the previous chapter that a major reason why Obama did so well among racial liberals in the primary was the lack of major substantive differences between himself and Senator Clinton in terms of broader ideology or non-racial issues. That presumably allowed the least racially resentful to vote their affective sympathies for African Americans without any adverse policy consequences—a cost-free racially liberal statement, if you will.

There were obviously much more meaningful policy differences between Obama and Senator McCain. Still, these differences should have made it *even more enticing* for racial liberals to vote for Obama than if they were casting a vote that merely expressed their positive affect for African Americans, as in the primary. As the fundamentals in the election forecasting models indicated, Barack Obama had the great benefit of running for president as a Democrat in an election year in which the Republican brand name was severely damaged. With less than 30 percent of the country approving of the incumbent Republican president and over four out of five Americans saying the nation was on the wrong track throughout the fall of 2008, the circumstances greatly favored any Democratic candidate. A vote for Obama thus provided the perfect political scenario for racial liberals: They could simultaneously express their support for a black candidate and vote with the prevailing partisan proclivities of the moment.

We should expect, therefore, that even with our base-model variables controlled for, Obama would capture the great majority of votes from the most racially liberal Americans. Figure 3.1 shows that this is precisely what happened. Although racial resentment was a much bigger factor in 2008 than in previous elections, much of this difference was produced by Obama's stout support from racial liberals. Indeed, with the familiar demographic and partisan control variables set to their means, our vote model predicts that over 90 percent of the most racially liberal respondents (and over 80 percent of racially liberal whites, as will be shown in chapter 5) supported Obama.

All the fundamentals that were so favorable to the Democrats, however, did not comparably expand the Democratic vote share among racial conservatives. This opposition to Obama among the racially resentful, and under performance among them relative to the pro-Democratic fundamentals, is to be expected from much prior research showing the detrimental effects of symbolic racism on white support for otherwise well-positioned black candidates. Indeed, the concept of symbolic racism was originally born out of a need to explain widespread white opposition to black candidates and race-targeted policies in the post–civil rights era. Most of the action, therefore, has usually occurred on the racially resentful side of the spectrum.

So racial resentment was more important in 2008 than in previous years. That unusual salience should have worked against Obama, since most Americans score on the conservative side of the resentment spectrum. Yet Obama's powerful performance among racial liberals offset much of that disadvantage. Race has historically created opposition to black candidates among whites, but he activated unprecedented support on the liberal side of the resentment spectrum—a phenomenon much less expected from prior research.

The Impact of Racial Resentment throughout the Campaign

There is still much to be explained about the dynamics of racial resentment through the campaign, though. For starters, figure 3.1 offers little insights into how racial resentment's impact on general election vote intention changed throughout the course of the campaign. Racial resentment had a stronger effect on support for McCain against Obama in the March CCAP than in the Fall ANES, seemingly indicating that its power dwindled with time. But two differences between the surveys prevent us from knowing exactly what caused that decline. The ANES was carried out over the two month time span from the beginning of September to Election Day, thereby making it impossible to detect changes in the effects of racial resentment over the course of the full election year. Moreover, differences in sampling methodology make the ANES and CCAP results not entirely comparable.

However, the CCAP's panel design does have desirable features for tracking differences in the impact of racial resentment over the course of the 2008 general election campaign. Over time, voters may change the standards they use to make their decisions. Campaign content and media coverage may influence such changes as a result of what social psychologists refer to as "priming," as indicated in chapter 2 (see Bartels 2006b and Kinder 2003 for reviews). For example, introducing the race-infused Willie Horton case into the 1988 campaign yielded a natural experiment on racial priming.[15] Researchers partitioned the 1988 ANES into different time intervals in order to demonstrate how the Horton issue primed racial resentment, thereby increasing its influence on both candidate evaluations (Mendelberg 2001) and presidential vote choice (Kinder and Sanders 1996).

However, such priming studies based on cross-sectional data run the risk of blurring reciprocal causality (Lenz 2009). On the one hand, priming race could increase the dependence of vote preference on the voter's level of racial resentment, as the priming hypothesis proposes. On the other hand, the new information could cause a shift in underlying racial attitudes to rationalize one's preexisting vote decision. If so, the enhanced relationship between racial predispositions and voting behavior might have nothing to do with the priming mechanism.

The robust individual-level stability of symbolic racism makes the racial priming results from these two Willie Horton studies (Kinder and Sanders 1996; Mendelberg 2001) much less vulnerable to this rationalization explanation. It is unlikely that voters changed their rather stable levels of racial resentment to rationalize their 1988 vote choices. Even so, the researchers were limited by having to compare pre-Horton with post-Horton respondents, and the two groups could have differed in other ways. In contrast, the 2008 CCAP's panel design allows us to test the effects of racial resentment, as measured in March, on the same panel respondents' vote choices in March, September, October, and November. Since their March responses to the racial resentment questions were especially unlikely to serve as rationalizations for their general election vote preferences in the fall, the panel design offers a big advantage in mitigating concerns about reverse causality.

The timing of the CCAP interviews also turned out to be fortuitous for examining whether any changes in the impact of racial resentment through the campaign affected Obama's prospects for victory. According to Pollster. com's compilation of daily national polling averages through the entire campaign, McCain led Obama only from late March to early April, holding a 45.5 to 44 percent lead during that time period.[16] This time frame perfectly parallels the CCAP's March interviews, which showed an analogous McCain lead among the full sample of 45 to 43.7 percent.[17] These national polls, of course, showed significant movement toward Obama during the fall of

2008. Similarly, Obama headed into Election Day leading among the same CCAP panelists among whom he trailed McCain back in March 2008.

The fact that Obama trailed McCain in late March 2008 in both the national polls and the CCAP is interesting. We showed in figure 3.1, for instance, that all other things being equal, Obama was predicted to receive about 90 percent of the most racially liberal vote in his March trial heat against McCain. Nevertheless, Obama was still trailing McCain among all respondents in this survey because he was losing about three-quarters of the vote from those with high resentment scores. The overall skew toward high levels of racial conservatism made it difficult to offset a poor performance among the most racially resentful. Because of the stability of voters' levels of racial resentment, that skew was unlikely to change. Obama, therefore, needed somehow to change the *relationship* between racial resentment and support for McCain in March in order to win.

There were three plausible ways the Obama campaign could change that crippling relationship between racial resentment and support for McCain. First, it could deactivate the impact of racial resentment among racial conservatives. As previously mentioned, the Obama campaign seemed to be actively pursuing that deactivation strategy by speaking about black responsibility and saturating white working-class areas with its messages of economic moderation. Moreover, the interviews for the March CCAP took place soon after the Reverend Wright story broke. Racial resentment, therefore, may have been at the high point of its influence during this time period. With Reverend Wright largely vanishing from the headlines by the fall of 2008, though, the racially resentful could have grown more supportive of Obama over time.

A second possibility was that Obama might actually increase his aggregate level of support by enhancing the impact of racial predispositions on vote preference. This strategy could work if he gained votes among racial liberals without suffering corresponding losses from racial conservatives. Recall from the previous chapter that stimulating Obama's support on this "second side" of symbolic racism led to the racialized momentum that won him the nomination. However, a similar trend of targeted activation was much less likely to benefit him in the fall campaign because Obama was already close to maximizing his support among racial liberals in March 2008.

Third, Obama might increase his aggregate level of support without altering the effect of racial resentment over the course of the campaign. That would occur if he managed to enhance his vote share among individuals of all resentment levels. Favorable campaign conditions such as his superior

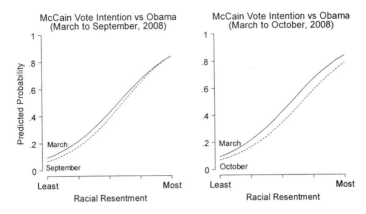

Figure 3.2. Support for McCain against Obama as a function of racial resentment. Probabilities were based on logistic regression coefficients in table A3.1 of the online appendix (http://www.press.uchicago.edu/books/tesler/). Predicted probabilities were calculated by setting all other variables to the mean respondent in each regression analysis. *Source*: March through November 2008 CCAP panelists.

resources, strong debate performances, and the crashing economy could have produced this pattern of increased support for Obama from March to October among those at all levels of racial resentment.

To determine how the effect of racial resentment on vote intentions changed throughout the campaign, figure 3.2 graphs its impact in March, September, and late October for CCAP panelists interviewed in all three waves.[18] The display's first panel shows that the effect of racial resentment, as measured in March, had actually risen slightly among CCAP panelists by September. Obama nevertheless increased his overall vote share because he performed about 5 points better in September among racial liberals. Interestingly, Obama hardly increased his predicted vote share at all among racial conservatives despite the fact that all of the September interviews took place after both Lehman Brothers filed for bankruptcy and the stock market began imploding. The upshot was that Obama increased his aggregate vote share during this time period among CCAP panelists, despite the rise in the impact of racial resentment, because racial liberals' support for him was activated.

How did the effects of resentment on the McCain-Obama matchup close to Election Day compare with those on the hypothetical matchup in the spring? The effects of racial resentment in October were almost entirely unchanged from March, as shown in the second panel of figure 3.2. Obama gained support, across the board, by about 6 to 8 percentage points at all levels of racial resentment. He even appreciably outperformed his March numbers among the most racially conservative respondents. That increased support over the course of the campaign, irrespective of racial resentment, explains how Obama's deficit among CCAP panelists in March turned into a lead in late October. Of the three possible avenues open to Obama for coping with the obstacle of racial resentment going into the fall campaign, then, the third proved successful. Obama increased his predicted vote share at every level of racial resentment.

The uniformity in the effects of racial resentment over time revealed in figure 3.2 is rather remarkable. Despite nearly one billion dollars in campaign spending, the economy crashing, and the diminished salience of race in the campaign from the high of Reverend Wright in March, the effects of racial resentment on support for McCain against Obama were almost identical across time. This continuity strongly supports our prior contention that the hopes and fears generated by Obama's role as the first black presidential nominee from a major political party *ipso facto* made racial predispositions readily accessible in the general election vote choice. Given the broad and deep natural accessibility of race, it appears that neither the campaigns nor the media could do much to alter its impact.

Short-Term Political Dynamics in Voting Behavior

If the impact of racial resentment was unchanged throughout the campaign year, then how did Obama manage to increase his vote share among Americans from March to October? Studies of voting behavior have long shown that the major functions of a campaign are to prime symbolic predispositions and/or short-term political factors like the election year fundamentals (going back to Berelson, Lazarsfeld, and McPhee 1954; Campbell et al. 1960; Miller and Shanks, 1996; more recently, see Hillygus and Jackman 2003; Bartels, 2006b; Vavreck 2009). For example, Gelman and King (1993) suggest that the answer to their aptly titled article "Why Are American Presidential Election Campaign Polls so Variable when Votes Are so Predictable?" is that presidential campaigns prime the election year fundamentals from which the forecasting models make predictions. We might expect, then, that the growth in Obama's vote share after March resulted from short-term political factors rather than racial resentment becoming more important as the campaign passed from the primary to the general election phase.

To test this expectation, we added three short-term factors widely discussed as influential in 2008 to the base model of vote intention used in table 3.1. The first factor added was George W. Bush's five-category approval rating from the March CCAP. Barack Obama ran his campaign as much, if not more, against President Bush as against Senator McCain. Indeed, it was difficult to change the channel in battleground states after Labor Day without seeing an Obama ad featuring a close linkage between Bush and McCain, either showing the two Republicans embracing or McCain boasting (several years earlier) that he had voted with the president more than 90 percent of the time. There was an obvious reason why the Obama campaign was putting so much effort into priming voters' evaluations of George W. Bush. As Bartels (2006b, 90) points out, the electoral consequences of priming effects "depend crucially on the partisan balance of the attitudes and perceptions being primed." With Bush nearing record low approval ratings throughout most of his second term in office, activating assessments of the president was bound to be a significant boon to Obama.

The second factor was the rapidly collapsing economy. The partisan balance of attitudes about the economy put relentless downward pressure on the incumbent Republicans. As previously mentioned, evaluations of national economic trends were at unprecedented lows in 2008.[19] Consequently, Obama ran many campaign ads hoping to stamp into the voters' memories McCain's comments that the "fundamentals of the economy are strong" and that "economics is not something I understand as well as I should." Obama should thus have substantially increased his aggregate vote share if he succeeded in making the economy salient.

The third short-term factor added to the model is the voters' support for the war in Iraq. Public opinion about the Iraq War was extremely polarized along partisan lines throughout Bush's second term in office (Jacobson 2007; Berinsky 2009). As such, it was sure to be a significant predictor of vote choice in 2008. It was also one of the defining issues of Obama's challenge to Hillary Clinton early in the primary season, as discussed in the previous chapter. Yet its impact may not have changed much throughout the course of the campaign. The media began paying less attention to the war as conditions on the ground began to improve in late 2007 (Project for Excellence in Journalism 2007). Moreover, the partisan balance in opinions about how to proceed in Iraq did not decisively favor either candidate. For example, 43 percent of March CCAP respondents said we should withdraw "immediately" or "by the end of the year" compared to 32 percent who thought "we should stay as long as it takes." Neither candidate, therefore, had much incentive to prime the war issue. We included the Iraq withdrawal variable in

Predicted Probability of McCain Vote Intention

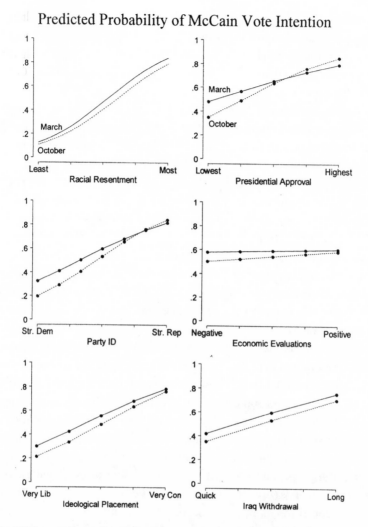

Figure 3.3. Support for McCain against Obama as functions of symbolic predispositions and short-term political factors. Probabilities were based on logistic regression coefficients in table A3.2 of the online appendix (http://www.press.uchicago.edu/books/tesler/). The points on the lines are the values at each interval of any categorical variables with <7 intervals. Predicted probabilities were calculated by setting all other variables to the mean respondent in each regression analysis. *Source:* March through November 2008 CCAP panelists.

our expanded model, but we did not expect it to explain Obama's increased vote share over time from March to October.

Changes through the campaign in the effects of both long-term political predispositions and short-term political factors on 2008 vote preferences are shown in figure 3.3. Most important for our purposes is that the effects of racial resentment shown previously in figure 3.2 are *not* substantially altered by adding presidential approval, economic evaluations, and opinions about Iraq to our base model, all else being equal. Indeed, the first panel of figure 3.3 again shows that Obama increased his support from March to October across the entire spectrum of racial resentment.

With these stable resentment effects once again established, we can now turn our attention to the short-term political factors in the three panels in the second column of figure 3.3. As just mentioned, Bush's extraordinary unpopularity had the Obama campaign hard at work to make him a more important factor in people's voting behavior. From our results, their efforts appear to have been extremely successful. Presidential approval produces the biggest priming effects during the campaign of any of the short-term forces tested. The difference between those "strongly disapproving" and those "strongly approving" of Bush's job performance was a 30-point advantage for Obama over McCain in March 2008, with all other factors held constant. That significant effect of Bush disapproval on vote preference back in March increased even further through the later campaign. By October, the same difference in assessments of Bush (i.e., in Bush's March disapproval ratings) had almost twice as much impact, increasing Obama's vote share by 50 points, as shown in the second panel of figure 3.3.

This effort to link McCain to Bush was particularly targeted toward, and fortunately for Obama, especially effective among Democrats who strongly disapproved of Bush's job performance. All else being equal, Obama increased his vote share from March to October by 13 points with those who most disapproved of Bush. In other words, the Obama campaign succeeded in linking McCain even more tightly to the electorate's already negative views of the Bush's presidency. The result of targeting Democrats and Bush unenthusiasts throughout the campaign was that the effects of partisanship and presidential approval shown in the second and third panels of figure 3.3 significantly increased from March to October. This targeted activation, in fact, appears to be the key difference between Obama trailing McCain in March and leading him on the eve of the election.

Much less expected, however, is that perceptions of how the economy had been performing over the previous year had only modest effects on vote intentions throughout 2008, as shown in the fourth panel in figure 3.3. Part of the apparent unimportance of the economy in the fall could be due to our using retrospective economic evaluations assessed in the March CCAP.[20] That measure, of course, does not take into account the financial meltdown that occurred in the fall. However, the poor economy had already been highly salient in the spring. Economic assessments in March were already dismal, and the economy at that time had become by far the most important national problem identified in surveys.[21]

Moreover, these assessments of the economy from March *did* significantly influence votes. They became much more important throughout the course of the campaign, too, influencing votes more heavily in October than March. But the impact of the economy on vote intentions was indirect, mediated by its more direct effect on presidential approval. The logic is this: Bush's job approval ratings were strongly related to economic evaluations—how poorly the economy was perceived as functioning. The correlation between the two variables among our CCAP panelists was .58. As a result, including both economic evaluations and presidential approval in the same model masks the indirect effect of the poor economy through its effects on Bush's reputation. Removing presidential approval from the vote intention model, therefore, substantially increased the impact of economic evaluations in March, and especially in October.[22] Indeed, the difference in national economic evaluations from "much better" to "much worse" in national economic evaluations now heavily reduced McCain's October predicted vote share, decreasing it by roughly 40 percentage points—an effect twice as big as its effect on March vote intention.

Finally for our short-term political factors, the final panel of figure 3.3 shows that Iraq was a minor player in the Obama surge that won him the presidency. Obama increased his predicted vote share from March to October by similar margins among CCAP panelists who thought we should withdraw from Iraq and with those who believed we should stay in Iraq "as long as it takes." That uniformly increased support for Obama from March to October, regardless of respondents' attitudes about Iraq, indicates that Iraq, like racial resentment, was not responsible for his growing popularity through the spring and fall.

Partisan Activation: The Hillary Clinton Primary Voters Return to the Fold

"The function of the campaign," according to Gelman and King (1993, 433–434), "is to inform voters about the fundamental variables and their appropriate weights." Conventional wisdom has long posited that partisan differences are one of the fundamental variables that are activated by presidential elections. This thinking dates back to Berelson, Lazarsfeld, and McPhee's

(1954, 292) classic finding that Roosevelt voters in 1944, who were initially hesitant to support Harry Truman four years later, came home to the Democratic Party at the end of the 1948 campaign because of "the reactivation of a previous tendency." Yet Gelman and King's (1993) analysis of the 1988 campaign showed that partisanship was the one fundamental variable whose impact did not change much throughout the election year. Bartels's (2006b, 93) analysis of priming effects in presidential elections from 1980 to 2000 similarly revealed "remarkably little evidence of partisan activation in recent general election campaigns."

The third panel in figure 3.3, however, shows substantial evidence of partisan activation, with especially concentrated gains for Obama among Democrats. As can be seen in the display, Obama increased his vote share among Democrats by about 12 points from March to October, with all other factors held constant. Aside from presidential approval ratings, partisanship shows the biggest priming effects of any variable in our model. To repeat our earlier contention, Obama's targeted activation of Democrats and anti-Bush voters in the fall campaign appears to be the main reason why McCain's lead among CCAP panelists in the spring turned into a deficit right before the election.

So why was partisan activation so much stronger in 2008 than in recent elections? These large priming effects stem from the fact that the anti-Bush Democrats activated by the campaign were primarily Hillary Clinton supporters, who had been hesitant to back Obama in March because of his race, returning to their partisan home. Most of Obama's increased vote share among CCAP panelists from March to October was, in fact, produced by a net gain of roughly 30 points from Clinton's primary voters.[23] Not surprisingly, Clinton's support in the primaries came overwhelmingly from Democrats. Strong Democrats accounted for 57 percent of her voters, with weak Democrats making up another 21 percent. An astounding 88 percent of CCAP panelists who supported Clinton in March also strongly disapproved of Bush's job performance. So when Clinton voters transitioned in great numbers to Obama from March to October, it naturally increased his predicted support both among Democrats and among those who were strongly opposed to the incumbent president.

Perhaps the reluctance of Clinton voters to support Obama in March really had little to do with race, though. A priori, one could argue that this hesitancy stemmed more from the contentious nominating contest than from Obama's racial background. Yet the results presented in figure 3.4 clearly

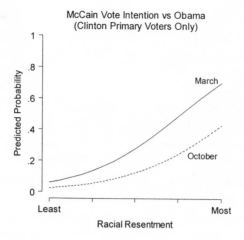

Figure 3.4. Support for McCain against Obama among Clinton primary voters as a function of racial resentment. Probabilities were based on logistic regression coefficients in table A3.3 of the online appendix (http://www.press.uchicago.edu/books/tesler/). Predicted probabilities were calculated by setting all other variables to the mean respondent in each regression analysis. *Source*: March and October 2008 CCAP panelists.

indicate that Obama's race was a critical factor in many Clinton voters' decisions to defect to McCain. The display shows the effect of racial resentment on Clinton primary voters' support for McCain against Obama in the late March CCAP panel, while holding our base-model variables constant. As can be seen in this graphic, there was little chance of Clinton voters on the racially liberal side of the scale defecting to McCain in March. Among the most racially resentful, though, Obama was expected to lose two-thirds of Clinton backers to McCain in that same early trial heat.

Figure 3.4 also shows that those initial intentions of some Clinton voters changed over time to Obama's advantage. More than a third of racially conservative Clinton voters who in March had said they would support McCain against Obama came around to the Democratic nominee by late October. Nevertheless, it is noteworthy that so many racially resentful Democratic primary voters turned to a Republican over a black Democrat in a year where the campaign fundamentals so decisively favored their party's nominee. It strongly supports the earlier contention that racially conservative Democrats were voting against Obama in the primaries more than they were voting for Hillary Clinton.

In sum, the widespread defections of racially conservative Clinton voters in March 2008 indicate that a considerable proportion of voters who should have been eager to vote for a Democrat because of both their partisanship and their evaluations of the incumbent Republican administration were not doing so because of Obama's race. The campaign's activation of those factors, however, brought many Democratic-disposed voters back. As a result of their coming back to the fold from March to October, his margin of victory fell back into the zone expected on the basis of election year fundamentals.

Concluding Remarks

We began by showing that despite the absence of racial appeals during the general election campaign, Obama-McCain vote preferences were more polarized by racial resentment than was the case in any other presidential elections since the Reagan era. The general election was also far more racialized than the trial heat between Clinton and McCain had been in the spring. Just having a black candidate seems to have produced a larger impact of racial predispositions. With more Americans scoring high than low in racial resentment, these greater racialized voting patterns in 2008 could have easily prevented Obama from winning, as many expected.

Yet Obama won. Our analysis of long-term symbolic predispositions and short-term political dynamics points to two central explanations for how Barack Obama won the White House despite the unusually large individual-level impact of racial resentment. The first is that he activated much greater support among racial liberals than had any other recent Democratic presidential candidate. A vote for Obama by racial liberals allowed them both to express their symbolic support for an African American and to evict the unpopular Republican Party from the White House. This strong performance on the "other side" of the symbolic racism dimension helps explain how he won even when the impact of racial resentment was at historic highs in a country where the majority falls safely on the racially conservative side of the resentment spectrum.

Powerfully activating support from the least racially resentful by itself was not enough to win, though. Obama would have lost if the election had been held among CCAP respondents in March 2008 despite his overwhelming support from racial liberals in that survey. The second key factor, then, was that he succeeded in activating Democratic partisanship and primed the election-year fundamental of presidential assessment, which in this case meant the broad and deep disapproval of the Bush administration.

Obama's relatively poor performance among racial conservatives was, therefore, seemingly offset by a combination of racial moderates who were inclined to vote with the prevailing short-term forces of the election year and racial liberals who were eager both to support a black candidate and to vote a damaged Republican Party out of power. The upshot is that racial resentment had a much larger effect on presidential voting at the individual level in 2008, but Obama's aggregate vote share still remained in line with predictions based upon election year fundamentals.

4

The Spillover of Racialization

And what you want to do to Joe the plumber and millions more like him is have
their taxes increased and not be able to realize the American dream of owning their
own business.

JOHN MCCAIN to Barack Obama during their
third presidential debate, October 15, 2008

It is now apparent that racial attitudes were a prime determinant of support
for and opposition to Barack Obama in both the primaries and the general
election. Beforehand many expected that Obama's candidacy would further
racialize the vote in 2008. Numerous studies had shown that public opinion is highly racialized both about black candidates (Kinder and Sears 1981;
Reeves 1997; though see Hajnal 2007 and Citrin et al. 1990 for instances of
deracialized voting in biracial contests) and race-targeted policies like affirmative action (Kinder and Sanders 1996; Sears, Van Laar, Carillo, and Kosterman 1997). Ostensibly non-racial issues that have become disproportionately associated with African Americans, such as welfare and crime, also
strongly evoke racial predispositions (Gilens 1999; Winter 2008; Hurwitz
and Peffley 1997).

The centrality of racial attitudes in 2008 is more remarkable, however,
when we consider the backgrounds of Obama's chief rivals for both the Democratic nomination and the White House. Chapter 2, for instance, showed
that racially liberal Democrats evaluated the racially liberal former first lady
significantly more favorably from 1992 to 2004 than had racially conservative Democrats. Absent Barack Obama's candidacy, then, there was little reason to expect racially conservative Democrats to cast their lot with a candidate like Hillary Clinton who had such a strong socially liberal background.

There was also little reason to think John McCain, perhaps the most
prominent Republican moderate of our time, would ever strongly evoke racial predispositions. Sears, Van Laar, Carillo, and Kosterman (1997), for example, show that racial attitudes were not significantly implicated in ANES
thermometer evaluations of other moderate presidential candidates such as

George H. W. Bush and Bill Clinton in 1992. Absent Barack Obama's candidacy, then, it is difficult to envision a scenario in which evaluations of Senator McCain would be racialized. Indeed we show below that racial attitudes were not strongly connected to McCain evaluations before he clinched the Republican Party's presidential nomination.

Despite the lack of any positive association of racial resentment with support for Hillary Clinton and John McCain before 2008, both of their campaigns against Barack Obama generated the most racialized presidential voting in the contemporary era. So what happened to the earlier nonracialized Hillary Clinton and John McCain? Could racial prejudice possibly continue to have negative effects on Clinton evaluations among Democrats, and insignificant effects on assessments of McCain by the entire electorate, when vote choices in their contests with Barack Obama were so decisively split by racial attitudes? Similarly, would an especially salient campaign issue like tax policy be evaluated primarily upon nonracial considerations once Barack Obama's position on the issue was so heavily spotlighted? We believe the answer to all of these questions is a resounding no.

Theoretical Background and Empirical Expectations

As touched upon in the previous chapters, mass communications can make political considerations more important in subsequent decision making by priming specific issues or attitudinal predispositions. Much of the research illuminating this priming mechanism has been devoted to studying the process of racialization, where priming race elevates racial predispositions to greater importance in political evaluations (see Mendelberg 2008 for a review). Racialization studies are by no means limited to race-specific evaluations like opinions about affirmative action and assessments of African American politicians who are strong black rights activists. Multiple studies, in fact, show that mass communications can make racial attitudes a more central ingredient of opinions even about ostensibly nonracial policies, such as welfare and Social Security (Gilens 1999; Mendelberg 2001; Winter 2008), and a stronger determinant of presidential evaluations even in all-white campaigns like 1988, 1996, and 2000 (Mendelberg 2001; Valentino 1999; Valentino, Hutchings, and White 2002).

This racialization even of political controversies that have no manifest racial content is thought to result in part from communications that make racial predispositions more accessible in subsequent political evaluations. Subtle, "implicit" racial cues like images of ordinary African Americans are often shown to be effective in activating these racial attitudes. The logic is that implicitly racial messages foster connections between racial predispositions and evaluations of political candidates or public policies without audience members consciously knowing that they are violating the strong societal norm of racial equality (Mendelberg 2001, 2008; Valentino, Hutchings, and White 2002; Winter 2008; though see Huber and Lapinski 2006).

The mechanism we propose for the racialization of normally nonracial attitude objects during Obama's 2008 campaigns is quite different from that in past studies. Implicit racial symbolism, for instance, was certainly not needed. Rather, racial predispositions were directly and overwhelmingly implicated in attitudes toward Barack Obama during his 2008 primary and general election campaigns.[1] As a result, prominently associating any political evaluation with his candidacy—in support or opposition—was likely to result in racialization. In other words, Barack Obama racialized evaluations of other objects via transfer of affect—racial predispositions were *transferred* from opinions about Obama to related political evaluations when there was a strong association between the two

We operationalize this process by examining correlations between respondents' favorability ratings of Barack Obama and their evaluations of other candidates or issues. A strong oppositional relationship obviously occurred between Obama and his major opponents for the nomination and White House. Situating policy preferences in opposition to Obama, however, was not nearly as organic. Yet, as the "Obama Tax Policy" of raising taxes on Americans in the top income bracket became more salient over the campaign, the connection between Obama and their opinions about tax policy should have become more automatic. For example, Winter (2008, 130) concludes that 1994 health care opinions were gendered—meaning gender attitudes were brought more heavily to bear on preferences than in the past—in part because of that policy's strong association with Hillary Clinton. Similarly, tax policy should have become racialized by October 2008 because of its connection to Barack Obama.

The 2008 campaign thus presents something of a natural experiment for testing this theory of the spillover of racialization. In order for the theory to be valid, racial attitudes should have become more important in evaluations of Obama's main rivals as his campaigns against them intensified. It is also critical to demonstrate that the racialization of McCain evaluations is not simply an artifact of racial predispositions becoming more important in evaluations of *all* Republican nominees, as representatives of the more racially conservative political party. Rather, McCain evaluations should exhibit a markedly different pattern of racialization from before to after he became the nominee than should other GOP candidates. Finally, we expect to see tax policy undergo a similar process of racialization, as tax and redistribution issues came to dominate campaign debates in the final month of the campaign. However, the effect of racial predispositions on tax policy preferences should only increase over time for panel respondents who knew Barack Obama's position on taxes by the end of the campaign.

Racialized Evaluations of Hillary Clinton Before, During, and After the Primaries

Recall from chapter 2 that there was a dramatic reversal in the association of racial resentment with evaluations of Hillary Clinton among Democrats in March 2008 (see fig. 2.5). The impact of racial resentment changed from significantly negative (1992 to 2004) to significantly positive during the 2008 primary season. Our interpretation was that Hillary Clinton's strong support among racially conservative Democrats in the primaries resulted more from her (and their) opposition to Obama than from their affinity for her. It is equally important for our theory of Obama-induced racialization to compare the impact of racial resentment on evaluations of Hillary Clinton among Republicans and Independents with its impact among Democrats and to examine how these effects changed during the campaign. If a forced choice between her and Obama was required to racialize her public image, we should see less increase over time in the effects of racial resentment among Independents and Republicans who for the most part did not have to choose between her and Obama in the primaries.

The OLS coefficients for racial resentment displayed graphically in figure 4.1 show that this is precisely what happened. Each coefficient (or point on the graph) represents the effect of moving from least to most resentful on Hillary Clinton's ANES thermometer ratings from 1992 to 2004 and her CCAP favorability in 2008 (both dependent variables are coded on 0–1 scales),[2] while holding ideology and demographic factors constant. The dissimilar measurement of these two Clinton evaluation scales again complicates direct comparisons, but the patterns of racialization are unmistakable nonetheless. From 1992 to 2004, racial resentment had a significant negative impact on evaluations of Clinton among Democrats, Republicans, and Independents. By December 2007, however, a substantial gap emerged between Republicans and Independents, on the one hand, and Democrats, on the other, in the effects of racial resentment on their assessments of Hill-

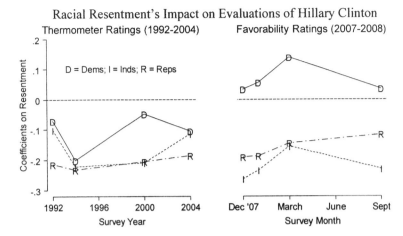

Figure 4.1. Impact of racial resentment on Hillary Clinton's thermometer ratings and favorability ratings by party identification. Points plot the OLS coefficients on racial resentment in table A4.1 of the online appendix (http://www.press.uchicago.edu/books/tesler/); each point represents either the effect of moving from least to most resentful on Clinton's thermometer ratings (coded 0–1) or her favorability ratings (coded 0–1). *Source*: 1992, 1994, 2000, and 2004 ANES; December 2007 and January, March, and September 2008 CCAP panelists.

ary Clinton. Racial resentment continued to be a strong negative predictor of opinions about Clinton in December 2007 for Republicans and Independents. Yet, at the same time, racial resentment had a small *positive* impact her evaluations by Democrats. This difference suggests that with Barack Obama situated as Hillary Clinton's main rival for the nomination, Democrats had to readjust their opinions of her in accordance with their racialized vote choices that we discussed in chapter 2. Independents and Republicans, however, likely maintained their previous racialized evaluation patterns because they could continue judging Hillary Clinton on her long record of social liberalism rather than as the last line of defense against Barack Obama winning *their* party's nomination.

In keeping with this contention, the correlation between Obama and Clinton favorability ratings was larger in December for Republicans and Independents than Democrats (r = .34 for Republicans, r = .38 for Independents, r = .13 for Democrats). In other words, Republicans and Independents evaluated Clinton and Obama more similarly than Democrats did. That disparity in Clinton-Obama favorability correlations between Democrats and Republicans/Independents grew considerably wider in March 2008, as the contest for the nomination got more contentious. Despite both candidates being ideologically similar Democrats, their favorability ratings were now *negatively correlated* for Democratic identifiers (r = −.15)—meaning Democrats viewed Clinton and Obama as opposites when the primaries became especially heated. Independents and Republicans, however, continued to mostly evaluate Obama in harmony with Clinton (correlations between Obama and Clinton's favorability ratings were r = .29 for Independents and r = .28 for Republicans).

Not surprisingly, then, figure 4.1 shows that racial resentment became an increasingly strong predictor of Democrats' favorable attitudes toward Hillary Clinton during the primaries. All else being equal, moving from least to most resentful in March 2008 increased support for Clinton by 14 percent of the favorability scale's range for Democrats. However, racial resentment remained a significant negative predictor of Independents' and Republicans' assessments of Hillary Clinton throughout the primary season, presumably because they were not forced to situate Obama and Clinton in opposition to each other to the same degree that Democrats had to.

So the intraparty nature of primary elections necessarily meant Democrats had to choose between these two candidates. However, they no longer viewed Clinton and Obama as opponents in September 2008. After the primaries were over, and Bill and Hillary Clinton forcefully endorsed Obama's candidacy at the Democratic National Convention, Democrats' evaluations of Clinton and Obama were once again positively correlated (r = .20)—meaning they were not evaluated in opposition to each other, as they had been in March 2008. The upshot, as the spillover-of-racialization theory predicts and figure 4.1 shows, is that racial resentment was no longer a significant positive predictor of Clinton favorability among Democrats in September 2008.

Taken together, these results clearly suggest that the impact of racial resentment on Hillary Clinton evaluations throughout 2008 depended on whether or not she was in a fundamentally oppositional relationship to Barack Obama at the time of the survey.

Racialized Evaluations of John McCain Before, During, and After the General Election Campaign

Changes in Racial Resentment's Impact on McCain Evaluations During the Election Year

If the effect of racial attitudes on political evaluations in 2008 depended primarily on how closely a candidate or issue was evaluated in contrast with

Barack Obama, then we should see a large increase in racial resentment's impact on evaluations of John McCain as his general election matchup with Barack Obama intensified. The American public, of course, increasingly contrasted the two general election candidates with one another as Election Day approached. For example, the correlation between Obama and McCain favorability ratings changed among CCAP panel respondents from –.02 in January to –.33 in March to –.75 in late October. With Obama and McCain increasingly evaluated as opposites by the electorate, we should see a corresponding increase in the effect of racial resentment on McCain evaluations.

This expectation is clearly borne out in figure 4.2. The display graphs the OLS coefficients for racial resentment's impact on McCain's CCAP favorability ratings throughout the election year. These coefficients again represent the change in favorability ratings associated with moving from least to most resentful, while holding our base control variables constant. Figure 4.2, therefore, shows that racial resentment had only a small independent impact on McCain's favorability ratings in December 2007 and January 2008. As a McCain-Obama general election was looking more inevitable by March 2008, though, racial resentment's profound negative impact on assessments of Barack Obama spilled over to positive evaluations of his likely opponent,

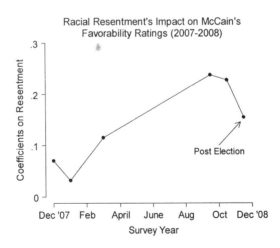

Figure 4.2. Impact of racial resentment on John McCain's favorability ratings. Points plot the OLS coefficients on racial resentment in table A4.2 of the online appendix (http://www .press.uchicago.edu/books/tesler/); each point represents the effect of moving from least to most resentful on McCain's favorability ratings (coded 0–1). *Source*: December 2007 and January, March, September, October, and November 2008 CCAP panelists.

McCain. Even with partisan, ideological, and demographic controls in place, moving from least to most resentful increased McCain's March favorability rating by 12 percent of the favorability scale's range.

The effect of racial resentment on evaluations of McCain continued to grow during the fall campaign as he and Obama were increasingly seen as opposed to each other. During the two months just before the election, moving from least to most resentful was predicted to increase one's opinion of John McCain by nearly one-quarter of the favorability scale's range. After the election was over, though, these same panel respondents predictably contrasted McCain less with Obama than they had just a few weeks earlier ($r = -.57$ in November to $r = -.75$ in October). The impact of racial resentment on McCain evaluations, therefore, also receded. Figure 4.2 shows that the effect of racial resentment on McCain's favorability rating diminished by about one-third between October and the postelection CCAP.

Racialization of McCain Occurred Earlier among Panelists Expecting a McCain-Obama General Election

Just above we discussed how Barack Obama and Hillary Clinton were viewed more in opposition to one another by Democrats than by Republicans or Independents who did not necessarily have to choose between the two candidates in the primaries. Likewise, respondents who during the primaries foresaw that Barack Obama would face John McCain in the general election should have differentiated the two candidates more than fellow panelists who did not yet perceive them to be in such an oppositional relationship.[3]

Hardly any of our panelists expected John McCain and Barack Obama to be the two parties' presidential candidates in December 2007.[4] However, by January 2008, 17 percent thought that they both would eventually become their parties' nominees. And as expected, McCain's and Obama's January favorability ratings were more strongly negatively correlated among CCAP panel respondents who thought the two would be the eventual nominees than among panelists expecting a different matchup ($r = -.24$ to $r = -.01$, respectively).

By our account, the sharper contrast between McCain and Obama in early 2008 among respondents correctly predicting the ultimate matchup should also have resulted in earlier racialization of McCain evaluations. Figure 4.3 reveals that those correctly predicting an Obama-McCain matchup did indeed racialize their evaluations of John McCain earlier than did their fellow panel participants. The figure graphs the OLS coefficients for racial

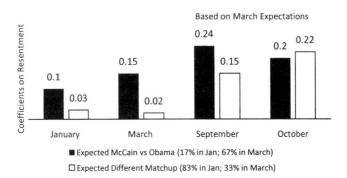

Figure 4.3. Impact of racial resentment on John McCain's favorability ratings by general election expectation. Columns plot the OLS coefficients on racial resentment in table A4.3 of the online appendix (http://www.press.uchicago.edu/books/tesler/). Each column represents the effect of moving from least to most resentful on McCain's favorability ratings (coded 0–1). The September and October columns show the impact of racial resentment by whom the panel respondents expected to become the Democratic and Republican nominees back in March 2008. *Source*: January, March, September, and October 2008 CCAP panelists.

resentment's effect on McCain's favorability ratings separately for panel respondents who correctly predicted a McCain-Obama contest at the time of the survey and for their less prescient counterparts. The effect of racial resentment was considerably bigger for the accurate predictors in January and March 2008 than it was for the other panelists. Yet, as we just mentioned, only a small fraction of the panel correctly predicted this matchup in January 2008. Because such a small percentage of the public actually thought McCain and Obama would compete against each other for control of the White House, racial resentment had only a modest effect on evaluations of McCain in January 2008, as figure 4.2 illustrated. The fact that Obama-McCain soothsayers changed from a small minority of respondents in January 2008 to the majority (67 percent) in March 2008 helps explain the large increase in racial resentment's overall effect on McCain evaluations over that period, as also shown in Figure 4.2.

Perhaps the earlier racialization of McCain's favorability ratings had nothing to do with Obama, though. Maybe those who expected this matchup were simply better at connecting their racial predispositions to McCain evaluations than the rest of the electorate to begin with. That seems unlikely because there was a large difference in racialization between those who accurately predicted the general election matchup and those who did not, either when correct predictors made up a small minority in January 2008, or when they constituted a clear majority in March 2008. The CCAP's panel design, however, allows us to empirically test this hypothesis by tracking respondents from both expectation groups throughout the election year. If individuals who expected the correct general election matchup back in March were simply better at connecting their racial predispositions to the Republican nominee than their fellow panelists, they should continue to rely more on racial resentment in evaluating John McCain throughout the entire campaign.

We suspect, however, that McCain's favorability ratings racialized earlier among respondents who expected him to face off against Obama in the general election because he was already seen by them as the last line of defense against a black president. If this "earlier racialization" hypothesis is true, then we should find only a negligible joint effect of racial resentment and March general election expectations on McCain's favorability ratings come the fall of 2008. Indeed, the visibility of presidential campaigns ensured that virtually every American would then know that Senator McCain was the final obstacle in Obama's quest for the White House.

The September and October results presented in figure 4.3 are highly consistent with this expectation. These columns show the effects of racial resentment on McCain's favorability ratings in September and October for panel respondents who had, or had not, thought in March that Obama and McCain would ultimately square off. As can be seen, incorrect predictors closed the relative gap in racial resentment effects on evaluations of McCain by September 2008. Regardless of how accurately our panel respondents had forecast the ultimate nominees back in March, all relied heavily on their racial predispositions to evaluate John McCain in September 2008. And by late October, the effect of racial resentment was essentially the same for the two expectation groups.

These results again strongly suggest that the racialization of Clinton and McCain in 2008 depended on how closely they were situated in opposition to Barack Obama. During the primary season, Democrats were forced to choose between Obama and Clinton, so they racialized evaluations of her more than did Independents or Republicans. Similarly, some forecast early on that McCain would be the ultimate opponent of Obama, and they racialized their McCain evaluations more than did those who did not see McCain and Obama as eventual opponents. This disparity in the effects of racial resentment between early Obama-McCain predictors and their less prescient counterparts, however, vanished as the general election campaign intensified.[5]

McCain Racialization Compared to Previous Republican Nominees

The increased racialization of McCain evaluations through the campaign could conceivably have been due to ideological considerations rather than to his opposition to Barack Obama. The racialization of Clinton evaluations during the primaries cannot have been due to nonracial ideological factors on which they were so similar. But the impact of racial resentment on Mc-Cain evaluations could have increased through the election year simply because he was running against a liberal Democrat, no matter what his race, because liberals and conservatives have long been divided over racial issues, as indicated in chapter 1. The growing racialization of McCain evaluations, then, could simply have been a byproduct of his newfound position as torch bearer for the more conservative political party.

A good test of this possibility is to compare the link of racial resentment to McCain evaluations with its link to evaluations of earlier Republican candidates who opposed *white* liberals. And in fact, McCain's trajectory was quite different from that of earlier Republican candidates. Figure 4.4 plots the effects of racial resentment on the thermometer ratings of the previous Republican presidential candidates before and after they won the party nomination.[6] The impact of racial resentment on evaluations of George H. W. Bush, Bob Dole, and George W. Bush was actually larger *before* they became the nominees, with controls on other predispositions and demographics. This postnomination decrease in the effects of racial resentment on evaluations of earlier Republican candidates was most likely produced by the rush to party solidarity after their nominations. Indeed, party identification showed large increases in impact on thermometer ratings after these earlier Republicans became the party's leaders.[7] This enhanced strength of partisanship probably came at the expense of racial resentment, since the two predispositions are highly correlated (Valentino and Sears 2005). The upshot is that the impact of racial resentment decreased for George H. W. Bush, Bob Dole, and George W. Bush after they became the GOP's presidential nominees.

Figure 4.4 shows, however, that the effect of racial resentment on Mc-Cain evaluations bucked this pattern of diminishing postnomination racial resentment effects for the previous GOP presidential candidates. In contrast

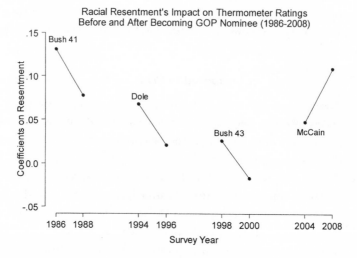

Figure 4.4. Impact of racial resentment on candidate thermometer ratings before and after becoming the GOP nominee. Points plot the OLS coefficients on racial resentment in table A4.4 of the online appendix (http://www.press.uchicago.edu/books/tesler/); each point represents the effect of moving from least to most resentful on candidates' thermometer ratings (coded 0–1). *Source*: 1986, 1988, 1998, 2000, 2004, and 2008 ANES; 1994–1996 ANES panelists.

with them, the impact of racial resentment on Senator McCain's thermometer ratings substantially *increased* from 2004 to 2008.[8] That increased racialization of McCain evaluations from 2004 to 2008, in contrast to the decreased effects of racial resentment on the three prior Republican candidates postnomination, would seem to be the result of his representing the last line of defense against the election of a black president, rather than simply opposition to a generic liberal Democratic candidate.

Racialized Evaluations of Hillary Clinton and John McCain in November 2009

We saw earlier that the distinctive support for Hillary Clinton among racially resentful Democrats receded after her contest with Barack Obama ended (see fig. 4.1). Racial resentment's effect on McCain favorability also diminished after the general election (see fig. 4.2). With this in mind, we once again asked CCAP panel respondents about their impressions of Clinton and McCain in our November 2009 survey. Based upon the trends in figures 4.1 and 4.2, we expected that the link of racial resentment to favorable evaluations of Hillary Clinton among Democrats, and to favorable evaluations of John McCain in the entire electorate, would continue to decline as the 2008 Democratic primary, in Clinton's case, and the 2008 general election, in McCain's case, faded further into history.

Figure 4.5 supports this expectation. The first display tracks the impact of racial resentment on Democrats' favorability ratings of Hillary Clinton from January 2008 to November 2009. The coefficients presented here differ slightly from those in figure 4.1 because the analysis now includes only panel respondents who were interviewed in all four of these surveys. However, the same pattern of highly racialized Clinton evaluations during her spring contest with Obama and then a falloff in these resentment effects afterward is apparent again. Racial resentment's positive impact on Clinton's favorability ratings reached its peak at the height of her primary battle with Barack Obama in March 2008 and then diminished in Sep-

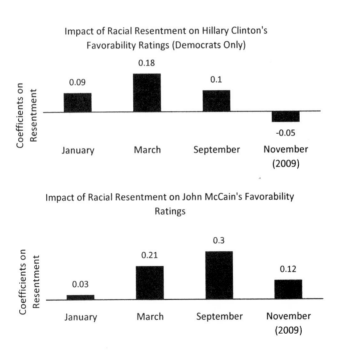

Figure 4.5. Impact of racial resentment on favorability ratings of Hillary Clinton (Democrats only) and John McCain (full-sample model). Points plot the OLS coefficients on racial resentment in table A4.5 of the online appendix (http://www.press.uchicago.edu/books/tesler/); each point represents the effect of moving from least to most resentful on candidates' favorability ratings (coded 0–1). *Source:* January, March, and September 2008 and November 2009 CCAP panelists.

tember after she strongly endorsed Obama's candidacy at the Democratic Convention.

At the end of 2009, Secretary of State Clinton, of course, was even more closely allied with Barack Obama as a loyal member of his administration. Not surprisingly, then, the first panel in figure 4.5 shows racial resentment had returned in November 2009 to its normal and longstanding negative impact on evaluations of Hillary Clinton among our Democratic panel respondents. That is, racial resentment once again resumed the association with Democrats' colder feelings toward Hillary Clinton that it had in every survey before fate happened to match her against the first black candidate with a realistic shot at winning the Democratic nomination.

The second display in figure 4.5 similarly shows a reduction in the impact of racial resentment on McCain's favorability ratings after he was freed of his opposition to Obama. By November 2009, a year after his defeat, McCain's linkage with racial resentment had almost returned to prenomination levels. As we saw in figure 4.2, racial resentment's positive impact on John McCain's favorability ratings steadily grew in size as his general election contest with Barack Obama intensified. Figure 4.5, however, shows that racial resentment's impact on our CCAP panelists' evaluations of McCain in November 2009 was now only about one-third the size it had been a year earlier during his general election campaign against Barack Obama.

The changing impact of racial resentment on assessments of Hillary Clinton and John McCain from early 2008 to late 2009 demonstrates the polarization of political evaluations associated with Obama according to racial liberalism or conservatism. The activation of racial resentment during their campaigns against Obama, along with the corresponding deactivation as those contests became an increasingly distant political memory, clearly indicates that the effect of racial attitudes on political evaluations can be substantially altered by how closely those assessments are related—either positively or negatively—to Barack Obama.

Barack Obama and the Racialization of Tax Policy in 2008

It would have seemed improbable that tax policy preferences could ever be as strongly associated with Barack Obama as opposition to John McCain was in the fall of 2008. General election vote choice, after all, is almost perfectly predicted by which candidate one likes better (Kelley 1983). It was also a cognitively much less demanding task to know that John McCain was Barack Obama's opponent for the White House than it was to understand

that President Bush's high-income tax cuts and Obama were in an oppositional relationship.

The McCain campaign did everything in its power, however, to make
voters aware of this oppositional relationship. After months of searching
for a unifying campaign message, McCain settled on attacking Obama's tax
policy in October. The final debate exemplified this strategy, as John Mc-
Cain introduced "Joe the Plumber" to America. Obama had made a televised
comment to Joe the Plumber about a need to "spread the wealth." McCain's
campaign seized on the comment to make the case that Obama's tax policy
would take money from the hardworking Joe the Plumbers of America and
use the revenue for economic redistribution. This tax policy frame dominated the final weeks of the campaign. McCain began referring to Obama
as "Barack the Redistributor" and Joe the Plumber quickly became a household name.[9] Jackman and Vavreck (2009) surmise that this instructive message from the McCain campaign contributed to substantial learning about
Obama's tax policy positions in 2008.

The result of such learning was that by October 2008, our respondents
situated their tax policy preferences in opposition to Obama's much more
directly than they had earlier in the year. The correlation between Obama's
favorability ratings and favoring a tax increase on Americans making over
$200,000 was .40 in December 2007, compared to .67 in October 2008—a
correlation comparable in absolute magnitude to the previously mentioned
negative association between Obama and McCain October favorability ratings ($r = -.75$). Thus, as Americans connected their tax policy preferences
more closely to Barack Obama during the general election campaign they
should have similarly connected their racial predispositions to opinions
about taxes via our spillover theory of racialization.

To test this, figure 4.6 graphs the effects of racial resentment on tax
policy preferences with our base-model control variables held constant. It
shows that the impact of racial resentment on tax policy positions indeed
increased through the campaign year of 2008. Of course tax policy was
already somewhat racialized before 2008 (see also Sears and Citrin 1985).
The first panel in figure 4.6 shows that all else being equal, moving from
least to most racially resentful decreased support for a top-bracket tax increase by roughly 25 percentage points in December 2007. With the McCain
campaign subsequently doing its best to link higher taxes to Barack Obama,
though, the impact of racial resentment on tax policy preferences jumped in
magnitude among the exact same panel respondents during the course of
the campaign. By October, moving from least to most resentful had become

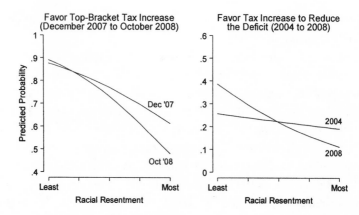

Figure 4.6. Support for tax increases as a function of racial resentment. Probabilities were based on logistic regression coefficients in table A4.6 of the online appendix (http://www .press.uchicago.edu/books/tesler/). Predicted probabilities were calculated by setting all other variables to their sample means. *Source*: December 2007 and March and October 2008 CCAP panelists; 2004 and 2008 ANES.

associated with about a 40-point decrease in support for raising taxes on high-income Americans.

The second panel in figure 4.6 shows that tax policy preferences were more racialized in 2008 than in 2004, at least as reflected in the one tax policy question similarly worded in both ANES surveys: a postelection item about increasing taxes to balance the budget.[10] This question did not evoke racial predispositions in 2004. Figure 4.6, however, shows that moving from least to most resentful decreased support for a tax increase to balance the budget by nearly 30 percentage points in 2008, again suggesting that the association with Obama had racialized his tax policy.

As with the racialization of evaluations of Hillary Clinton and John Mc-Cain, not all subgroups should have situated their tax policy preferences in opposition to Barack Obama as closely as others. For example, panel respondents who were aware of Obama's tax policy position should have connected their tax policy preferences to Obama more strongly than those who did not know that Obama wanted to raise the top-income tax rate. Indeed, the correlation between supporting a top-bracket tax increase in October and Obama's October favorability rating was .73 for those aware of his position and only .20 for those who did not know Obama favored raising taxes on Americans making over $200,000. If the association with Obama was driving the growing racialization of tax policy preferences, then the impact of racial resentment on these opinions should have increased more powerfully during the course of the campaign for panel respondents who knew Barack Obama's position on the issue.

Figure 4.7 tests this hypothesis by assessing the effects of racial resentment on tax policy preferences in December 2007 and October 2008 for those who knew Obama's position on taxes by the end of the campaign, compared to those who did not know his tax policy position. The results presented in the display are consistent with our expectations. The effect of racial resentment on tax policy preferences among panel respondents aware of Obama's tax policy increased in October by about two-thirds its original December value. However, the negative impact of racial resentment on tax policy preferences for those *unaware* of Obama's tax policy position in October actually *decreased* during the campaign, as shown in the second panel of figure 4.7. Knowing the link between Obama and his tax policy, then, was absolutely essential for the racialization of taxes during the 2008 campaign.

Since Obama's tax policy position was such a high-profile campaign issue, only about 15 percent of our October CCAP panel respondents did not know Obama favored a top-bracket tax increase. The racialization of tax policy among the 85 percent who knew Obama wanted to increase taxes on high-income Americans overshadowed the lack of an effect among the small, less-knowledgeable minority. The upshot was a significantly enhanced overall

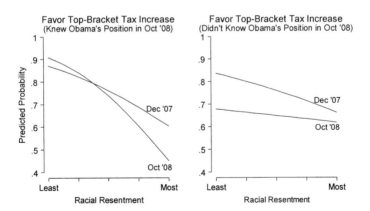

Figure 4.7. Probability of favoring a top-bracket tax increase as a function of racial resentment and knowledge of Obama's position. Probabilities were based on logistic regression coefficients in table A4.7 of the online appendix (http://www.press.uchicago.edu/books/tesler/). Predicted probabilities were calculated by setting all other variables to their sample means. *Source*: December 2007 and March and October 2008 CCAP panelists.

impact of racial resentment on tax policy preferences over the course of the election year.

Concluding Remarks: Growing Polarization of Public Opinion by Racial Attitudes?

These results could have profound implications for American politics during the Obama presidency. They suggest that any issue Obama takes a public stance on might soon become polarized according to racial predispositions. Race is probably the most visceral issue in American public life. As such, increased polarization of the electorate according to racial attitudes could make the contemporary political discourse even more vitriolic than the earlier rancorous atmospheres under Presidents Bill Clinton and George W. Bush. Such a racialized environment would have the potential to make reaching common ground on public policy an even more difficult task in the age of Obama. That was hardly the vision of an Obama presidency envisaged by those hoping it would bring in a post-racial less-polarized nation.

Of course, the same Obama-induced racialization uncovered in the campaign would only continue into the future if President Obama's evaluations remained as racialized as Candidate Obama's were in 2008. There are several plausible factors that could mitigate these effects during his tenure in the White House. However, the final chapter also presents substantial new post-election evidence suggesting that both support for and opposition to Obama during the first year of his presidency remained extraordinarily racialized.

That new evidence from the Obama presidency is consistent with a number of results from the campaign indicating that it could be very difficult to deactivate racial predispositions in assessments of Barack Obama. Despite nearly one billion dollars in campaign spending, the economy crashing, and three polished debate performances in which he was clearly viewed as a stronger leader than his opponent,[11] the effect of racial resentment on McCain-Obama vote preference was virtually unchanged from March 2008 up until Election Day, as seen in chapter 3. Similarly, racial attitudes continued to have an enormous impact on evaluations of Barack Obama throughout the election year. In fact, racial resentment's impact on Obama evaluations for CCAP panel respondents was nearly identical in December 2007 and October 2008.[12] Likewise, and in spite of roughly 70 percent of Americans approving of Obama's job handling the White House transition at the end of November,[13] the impact of racial resentment was not at all diminished in postelection evaluations of Obama by either the CCAP panelists interviewed throughout November 2008 or in the ANES postelection survey.[14]

We have suggested that the continuity of these effects on both support for and opposition to Barack Obama, in the face of changing campaign contexts and differentially racialized informational environments, stemmed from the accessibility of racial attitudes evoked by Obama's position as the first black candidate who could realistically win the presidency. After his victory, Obama occupied an even greater symbolic title as the first black president. The hopes and fears evoked by that symbolism could well have made racial predispositions highly accessible in evaluations of Obama from his earliest days in office. If so, any contentious policies that he took a strong position on might become increasingly polarized by racial attitudes in the years ahead.

5

The Racialized Voting Patterns of
Racial and Ethnic Minorities

"Obama simply has a problem that he happens to be black."

ADELFA CALLEJO, *on Obama's inability to make inroads with
Latino voters, February 27, 2008.*[1]

The demographic composition of the American electorate is rapidly changing. According to national exit polls, 89 percent of presidential voters in 1976
were white, with whites still comprising 87 percent of the national electorate in 1992. This white proportion had precipitously fallen to just 74 percent
by 2008, though. The reason is twofold. First, the black proportion of the
electorate increased substantially in the 2008 election. African Americans
accounted for only 9 percent of the national electorate in 1976 and 8 percent
in 1992, but in 2008, this number grew to 13 percent. The second reason
is an even more dramatic upsurge in the Latino fraction of the vote, from
1 percent in 1976, to 2 percent in 1992, to 9 percent in 2008.

This surge in minority voting was politically crucial for Obama's prospects in 2008. First, the proportion of white voters was even smaller in
the 2008 Democratic primaries. With African Americans accounting for
roughly one-fifth of Democrats, only about two-thirds of the party's primary
votes were cast by white Americans. That plainly was of great potential advantage to a black candidate for the Democratic nomination. Second, the
rapidly increasing Latino vote is particularly noticeable in some potentially
crucial swing states in the Electoral College, such as Florida, New Mexico,
Colorado, Nevada, and Arizona. A strong showing with Latinos, then, could
have easily tipped the general election balance in Obama's favor.

Any comprehensive account of how Barack Obama won the nomination
and the White House must, therefore, include analyses of African American
and Latino voters. That point was certainly not lost on astute political commentators in the media. Considerable attention was paid to racial and ethnic
voting patterns before the primaries began. Obama simply could not win
the nomination without overwhelming support from African Americans.
In almost any election in which a black Democrat has a white opponent,

blacks usually vote almost uniformly for the African American candidate (Hajnal 2007). But 2008 had the potential for being a little different. Speculation abounded in 2007 about whether African Americans' strong support for Hillary Clinton in most national polls throughout that year would continue when the votes were actually cast in 2008. Some African Americans at the time were even describing Obama as not authentically black enough (Walters 2007). Moreover, African Americans had a longstanding loyalty to President Clinton, sometimes called "the first black president," that generalized to his wife.[2] And there were serious concerns among black voters about Obama's viability as a candidate.

Hillary Clinton's popularity with Latinos generated similar interest during the primaries. Bill Clinton had also been highly popular among Latinos. Yet some suspected that Obama's inability to wrestle the Latino vote away from Senator Clinton might have also stemmed from elevated tensions between African American and Latino communities (Arrillaga 2008; Reno 2008; Nagourney and Steinhauer 2008). After the general election, however, analysts quickly turned their focus to Obama's strong *support* from Latino voters. How, for instance, did he manage to outperform John Kerry's 2004 performance by 14 percentage points among Latino voters, assuming one can trust the exit polls to estimate that correctly? And what might that substantial Latino movement to the Democratic Party from 2004 to 2008 mean for partisan politics in the years to come?

Challenges in Analyzing Racial and Ethnic Minorities' Vote Preferences in 2008

To begin with, sampling issues complicate our analyses of racial and ethnic minorities' voting behavior, especially that of Latinos. For starters, the sampling frames differ across the three surveys we depend on in this chapter's Latino analyses. The CCAP is a registered voter sample. The 2008 ANES's Latino oversample additionally includes people who are not registered to vote, but only if they are citizens. And the 2004 National Politics Study (NPS) samples the entire Latino population.[3] The NPS, therefore, includes a large proportion of foreign born respondents and noncitizens.[4] Second, we suffer from the standard problem of worryingly small numbers of cases, though less worrisome than usual because of the unprecedentedly large CCAP sample and the 2008 ANES's oversample of Latinos. But still, analyzing just Democratic primary voters in the CCAP reduced its Latino subsample to only about 300 cases. Our comparison of general election voting behavior in the 2004 NPS with the 2008 ANES also leaves us with less than 400 Latinos who voted in each survey. Finally, these three surveys yielded considerably different estimates of Latino support for the Democratic presidential candidates. And the estimates in all three surveys differ significantly from the Latino vote shares reported in presidential exit polls: compared to the exit polls, the 2008 ANES and the 2004 NPS *overstated* Latino support for the Democratic candidate by 7 and 8 percentage points, respectively, while the CCAP *understated* Obama's two-party vote share among Latinos by 6 points.[5] Taken together, our surveys' differing sample frames, smaller Latino sample sizes, and variability in estimated vote shares necessarily leave us cautious about our Latino results.

The Nature and Origins of Symbolic Racism by Race and Ethnicity

Our primary objective in this chapter is to determine how racial attitudes affected these minority voting patterns throughout 2008. However, our key variable, symbolic racism, was originally conceptualized and has always been used as a measure of white prejudice against African Americans. It is theorized to be based, among whites, in a blend of early socialized negative feelings about blacks with traditional conservative moral values. Does the construct have such underpinnings for Latinos? There is good reason to believe that it might. After all, through schools and the media, U.S.-born whites and Latinos are both exposed during their childhood and adolescent years to the same prevalent stereotypes about African Americans (Gilens 1999; Entman and Rojecki 2000; Blinder 2007). Yet, besides research showing that symbolic racism had similar correlates for white, Latino, and Asian undergraduates at UCLA (Sears, Haley, and Henry 2008), little is known about its meaning and underpinnings for minority groups that are dominated by relatively recent immigrants.

Even less is known about the determinants of African Americans' responses to the racial resentment measures. The four items in the racial resentment battery present an entirely different task for black respondents than for interviewees from other racial and ethnic groups. For African Americans, these survey questions are tapping attitudes about their own group, that is, their *in-group*. Because all other races and ethnicities are evaluating African Americans as an out-group, one might suspect black respondents' answers to these questions could have markedly different origins than is the case for Latinos and whites.

Table 5.1. Summary statistics for racial resentment by race and ethnicity

	N	Mean	SD	Cronbach's α
Whites				
2008 ANES	1,047	.646	.231	.772
March CCAP	11,108	.664	.258	.839
Latinos				
2008 ANES	434	.598	.209	.613
March CCAP	873	.591	.269	.812
African Americans				
2008 ANES	512	.477	.212	.495
March CCAP	1,406	.368	.222	.647

Since so little is known about the nature of symbolic racism among Latinos and African Americans, we start with a brief examination of both the extent of their racially resentful responses and what exactly these responses seem to mean to them. Table 5.1 presents a basic summary of racial resentment scores for whites, Latinos, and African Americans. As can be seen, white Americans score about 6 percentage points higher in racial resentment than Latinos. Yet both groups are, in the aggregate, on the resentful side of the spectrum. The racial resentment scores of about .65 for whites and .60 for Latinos are well above the .50 midpoint. In contrast, African Americans have much lower levels of racial resentment than either their white or Latino counterparts. Averaging across the two surveys, their mean resentment levels are 23 points lower than whites' and 17 points below their Latino counterparts.[6] We mentioned earlier that the racial resentment battery was designed to distinguish between *whites* who are generally sympathetic and unsympathetic to blacks (Kinder and Sanders 1996). If we apply this distinction to *all* racial and ethnic groups, the average resentment scores above .50 for whites and Latinos mark them as predominantly racially resentful, whereas African Americans' scores below this midpoint classify them as racially sympathetic.

But does symbolic racism actually mean the same thing for different races and ethnicities? One way to address that question is to compare its underpinnings across groups. Several previous studies have examined the multiple components of symbolic racism for white Americans (Sears, Van Laar, Carillo, and Kosterman 1997; Sears and Henry 2003, 2005; Tarman and Sears 2005). These earlier examinations have largely confirmed the original theory that the origins of symbolic racism for white Americans lie in a blend of antiblack affect and beliefs that blacks violate traditional conservative values such as individualism, obedience, and social morality.

To determine whether racial resentment has similar origins for Latinos and African Americans, we compared the relationships of racial resentment with racial affect and traditional conservative values across these groups. The large oversamples of Latinos and African Americans in the 2008 ANES permit such a comparative analysis. Moreover, this survey's rich array of questions allows us to operationalize racial affect in the forms of group feeling thermometers, racial stereotypes, and Pettigrew and Meertens's (1995) affective prejudice questions about how often one feels admiration and/or sympathy for blacks. We can also effectively operationalize the respective conservative values of obedience and social morality with standard ANES measures of authoritarianism and moral traditionalism (see appendix for question wording and variable measures).

Table 5.2 presents both the bivariate correlations and multivariate standardized regression coefficients reflecting the relationship that each of these variables has with racial resentment. The results for white Americans comport quite well with previous research. White racial resentment has origins in both antiblack affect and traditional conservative values. All of our racial attitude measures—most especially antiblack affect—are sizable and significant components of white racial resentment in the multivariate model. Even with the other racial attitudes and conservative values in the model held constant, moving from lowest to highest in black affect decreased white racial resentment by 41 percent of the scale's range. Each traditional conservative value is also significantly related to symbolic racism for white Americans.

Among Latinos, symbolic racism also appears to have origins in antiblack affect and beliefs about social morality. Table 5.2 shows that antiblack affect, stereotypes about African Americans, and moral traditionalism are all significant predictors of racial resentment for Latinos. Although Latinos' and whites' racial resentments have similar correlates, symbolic racism is better organized by our model among white Americans. The predictors in table 5.2, for instance, explain 40 percent of the variance in white racial resentment but only 16 percent of the variability in Latino responses. Similarly, table 5.1 showed that the internal consistency of the racial resentment scale is also higher for whites than for Latinos (the Cronbach's alphas for whites are .77 and .84, and for Latinos .61 and .81). Both findings indicate that symbolic racism is a more coherent and crystallized belief system for whites than it is for Latinos.

African Americans, interestingly enough, prove to be quite a different story. The model that works well for whites does not work at all well for blacks. Overall, the racial affect/conservative values model explains even less of the variance in racial resentment for African Americans (13 percent)

Table 5.2. Origins of symbolic racism by race and ethnicity (affect and values model; OLS regression)

	Whites		Latinos		African Americans	
	Beta	r	Beta	r	Beta	r
Attitudes about Blacks						
Black Affect	−.330**	−.426**	−.246**	−.227**	−.153**	−.157**
Negative Stereotypes	.147**	.251**	.123*	.217**	.130**	.013
Attitudes about Whites						
White Affect	.112**	.087**	.150**	.017	.077	.092*
Negative Stereotypes	−.093**	−.103**	.020	.026	−.169**	−.174**
Conservative Values						
Moral Traditionalism	.184**	.382**	.231**	.248**	.045	.021
Authoritarianism	.119**	.324**	.100*	.154**	.000	.078
Ideological Conservatism	.162**	.362**	.042	.111*	.020	.072
Demographics						
Education	−.094**	−.206**	.052	.009	−.269**	−.297**
Age	−.052*	.066**	.008	.026	.002	.033
Male	−.076**	.040	.026	.052	−.027	−.045
South	.122**	.201**	.060	.105*	.087*	.130**
Observations	935		403		461	
Adjusted R²	.398		.157		.132	

Source: 2008 ANES.

Note: Beta represents the OLS standardized multiple regression coefficients; r represents bivariate correlations. All variables are coded 0–1, with 1 representing higher values of each variable.

* $p < .01$; ** $p < .001$

than for Latinos (16 percent), and far beneath that for whites (40 percent). Moreover, symbolic racism appears to have completely different origins for blacks. True, antiblack affect is significantly related to African Americans' scores on the racial resentment scale, but the correlation is more than two times greater for whites and 50 percent larger for Latinos. Also unlike whites and Latinos, stereotypes about *whites* actually yielded the largest standardized coefficient of any racial variable for African Americans.[7] Moreover, none of our indices of conservative values—moral traditionalism, authoritarianism, and ideological self-placement—is significantly related to black racial resentment, even at the bivariate level. A further contrast with whites and Latinos is that education is the one coefficient that stands out for African Americans in table 5.2. All else being equal, a change in education level from dropping out of high school to pursuing postgraduate studies decreased African Americans' racial resentment by 23 percent of the scale's range—a difference greater than the divide between black and white Americans' mean resentment scores in the 2008 ANES.

This large education effect for African Americans is informative. Sniderman and Piazza (2002, 42–43) found formal education to be a sizable positive predictor of their four forms of African American racial solidarity, with educational attainment having its biggest impact on feelings of black pride and Afrocentrism. Similarly, Sears, Haley, and Henry (2008) show a significant strengthening of group consciousness among black undergraduates at UCLA during the course of their college years.[8] Group consciousness and group interests have long been well-known, systematic determinants of African American public opinion and political behavior (Gurin, Hatchett, and Jackson 1989; Dawson 1994, 2001; Tate 1994; Kinder and Sanders 1996; Sears and McConahay 1973; Sears and Savalei 2006; Sniderman and Piazza 2002; Harris-Lacewell 2004). It is possible, then, that the strong association of greater education with lower racial resentment scores among African Americans is explained by the higher group consciousness shown by more educated blacks.

The large oversample of African Americans in the 2004 NPS allowed us to test the hypothesis that higher racial resentment scores for African Americans have their origins in weak feelings of group interests and racial solidarity. The survey includes only two items from the racial resentment battery, but it has two other questions that are nearly identical in content to the omitted resentment items.[9] Although the NPS lacks the ANES's comprehensive measures of black affect and traditional values—factors that are apparently central to racial resentment among whites and Latinos but not African Americans—it contains exceptional measures of group identity and racial competition with whites (again, see appendix for question wording and variable measures).

The relationships between these group consciousness variables and symbolic racism among African Americans are shown in table 5.3. As can be seen, group-based racial attitudes (feeling closer to blacks than to whites and believing African Americans work harder than white Americans) are significantly associated with racial resentment among African Americans. However, weak feelings of group interest and racial solidarity relate to symbolic racism even more strongly for black respondents. All else being equal, a combined change from believing that African Americans have a shared fate and that blacks are in competition with whites for jobs and political influence, on the one hand, to possessing the weakest feelings of both linked fate and group competition, on the other, increased racial resentment scores among African Americans by over 30 percent of the scale's range.[10] These large effects help the group consciousness model explain much more of the variance in racial resentment scores among African Americans than the affect and values model typically employed in analyses of the origins of sym-

Table 5.3. Origins of symbolic racism for African-Americans (group consciousness model; OLS regression)

	Beta	r
Group-Based Racial Attitudes		
Closer to Blacks than Whites	−.110**	−.263**
Blacks Work Harder than Whites	−.125**	−.191**
Group Interests		
Linked Fate	−.214**	−.355**
Black-White Competition	−.229**	−.324**
Conservative Values		
Ideological Conservatism	.105**	.197**
Demographics		
Education	−.209**	−.246**
Age	.022	.022
Male	−.037	−.050
South	.060	.079*
Observations	726	
Adjusted R^2	.270	

Source: 2004 NPS.

Note: Beta represents the OLS standardized multiple regression coefficients; r represents bivariate correlations. All variables are coded 0–1, with 1 representing higher values of each variable.

* $p < .01$; **$p < .001$

bolic racism among whites (27 percent in the NPS to 13 percent in the ANES, respectively).

We would certainly not claim this to be a definitive analysis of the origins of symbolic racism among members of ethnic and racial minority groups. But it does appear from this exploratory analysis that symbolic racism among Latinos, just as among whites, has its origins in a blend of antiblack affect and traditional conservative values. However, the symbolic racism belief system seems to be more highly crystallized among whites than among Latinos. And racial resentment has an entirely different meaning for African Americans. Black responses to the racial resentment questions are largely a function of negative attitudes toward their racial in-group combined with weak in-group consciousness, rather than with traditional conservative values.

Effects of Racial Resentment Through the Primary Season by Race and Ethnicity

Now that we have a working understanding of the meanings of racial resentment among Latinos and African Americans, we can test whether it had the same effects on their voting behavior during the primaries as it had among whites. Our full-sample analyses in chapter 2 showed that Obama's large increase in support among the entire Democratic primary electorate from December 2007 to March 2008 came disproportionately from the liberal

side of the resentment spectrum (see fig. 2.2). The least resentful, for instance, increased their predicted support for Obama by over 30 percentage
points during that time period, while the most resentful remained opposed
to Obama at a relatively constant rate throughout the primary season. We
described that pattern as reflecting Obama's racialized momentum, whereby
he increased his aggregate vote share primarily with enhanced support over
time from racial liberals.

Hillary Clinton's victories in California and Texas fueled the suspicion
that Latinos' racial attitudes were dealing an even more devastating blow
to Obama's prospects than they were even among whites. However, Latino
panel respondents actually showed a very similar pattern of momentum as
had whites. Figure 5.1 graphs the effect of racial resentment on Obama vote
choice in December 2007 and January and March 2008, for whites, Latinos, and African Americans while holding the rest of the variables in our
base-model constant. As can be seen in the first panel of the display, Obama
doubled his predicted vote share among the least racially resentful whites
from 35 percent in December 2007 to 70 percent in March 2008. Obama's
activation of white racial liberals, by our account, occurred because these
individuals were unencumbered in voting their affective sympathies for an
African American candidate after he had presented himself as a viable and
electable alternative to Hillary Clinton in the early primaries.

The second panel of figure 5.1 shows that Obama's growing support from
Latinos during the primary season also came disproportionately from those
low in racial resentment. All else being equal, Obama increased his support
during that time span by 23 points among the most racially liberal Latinos
but only increased his vote share by 7 points among their most racially conservative counterparts. Nevertheless, Obama still could not win over low-
resentment Latino panelists to the same degree that he mobilized unresent-
ful whites. Obama's poorer performance among Latinos with racial predispositions favorable to his candidacy may well have stemmed from the fact
that these individuals were not as unfettered as white racial liberals were in
voting their affective sympathies for an African American candidate. Barreto et al. (2008, 755) hypothesize that Hillary Clinton won the Latino vote
in the primaries for the following reasons: "(1) higher name recognition and
support of Bill Clinton; (2) endorsements from major Latino officials; (3) vig-
orous outreach to, and mobilization of, Latino voters." These factors could
have easily prevented the most racially sympathetic Latinos from voting for
Obama at the same rates as white racial liberals.

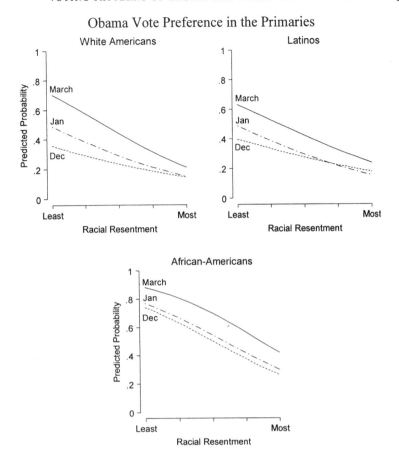

Figure 5.1. Vote preference for Obama in the primaries as a function of racial resentment (1=Obama, 0=other Democrat). Probabilities are based on logistic regression coefficients in table A5.1 of the online appendix (http://www.press.uchicago.edu/books/tesler/). Predicted probabilities were calculated by setting all other variables to the mean respondent in each separate analysis. *Source:* December 2007 and January and March 2008 CCAP panelists.

Meanwhile, racial resentment had a similarly large effect on African Americans' votes in the Democratic primaries. Yet the group's pattern of overall support for Obama was different than it was for their white and Latino counterparts. First, the impact of racial resentment on primary vote choice was noticeably stronger for black panel respondents in December than it was for whites and Latinos. The third panel in figure 5.1, for instance, shows that moving from least to most resentful decreased Obama's share of the black vote in December 2007 from 74 to 26 percent—an effect roughly two times larger than racial resentment's impact for whites and Latinos in December. Such a large resentment effect from the onset of the primary season would be expected if symbolic racism among African Americans were based in weak feelings of black group consciousness, as our earlier findings suggested. Dawson's (1994) examination of support for Jesse Jackson in the 1984–1988 National Black Election Panel Study, for instance, showed that "the variables associated with racial group interest best predict warmth toward Jackson" (144). Beliefs that African Americans have a common fate and that whites have too much political influence were both significantly related to greater black support for Jesse Jackson's 1984 and 1988 nomination bids. We similarly interpret the large effect of racial resentment on blacks' primary votes as an indicator of his greater support among African Americans with strong senses of group consciousness.

Conceptualizing high racial resentment scores among African Americans as reflecting weak racial solidarity more than racial animosity also helps explain the different trends in support for Barack Obama exhibited through the primary season among blacks compared to other races/ethnicities. Obama's expanding share of the black vote during the primaries did not come disproportionately from the left-hand side of the resentment spectrum, in contrast with the white and Latino vote. Instead, figure 5.1 shows that he proportionately increased his predicted black vote during the primaries by about 15 percentage points across the entire resentment spectrum. If high racial resentment scores mainly reflect weak feelings of in-group solidarity for African Americans, then Obama's growing support from African Americans during the primaries should look different from the momentum patterns of white and Latino voters. Simply put, the racial animus behind resentful whites and Latinos should more strongly motivate opposition to a black candidate, despite his momentum, than the mere lack of racial solidarity.

Despite these different patterns of racialized momentum exhibited throughout the primary season, the main story is that the effects of racial resentment were quite similar for each group by the end of the primaries. No other factor, in fact, had nearly as big an impact on all three groups' primary voting behavior as racial resentment. For whites and Latinos this impact reflected both race-based support and opposition to Obama's candidacy. Among African Americans, though, strong in-group attachment was the primary ingredient in generating overwhelming support for Obama.

Black-Brown Animus in Primary Voting Behavior?

Barack Obama performed better in the primaries with white voters than with Latinos in nearly every state that has a sizable Hispanic population.[11] That difference in his white and Latino vote shares was exacerbated by the fact that he performed especially poorly with Latinos in the two states with the most Hispanic residents, California and Texas (about 12 percentage points higher among whites than Latinos in both cases). These ethnic voting patterns provided fodder for journalistic conjecture that Hillary Clinton's success with Latino voters might have been due to her main rival's racial background. Repeated claims by Clinton consultants, Sergio Bendixen and Adelfa Callejo, that many Latinos would simply refuse to vote for an African American further fueled such media speculation during the primaries and added to the Clinton camp's argument that Obama would lack viability as a nominee. Yet, while this so-called black-brown divide made for a compelling news narrative, it did not have much basis in historical precedent. Latino voters, on the contrary, had a long history of overwhelmingly supporting African American candidates in state and local elections before 2008 (Barreto et al. 2008).

Obama's better primary showing with white Americans than Latinos in 2008 was not rooted in any special race-based reluctance to vote for a black candidate, according to our evidence. Figure 5.1 already showed that the biggest gap between our white and Latino CCAP panelists was among racial liberals. If Latinos' racial animus was responsible for the white-Latino gap in Obama support, this difference should instead have occurred primarily among racial conservatives. Obama's inability to activate Latino racial liberals as powerfully as he mobilized white racial liberals was more likely a product of both the longstanding goodwill the Clintons had developed with Latinos and Hillary Clinton's prominent endorsements from Latino officials.

Our contention, then, is that Hillary Clinton's stronger performance among Latinos than whites stemmed more from pro-Clinton sentiments than antiblack attitudes. That position was substantiated by general election vote preferences throughout the campaign. Examining the Obama-McCain vote intentions of Clinton supporters is perhaps the most straightforward measure of whether individuals were principally voting for Clinton or against Obama in the primaries. Voters who pulled the lever for Clinton simply because they liked Hillary Clinton more should not have defected from Obama to McCain in November. If, however, they were voting for Hillary Clinton because of Barack Obama's racial background, then they might have defected from the Democrats in the general election.

By that standard, Latinos voted more *for* Hillary Clinton than did white Americans. In the March CCAP trial heat, Obama performed about 10 percentage points better against McCain among Latino Clinton supporters than he did among white Clinton supporters.[12] This pattern of greater Democratic loyalty from Clinton's Latino supporters than from her white voters was again on display in two Pew polls taken in July 2008: 77 percent of Hispanics who had voted for Clinton preferred Obama over McCain, compared to only 71 percent of whites.[13] Latino Clinton voters were more likely to stick with Obama than were comparable whites, contrary to the idea of a special antiblack antagonism among Latinos—a conclusion borne out by the 67 percent of the Latino vote that went to Obama in the general election, according to the exit polls.

To be sure, racial resentment was still deeply implicated in the primary vote choices of Latinos. All else being equal, figure 5.1 shows that moving from least to most resentful decreased Obama's primary vote share by over 40 percentage points. Contrary to the black-brown divide narrative, however, these racialized voting patterns were no greater among Latino voters than they were among whites.

The Effects of Racial Resentment in the General Election among Whites and Latinos

"The relative homogeneity of black public opinion," according to Michael Dawson (2001, 44), "has been generally considered one of the few certainties of modern American politics." Such uniformity in African American partisan political behavior was never more apparent than in the 2008 general election. Unlike the primaries where Barack Obama received only 59 percent of the black vote in the December 2007 CCAP, there was almost no variation in the general election vote choices of African Americans. The national exit polls, for instance, estimated that Obama received 95 percent of the black vote. Similarly, in the 2008 ANES only 7 out of the 525 black respondents who reported their vote intentions for one of the two major candidates selected John McCain. Such homogeneity leaves little variance left to be explained by racial resentment. It necessarily limits our analyses of general election vote choice by race and ethnicity to whites and Latinos.[14]

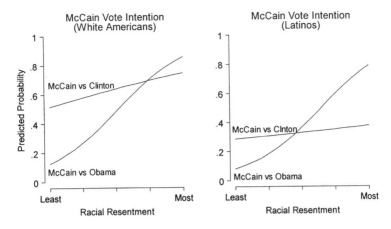

Figure 5.2. McCain vote intention as a function of racial resentment. Probabilities were based on logistic regression coefficients in table A5.2 of the online appendix (http://www .press.uchicago.edu/books/tesler/). Predicted probabilities were calculated by setting all other variables to the mean respondent in each separate analysis. *Source*: March 2008 CCAP.

In the March CCAP trial heat, Obama received only 56 percent of the Latino two-party vote share in his early matchup with the presumptive Republican nominee, John McCain—a number far lower than the 67 percent reported in general election exit polls. The March trial heat is quite informative, though, because it provides further confirmation of the sharply differing influence of racial attitudes in the Democratic candidates' matchups with McCain depending on whether the black man, Obama, or the white woman, Clinton, was considered as his ultimate opponent.

Figure 5.2 presents the effects of racial resentment in these two trial heats for whites and Latinos. The impact of racial resentment on support for McCain against Obama was nearly identical for whites and Latinos, again contrary to the brown-black hostility narrative. All else being equal, moving from least to most resentful increased McCain's white and Latino vote shares against Obama by roughly 70 percentage points. The Clinton matchup, however, did not strongly evoke racial predispositions among either group. Moving across the racial resentment spectrum only increased McCain's predicted vote share against Clinton by 23 points among whites and 9 points among Latinos. It certainly appears from this evidence that racial attitudes were a much bigger component of white and Latino vote preferences for John McCain over Barack Obama than they would have been if McCain's opponent had been white.

The larger effect on McCain-Obama vote preferences for both whites and Latinos occurred because the two sides of racialization that we documented in chapters 2 and 3 were operating for both groups. The archetypical "two sides" result should show Obama performing better than a similarly situated white Democrat like Hillary Clinton among racial liberals, but being less popular than her among the racially resentful. That result was produced in the CCAP trial heat comparison for both Latinos and whites, as figure 5.2 clearly shows. However, figure 5.2 also shows that Hillary Clinton's popularity with Latinos caused these differences in support between her and Obama against McCain to be greater on the racially liberal side of the scale for whites and on the racially conservative side for Latinos. Yet all else being equal, racially liberal Latinos were still considerably more likely to chose Obama over McCain than Clinton over McCain despite her tremendous support from the Latino community as a whole. These results suggest that the unusual hold Obama had on racial liberals held for both whites and Latinos alike.

The CCAP's panel design and large sample size also allowed us to repeat our chapter 3 analyses of racial resentment and vote intention from March to October 2008 separately for whites and Latinos. Despite the CCAP's overall sample size, though, we are still limited to only about 400 Latinos voters who responded to both survey waves.

These monthly results of racial resentment on vote choice for whites and Latinos are displayed in figure 5.3. The figure graphs the effects of racial resentment on McCain vote intention in March and October for both groups with our base control variables held constant. The first panel of the display shows that our whites-only results are almost identical to those from the full-sample model presented in chapter 3 (see fig. 3.2). Specifically, the impact of racial resentment is unchanged from March to October, with Obama increasing his predicted vote share during that time period among whites of all racial predispositions. Such continuity in effects presumably occurred because Obama's role as the first black nominee from a major party made racial predispositions chronically accessible in the general election vote choice. As such, it was difficult for either Obama's concerted efforts to deactivate "racial aversion" or the crashing economy to reduce the impact of racial resentment on white voting behavior.

Latinos, however, appeared to be slightly more responsive to the changing political environment from March to October 2008. The second panel in figure 5.3, for instance, shows that McCain was predicted to win 76 percent of the most racially conservative vote from our Latino panelists in March

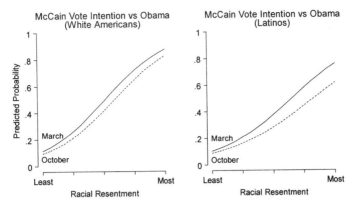

Figure 5.3. Support for McCain against Obama as a function of racial resentment. Probabilities were based on logistic regression coefficients in table A5.3 of the online appendix (http://www.press.uchicago.edu/books/tesler/). Predicted probabilities were calculated by setting all other variables to the mean respondent in each separate analysis. *Source*: March and October 2008 CCAP panelists.

compared to just 62 percent of the racially conservative Latinos in October. This enhanced support for Obama over time from racially conservative Latinos reduced the overall effect of racial resentment: moving from least to most racially resentful cost Obama 65 percentage points among Latinos in March and only 53 points in October.[15] Although the smaller Latino sample sizes limit our ability to make strong analytical claims about this change, perhaps racial predispositions were less accessible in Latinos' assessments of Obama than they were for whites. If so, Latinos might have been more receptive to changing national and economic conditions, thereby reducing race-based opposition to Obama's candidacy.

Given the limited number of Latinos in the CCAP, we are fortunate in being able to replicate these analyses with the fall ANES's Latino oversample. There we found a slightly larger racial resentment coefficient on vote intention among Latinos than among whites.[16] Yet, because Obama received over three-quarters of the vote from Latinos in that survey and just 46 percent of the white vote, the relationships between racial resentment and support for John McCain differ considerably across the two groups. Figure 5.4 graphically compares these resentment coefficients for whites and Latinos, holding the other base-model variables constant. Our model predicted Obama to receive a majority of even the most racially resentful Latino vote, but only about one-quarter of the vote from the most racially conservative whites. This overwhelming Latino support for Obama in the ANES limited

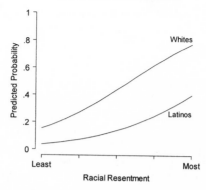

Figure 5.4. Support for McCain against Obama as a function of racial resentment. Probabilities were based on logistic regression coefficients in table A5.4 of the online appendix (http://www.press.uchicago.edu/books/tesler/). Predicted probabilities were calculated by setting all other variables to the mean respondent in each separate analysis. *Source*: 2008 ANES.

the substantive impact that racial resentment had on their respondents' vote choices—a "floor effect," if you will. So, while the resentment coefficient is slightly larger for Latinos than whites in the ANES, figure 5.4 shows that moving from least to most resentful increased McCain's share of the two-party vote by about 60 points with whites and 40 points with Latinos.

Despite our caution in interpreting the Latino results, we believe that there are a number of suggestive findings here. First, the effect of racial resentment on the McCain-Obama matchup was much greater than its effect on the McCain-Clinton trial heat for both whites and Latinos. That suggests the presence of an African American candidate made racial attitudes much more accessible for both whites and Latinos than they would have been in a matchup between McCain and a white Democrat like Hillary Clinton. Second, the two sides of racialization were evident in both groups. Latino and white racial liberals were more supportive of Obama than Clinton, with Clinton performing better against McCain among racially resentful members of both groups. Finally, by the end of the campaign, Latinos were considerably more pro-Obama than whites were, in both the ANES (September and October) and the CCAP (October).

While we do not know what caused his overwhelming popularity among Latinos in the ANES, the CCAP results indicate that his growing Latino support over time in that survey came disproportionately from the racially resentful. Recall that white Americans' resentment effects remained constant throughout the general election campaign. In contrast, racial opposition to Obama among Latinos was apparently deactivated to some extent during the campaign. Perhaps new information like the economic crash or Obama's strong debate performances mitigated the impact of racial resentment among Latinos. That would be consistent with our earlier evidence suggesting that the symbolic racism belief system is considerably less coherent and crystallized for Latinos than for whites. If these speculations are correct, they would contradict the impression among some that Latinos were more hostile to blacks than even whites were in their voting behavior. Rather, racial resentment may not be quite as accessible for Latinos as it is for white Americans.

Racial Resentment and Increased Democratic Support from Latinos from 2004 to 2008

Barack Obama's dominance among Latino voters was perhaps the most discussed result in the 2008 national exit polls. His 67 percent vote share from the group was 14 points better than John Kerry's showing in 2004. In contrast, Obama only outperformed Kerry by 2 percentage points among white Americans. That disproportionate movement by Latinos to the Democratic candidate, combined with both the group's expanding share of the national electorate and their strategic location in the Electoral College swing states of Colorado, Nevada, New Mexico, Arizona, Florida, and perhaps at some point even Texas, had pundits immediately talking about a new Democratic majority coalition in presidential elections.

For our purposes, it is important to understand the role of racial predispositions in the movement of Latinos to the Democratic Party from 2004 to 2008. Did they shift *because of* liberal predispositions or *in spite of* conservative predispositions? Our best test is to compare the relationships between racial resentment and Republican vote intention in the 2004 NPS and 2008 ANES. Unfortunately, the comparison is not quite ideal. Both surveys have less than 400 Latino voters to analyze and we have to shorten our ANES resentment scale to the two items included in the NPS in order to make the results comparable.[17] Moreover, the 2004 NPS and the 2008 ANES report significantly greater Latino support for the Democratic candidate than did the national exit polls in those years. Since these surveys both overstate Latino support for the Democratic candidate by similar margins, though, the enhanced Democratic vote share from the 2004 NPS to the 2008 ANES

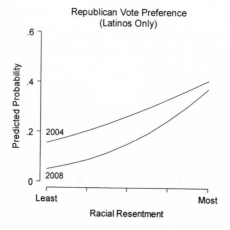

Figure 5.5. Republican vote preference as a function of racial resentment. Probabilities were based on logistic regression coefficients in table A5.5 of the online appendix (http://www.press.uchicago.edu/books/tesler/). Predicted probabilities were calculated by setting all other variables to the average Latino voter in the 2004 NPS. *Source*: 2004 NPS; 2008 ANES.

closely approximates the 14-point increase from 2004 to 2008 in the exit polls that received so much attention.

That said, figure 5.5 suggests that the increased Democratic vote share among Latinos in 2008 was not evenly spread across the racial resentment spectrum. The display graphs the effects of racial resentment (2-item scales) on Republican vote intention among Latino respondents in the 2004 NPS and 2008 ANES. All else being equal, Obama performed about 10 to 13 points better in the 2008 ANES than John Kerry did in the 2004 NPS on the racially liberal side of the scale. The predicted Democratic vote share, however, was less than 5 percentage points bigger in 2008 than it was in 2004 at the most racially resentful end of the spectrum.

The smaller Latino sample sizes in these two surveys again prevent us from interpreting this result too confidently.[18] However, Obama's ability to outperform previous Democratic candidates by activating the left-hand side of the resentment spectrum should now be a familiar pattern. Chapter 2, for instance, showed that the main difference between support for Jesse Jackson in the 1988 primaries and for Barack Obama in 2008 was Obama's much better performance among racial liberals. Similarly, chapter 3 showed that Obama activated racially liberal support in the general election more powerfully than any recent Democratic nominee had. Figure 5.2, of course, also showed that Obama outperformed Hillary Clinton against John McCain among both white and Latino racial liberals. And we similarly show in chapter 8 that President Obama was more popular with white racial liberals in April 2009 than even the highly rated President Clinton was during his presidency.

It should come as no surprise, then, that these preliminary results suggest that the much discussed movement of Latinos to the Democrats from 2004 and 2008 came disproportionately from those with lower feelings of resentment toward African Americans. As was also shown in figure 5.2, it appears from this 2004 to 2008 comparison that the second side of racialization was not just operating for white Americans, but that Obama had a special appeal to low-resentment Latinos as well.

Concluding Remarks

Because we have presented a number of findings in this chapter, it might be well to summarize them briefly. First, many pundits and black leaders going into the campaign had suspected that Barack Obama, with an African father and a white Kansan mother, born in Hawaii and reared in a variety of places including Indonesia, might not seem to fit the model African American prototype sufficiently to be fully accepted by black voters, especially since many retained a loyalty to the Clintons. On the other hand, black Democratic candidates have historically swept the black vote. Consistent with that history, Obama overwhelmingly won the black vote in the primary season, performing best among African Americans with the highest levels of in-group consciousness.

The Latino vote yields a somewhat more complex story, but more complicated because of some uncertainties generated by differences across samples than because the results are unclear. Most important, despite doubts about Latino support generated for Obama by their heavy vote for Clinton in the California and Texas primaries, in the end Obama did just as well if not better than previous Democrats among Latinos. Second, and perhaps in the long run equally important, the role of symbolic racism among Latinos was similar to its role among whites: Obama won big among racial liberals but did less well among racial conservatives. The roots of symbolic racism also lay in a similar combination of racial affect and conservative values for Latinos and whites.

However, Latinos did depart in some noticeable ways from the white model. Symbolic racism/racial resentment was substantially less crystallized among Latinos than among whites, perhaps reflecting some slow po-

litical acculturation in a group with many not far removed from immigration. Perhaps for that reason, the impact of racial resentment on the general
election vote diminished toward the end of the campaign among Latinos, in
contrast to whites.

The multiple complications involved in analyzing these effects of racial
resentment by race and ethnicity necessarily make the results and analyses
in this chapter less authoritative than those presented in the other chapters.
Nevertheless, there are a number of important findings that we hope will
spawn future comparative studies of symbolic racism. The first is that the
explanatory power of racial resentment is not limited to whites. The effects
of racial resentment, for instance, were comparable for whites, Latinos, and
African Americans in the Democratic primaries. Racial resentment's large
negative impact on black support for Obama combined with evidence indicating that the origins of symbolic racism for African Americans reside in
weak feelings of group consciousness suggest that the construct could be a
useful tool in explaining multiple facets of black public opinion.

Even more importantly, the sizable impact of racial resentment on Latino voting behavior in 2008 make it absolutely essential to apply symbolic
racism to studies of Latino public opinion and voting behavior in the age of
Obama. With Latinos considered by many to be the most vital voting demographic in future national elections, their opinions should carry special
weight during the Obama presidency. Racial resentment seems to be one of
the most important ingredients in Latinos' opinions about Barack Obama,
just as among whites. As such, a detailed investigation of Latinos' racial attitudes and the accessibility of their racial predispositions in Obama-related
political evaluations would be invaluable in understanding American partisan politics during his presidency.

6

The Paradox of Gender Traditionalists' Support for Hillary Clinton

It would have been naïve for me to think that I could run and end up with quasi-front-runner status in a presidential election, as potentially the first African American president, and that issues of race wouldn't come up, any more than Senator Clinton could expect that gender issues might not come up.

BARACK OBAMA, *The Breakthrough*[1]

Hillary Rodham Clinton had been a preeminent target of the antifeminist backlash long before she announced her intention to seek the Democratic presidential nomination. In 1980, her husband's defeat for reelection as governor of Arkansas in 1980 was blamed in part on defectors troubled by the feminist persona of "Hillary Rodham." In response, she officially became "Hillary Clinton."

That feminist image of her was perhaps permanently implanted in America's collective consciousness during Bill Clinton's 1992 campaign for the presidency. Indeed, the first lady of Arkansas became a national lightening rod for gender conservatism following these famous comments from the campaign trail in March of that year: "I suppose I could have stayed home and baked cookies and had teas, but what I decided to do was to fulfill my profession which I entered before my husband was in public life." The statement clearly struck a nerve in a nation still deeply divided between proponents of traditional marital roles and supporters of gender equality in the workplace. Political commentators long after those early days of her husband's bid for the Democratic nomination continued to describe Hillary Clinton as one of the most polarizing figures in American politics. And much of that perceived polarization was ascribed to her feminism.

Attitudes about gender roles, not surprisingly, have indeed factored prominently into this public divide over Hillary Clinton. Winter (2008), for instance, found her to be a particularly gendered figure in the 1994 ANES—meaning that attitudes about the woman's movement and traditional gender roles significantly influenced assessments of the then-first lady. We conducted a similar analysis with measures of modern sexism in the 2004

ANES. Modern sexism, which is modeled after contemporary conceptualizations of racial prejudice such as symbolic racism and racial resentment,
taps into subtle biases against women that often go unnoticed (Swim et al.
1995; Swim and Cohen 1997). Like symbolic racism, modern sexism is operationalized with questions about the severity of discrimination and antagonism toward demands for equality (see appendix variable measures). Also,
like the relationships between symbolic racism and resistance to black candidates noted earlier, this measure of gender conservatism has been shown
to predict opposition to women seeking elected office (Swim et al. 1995).

As expected, we found a substantial relationship between modern sexism and negative evaluations of Hillary Clinton in the 2004 ANES. Even
with partisan, ideological, and demographic controls in place, moving from
highest to lowest in modern sexism was associated with a 15 degree decrease
in her 0–100 thermometer ratings. Eleven other political figures were evaluated in the same survey. Only *positive* assessments of Dick Cheney, who
is often portrayed in a particularly chauvinistic light, were shaped to the
same degree by modern sexism that negative opinions of Hillary Clinton
were.[2] These exploratory results confirm what most observers of politics
would have already suspected—Hillary Clinton was one of the most gendered politicians in America before she sought the Democratic presidential
nomination.

A Gendered Campaign Context

One might also suspect that Hillary Clinton's polarization of Americans
with conservative positions on women's roles versus those with more egalitarian positions would be more salient than ever in the 2008 Democratic
primary. We saw in chapter 2 that Barack Obama's position as the first African American with a realistic chance of winning the White House generated
tremendous support in the primaries from racial liberals and comparable
opposition from the racially resentful. In similar fashion, Hillary Clinton's
analogous history-making situation as the first viable female candidate for
the presidency could easily have been expected to activate gender-specific
attitudes such as modern sexism.

Aside from the historical significance of her quest for the nomination,
modern sexism may have been further activated by the campaign itself. As
we now know, the impact of racial resentment can either be enhanced or
mitigated depending upon whether political evaluations are made in racialized or race-neutral informational environments (Kinder and Drake 2009;

Valentino, Hutchings, and White 2002; Mendelberg 2001; Kinder and Sanders 1996). It is logical to suspect, then, that the influence of modern sexism on 2008 primary vote choice could be primed by the prevalence of gender-oriented campaign content.

Both the campaign and the media's coverage of it were undoubtedly gendered by the time the first primary votes were cast in New Hampshire. Hillary Clinton was almost universally counted out of the nation's first primary contest after Barack Obama's stunning 8-point victory in the Iowa caucuses on January 3, 2008. Her 20-point lead over Obama in the New Hampshire polls only one month earlier had become a 7-point deficit in January 6 polling averages, just two days before the primary election.[3] Gender quickly displaced Obama's ostensibly inexorable momentum from the Granite State's headlines, though.

The January 5 debate in New Hampshire between the Democratic candidates was widely interpreted to contain significant gender hostility. Despite her third-place showing in Iowa, both Obama and John Edwards targeted their attacks at Hillary Clinton. The "pile-on" came across to some as a rehash of "no girls allowed" grade school clubhouse rules. Moreover, during a response by Clinton to a question about the likability gap between herself and Obama—a gap which may itself have been partially created by gender stereotypes about women in positions of power—Obama haughtily chimed in, telling her, "You're likable enough, Hillary." Several viewed Obama's comments as a clear case of gender condescension. Paul Begala, for instance, thought the moment made Obama look like "an ex-husband that was turning over the alimony check."[4] Obama claimed that the remark was meant to be supportive, but later acknowledged that both the seemingly condescending tone with which it came out and the "Edwards pile-on" probably contributed to his poor performance with female voters in the New Hampshire primary (Balz and Johnson 2009, 142).

Gender became even more salient in the campaign two days later. On the morning before the polls opened in New Hampshire, Clinton got choked up and teary eyed in response to a question about "how she does it." Emotional reactions are often interpreted in gendered terms, whereby women's emotional expressions are attributed to their female dispositions while the same emotional sentiments from men are interpreted as more rational responses to situational conditions (Shields 2002). Her teary response was a prototypical case in point, almost certain to make gender more prominent in the campaign. Moreover, there is a long history of the media tying emotionality to women and providing more coverage of emotional moments by female political figures than their male counterparts (Falk 2008). Not surprisingly, then, Jacobs and Gruszczynski (2009) concluded from their content analyses that Hillary Clinton's gender played a large role in the amount of coverage her emotional incident received compared to the minimal coverage given an analogous moment by one of the Republican presidential favorites, Mitt Romney, just a few weeks earlier.

By the eve of the primary, then, gender had seized center stage in New Hampshire. Indeed, famed women's rights activist, Gloria Steinem, wrote an op-ed in the *New York Times* on the morning of the election, titled "Women are Never Frontrunners," decrying sexist portrayals of Hillary Clinton during the campaign. Many, therefore, assumed that Clinton's unexpected victory in New Hampshire was due to female voters' breaking heavily for her in protest of this suspected sexist treatment.[5]

We would be a little more cautious. Such accounts as the *Guardian's* "Hill's Angels—How Angry Women of New Hampshire Saved Clinton: Female Voters Enraged by Coverage Following Iowa Rout"[6] made for a plausible and provocative news narrative. But it is difficult to determine whether Clinton actually won this primary because women were fed up with gender-based biases against her candidacy. However, we can say with a great deal of confidence that both the campaign's content and the media's coverage of it had become especially gendered in the nation's first and perhaps most visible primary contest.

Gender Conservatism and Primary Vote Choice

The stars seemed to have been perfectly aligned, then, for gender attitudes to significantly influence primary vote choice. After all, we had the first viable female presidential candidate, who herself had a long history of polarizing Americans with egalitarian versus traditionalist predispositions on women's roles, running in a gendered campaign context.

These factors appear to make the results presented in figure 6.1 all the more astonishing. The three panels in the display graph the bivariate relationships—meaning there are no control variables included in the model—between various measures of gender conservatism and primary vote preference for Hillary Clinton. Believe it or not, figure 6.1 clearly shows that gender *conservatism* was positively correlated with support for Hillary Clinton in the primaries. Moving from the lowest to the highest score on the modern sexism scale, for instance, increased her predicted share of the Clinton-Obama primary vote by 18 points among those recalling their

Clinton Vote Preference in the Primaries

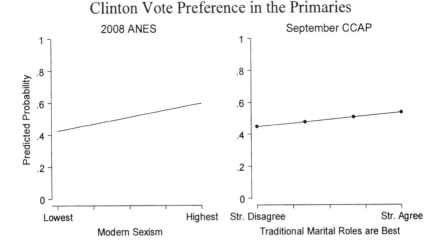

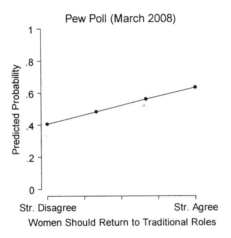

Figure 6.1. Hillary Clinton vote preference in the primaries as a function of gender attitudes (bivariate relationships; 1=Clinton, 0=Obama). Predicted probabilities are based on logistic regression coefficients in table A6.1 of the online appendix (http://www.press.uchicago .edu/books/tesler/). *Source*: 2008 ANES; September 2008 CCAP; March 19–22, 2008, Pew Poll.

primary votes in the 2008 ANES.[7] Hillary Clinton was winning the gender traditionalists, not the feminists.

The other two surveys we employ in our analysis here of gender conservatism and primary vote choice asked if traditional husband and wife roles are best (the September CCAP) and if women should return to their traditional roles (a Pew Poll conducted in March 2008).[8] Questions about gender roles such as those two are generally classified as measures of old-fashioned sexism (Swim and Cohen 1997). Traditional views of gender roles were also positively associated with support for Hillary Clinton. The second and third panels in figure 6.1 show that strongly supporting traditional gender roles increased Clinton's primary vote share by 12 and 23 percentage points in the CCAP and Pew surveys, respectively.

These relationships of support for Hillary Clinton in the primaries to gender *traditionalism*, measured with either modern or old-fashioned sexism, are not of trivial magnitude. To put their substantive importance in a broader context, we compared the association of gender conservatism to Clinton support with other bivariate relationships in the March 2008 Pew Poll. Gender conservatism was a stronger predictor of Clinton support than many other plausible variables. The roughly 20-point increase in Hillary Clinton's vote share associated with moving from least to most sexist in the ANES and Pew surveys is greater than the increases in her vote share associated with moving from youngest to oldest (43 to 56 percent), male to female (42 to 53 percent), and liberal to conservative (42 to 55 percent). Moreover, these effects of modern and old-fashioned sexism on support for Clinton in the ANES and Pew surveys rival the impact of moving from highest to lowest in educational attainment (37 to 63 percent), and they are not even that far removed from differences in rates of support for Clinton between African Americans and other voters (17 to 53 percent).

In sum, whether using measures of modern or old-fashioned sexism, it is apparent that Hillary Clinton performed substantially better against Barack Obama among those with conservative positions on women's issues.

Explaining the Paradox: Racial and Gender Conservatism in Primary Vote Choice

There have been few ironies in American political history as profound as Hillary Clinton's base of support in the primaries coming from citizens with traditional views about gender roles. For our purposes, though, this surprising result presents a fruitful research puzzle: How could the longstanding poster child for the antifeminist backlash, running in a gendered campaign context to be the first female presidential nominee of a major political party, perform significantly better at the polls among gender traditionalists?

This paradox is not as perplexing as it first seems, however. It is easily understood if we take into account the fact that racial liberals also tend to have egalitarian positions on matters of gender, and gender traditional-ists tend also to be conservative on racial issues. Racism and sexism were unfortunately often treated as independent in the one-dimensional media accounts that regularly pitted the two societal ills against each other dur-ing the primaries. In reality, though, there is a significant relationship be-tween racial resentment and gender traditionalism that must be taken into account. There was a powerful correlation between racial resentment and modern sexism among Democrats in the 2004 ANES ($r = .45$). Likewise, racial resentment was significantly correlated with the measures of gender conservatism used in our 2008 analysis of primary vote choice among ANES and CCAP Democratic primary voters ($r = .31$ and $r = .25$, respectively).

Recall from chapter 2 that racial resentment was overwhelmingly im-plicated in primary support for Hillary Clinton against Barack Obama. But these attitudes about blacks are also significantly correlated with gender pre-dispositions. Therefore, the bivariate relationships of gender conservatism with Clinton support displayed in figure 6.1 are likely to have misattributed some of this large effect of racial resentment to gender conservatism. In fact, the positive relationships between support for Hillary Clinton and sexism may not actually be a product of attitudes about gender per se. Rather, they may merely be artifacts of conflating support for traditional gender attitudes with symbolic racism.

This relationship between racial and gender conservatism must be taken into account in order to understand the *independent* effects of attitudes about race and gender. To do so, both variables need to be included in regression models predicting individual-level vote choice. If the effects of gender con-servatism are just an artifact of its positive relationship with racial resent-ment, we would expect that the association between sexism and voting for Hillary Clinton would disappear after we control for racial resentment in our models of primary vote choice.

This expectation is clearly borne out in figure 6.2. The display graphs out two separate relationships: The first is the effect of gender predispositions while holding racial resentment constant. The second is the effect of racial resentment with gender attitudes held constant. Simply adding racial resent-ment to our ANES and CCAP vote models dramatically alters the relation-ship between gender conservatism and support for Hillary Clinton. There is no longer a positive relationship between gender conservatism and Clinton vote preference after we control for racial predispositions. More specifically, the previously discussed 18-point *increase* in Clinton's ANES vote share asso-

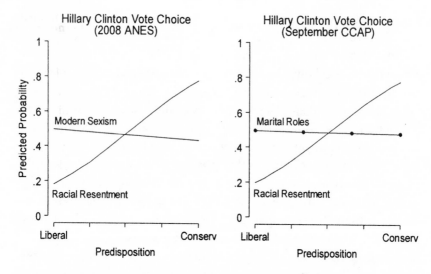

Figure 6.2. Hillary Clinton vote choice as a function of gender attitudes and racial resentment (1=Clinton, 0=Obama). Probabilities were based on the logistic regression coefficients in table A6.2 of the online appendix (http://www.press.uchicago.edu/books/tesler/). Predicted probabilities were calculated by setting the other variable to the mean respondent included in each separate analysis. *Source*: 2008 ANES; September 2008 CCAP.

ciated with moving from lowest to highest on the modern sexism scale now shows a 6-point *decrease* in her overall level of support once racial resentment is held constant. Similarly, the 12-point increase in Clinton's CCAP vote share induced by a change from strongly disagreeing to agreeing with the statement that traditional marital roles are best shows a 2-point *decrease* once racial resentment is controlled.

The March Pew Poll did not include the racial resentment items. Unfortunately, we therefore cannot conduct a parallel analysis of gender traditionalism in that survey using controls for racial resentment. The results from the ANES and the CCAP, however, strongly suggest that the sizable relationship produced in the Pew Poll between endorsing traditional gender roles and voting for Hillary Clinton was also an artifact of conflating racial and gender conservatism.

The correlation between racial and gender conservatism thus explains the paradox of Hillary Clinton's greater support from respondents high in either modern or old-fashioned sexism. Figure 6.2 shows the more logical result that Clinton performed slightly worse among gender traditionalists, once the conflation of attitudes about race and gender is taken into account.

Why Racial Attitudes Trumped Attitudes about Gender in Primary Vote Choice

While the results displayed in figure 6.2 resolve the sexist support for Clinton paradox, they raise another interesting question: Why were attitudes about race, rather than attitudes about gender, the prime determinants of vote choice in the primaries? We saw in that display that moving from least to most racially resentful produced a 60-point increase in support for Hillary Clinton against Barack Obama in both the ANES's and CCAP's retrospective assessments of primary vote choice. Moreover, even single-item measures of affect toward African Americans, such as either thermometer ratings or reported feelings of sympathy for blacks, were strong predictors of primary support for Obama in the 2008 ANES. Modern sexism, thermometer ratings of feminists, and endorsement of traditional marital roles, however, all had virtually no *independent* impact on voting behavior in the primaries after we controlled for racial resentment. Racial attitudes were ultimately so much more central than gender-based predispositions that the correlation between the two produced the great irony of gender traditionalists' support for Hillary Clinton in bivariate relationships.

A CBS News Poll conducted in March 2008 helps shed some light on why racial attitudes so decisively trumped gender attitudes in primary vote choice.[9] In keeping with the history-making gender and racial dynamics of the ongoing Democratic primary, CBS asked a number of questions about racism and sexism in that survey. By mid-March, the writing was on the wall: Barack Obama was probably going to win the Democratic nomination. Obama held a large lead over Clinton in respondents' expectations about which candidate would become the party's presidential nominee—53 percent to 31 percent in this CBS survey. Perhaps because of these expectations, more respondents said that female candidates face greater obstacles in presidential politics than male African American candidates do (39 percent to 33 percent). However, despite the fact that it looked like the black man would defeat the white women in their epic battle for the nomination, four times as many respondents picked *racism* over *sexism* when asked which of the two is a more serious problem in America (42 percent to 10 percent). Even white, female, Clinton voters believed racism was a much more serious problem than sexism (42 percent to 14 percent).[10]

To be sure, widespread opinions that racism is a more serious problem than sexism could itself be a major indicator of the ongoing impediments faced by women. Both modern conceptualizations of racism and sexism, after all, are operationalized with items about the impact of discrimination on racial and gender inequality. Yet these differences in societal perceptions help explain why attitudes about race were so much more accessible during the 2008 primaries than attitudes about gender.

America carries around very visible racial scars that are centuries old. These are the wounds of slavery, the Civil War, Reconstruction, Jim Crow, the civil rights movement, the black power movement, and the urban rebellions of the 1960s. These are the wounds that have long made race, rather than gender, the most visceral and divisive issue in all of American politics. Many of these wounds are still open. They can be found in the profound levels of social and residential segregation of the races. They are also evident in the striking differences between African Americans and white Americans in poverty, unemployment, and especially wealth.[11]

The enhanced salience of the color line throughout American history inevitably means that racism will be looked upon by the public as a more serious societal problem than sexism for the foreseeable future. That long and powerful history of American race relations also likely means that the hopes and fears produced by the possibility of a black man in the White House far overrode the symbolism of Hillary Clinton's bid to become our nation's first female president. It is not too surprising, then, that the central cleavage for voters in the 2008 Democratic primary was race and not gender.

Concluding Remarks: The Immeasurable Impact of Sexism in the Democratic Primaries

The fact that attitudes about women's roles did not strongly influence individual-level primary vote choices in no way implies that gender or sexism was not important in Barack Obama's victory over Hillary Clinton. Gender could have affected the contest in ways that are not as easily quantifiable as our analyses of attitudinal impacts. Susan Carroll's (2009) article, "Reflections on Gender and Hillary Clinton's Presidential Campaign: The Good, the Bad, and the Misogynistic," provides two very plausible, yet difficult to measure, ways that sexism could have cost Hillary Clinton votes.

One of these avenues was the media's campaign coverage. The charge of gender bias in Democratic primary reporting is a familiar one. The *New York Times*, for instance, ran a story shortly after Senator Clinton suspended her campaign entitled, "Media Charged With Sexism in Clinton Coverage."[12] The article featured a content analysis by George Mason professor, Robert Lichter, showing that until the Reverend Wright controversy in March, the coverage of Obama during the primaries on the three broadcast networks was far more favorable than their reporting on Hillary Clinton.

If sexism did, in fact, influence the differential media frames and tones applied to the Clinton and Obama campaigns, its effects on primary votes would probably be difficult to pick up in our individual-level analyses of gender attitudes. We showed in chapter 3 that favorable short-term political circumstances occurring from March to October 2008 helped increase Obama's predicted vote share among panel respondents of all racial resentment levels. In like fashion, unfavorable media coverage of Clinton rooted in sexism during the primary season could have depressed support for her candidacy among citizens of all gender predispositions.

The second factor identified by Carroll (2009) is how sexism and gender stereotypes influenced the Clinton camp's campaign strategy. Women running for elected office must counter the powerful and prevalent stereotype that they do not possess the same leadership qualities as men. The imperative to mitigate gender stereotypes about not being "tough enough" is surely amplified when the job description includes commander in chief of the military. As Carroll points out, though, if female candidates stress their qualifications and assertiveness in an effort to offset the stereotype of being less competent to hold leadership positions, they run the risk of turning off voters by appearing too masculine or not "nice enough." This could be one of the reasons why Clinton decisively outperformed Obama in questions about leadership traits, but was running comparable deficits against Obama in measures of likability.[13]

Carroll describes this need to strike a balance between being "tough enough" and "nice enough" as the Catch-22 of female political candidacies. We would describe this Catch-22 throughout the primaries as the "Clinton Bind." Her bind was that if she presented herself as too masculine in order to counter societal stereotypes about women, she would have to worry about Barack Obama condescendingly telling her that she was not likable enough. On the other hand, if she presented herself as too feminine in an effort to mitigate societal aversion to assertive women, she might have to worry about commentators saying, as Dick Morris did after the New Hampshire incident, that she will cry if she does not get her way in negotiations with Congress or Iran.[14]

Aside from her emotional moment in New Hampshire, the Clinton campaign seemed to clearly privilege the "tough enough" side of that spectrum. Or as Clinton's chief strategist, Mark Penn, put it, "Being human is overrated."[15] Instead, one of Penn's earliest campaign memos from 2006 cites

Margaret Thatcher as the role model for her candidacy—"and the adjectives used about her (Iron Lady)," he writes, "were not of good humor or warmth, they were of smart, tough leadership."[16] Judging by this memo it appears that Hillary Clinton's need to counter common stereotypes about female competence for leadership positions may have been partly responsible for her campaign's decision to base her appeal on experience in a political atmosphere that was so desperate for change. Like her unfavorable media coverage, this overcompensation at the expense of "good humor or warmth" could have depressed her vote margins among citizens of all gender predispositions. Moreover, Clinton's counter-stereotypical behavior may have deactivated gender conservatism, thereby contributing to the null independent relationships presented above between attitudes about gender and vote choice in the 2008 Democratic primaries.

These immeasurable factors could have easily made gender a much greater impediment for Hillary Clinton than race was for Barack Obama in their quests for the Democratic nomination. From an individual-level attitudinal standpoint, though, the results presented could not be more definitive: Race, rather than gender, was the driving force of Americans' vote choices in this historical contest.

7

Beyond Black and White
Obama as "Other"

All of these articles about his boyhood in Indonesia and his life in Hawaii are geared
towards showing his background is diverse, multicultural . . . It also exposes a very
strong weakness for him—his roots to basic American values and culture are at best
limited. I cannot imagine America electing a president during a time of war who is
not at his center fundamentally American in his thinking and in his values.

MARK PENN, chief campaign strategist, in a memo to
Hillary Clinton, March 19, 2007.[1]

As we have discussed throughout the book, attitudes about African Americans have factored prominently in American partisan politics for decades
now. We also mentioned in the first chapter that this organization of partisan politics around racial issues stemmed largely from elite-level differences
in the two parties' support for 1960s civil rights initiatives (Carmines and
Stimson 1989). Yet, despite the visibility of both Islamic terrorism following
September 11 and the Bush administration's forceful response to the attacks,
attitudes about Muslims did not shape partisan politics during Bush's presidency the way that attitudes about African Americans have in the post–civil
rights era.

Our conclusion about the peripheral role of attitudes about Muslims is
based on analyzing a fair amount of data from the Bush era. However, to
maintain our focus on 2008 we will mention these findings only in passing
rather than reviewing them in detail. For instance, we examined thermometer ratings of Muslims in the 2004 ANES and found that they did not
have significant independent effects on presidential vote choice, evaluations
of the president, or even opinions about going to war with the predominantly
Islamic nation of Iraq—a policy that had become highly polarized along party
lines by 2004 (Jacobson 2007; Berinsky 2009). Nor were favorability ratings
of Muslims and Muslim Americans significant predictors of presidential approval (after controlling for partisanship and ideological self-placement) in
a series of polls commissioned by the Pew Forum on Religion and Public

Life during Bush's presidency.[2] Other research has shown that ideology and party identification were only modest determinants of attitudes about Muslims during the Bush presidency (Kalkan et al. 2009). Consistent with those results, we found that affect toward Muslims did not heavily influence political evaluations even when partisan and ideological predispositions were not included as predictors in the regression model.[3]

An August 2007 survey from the Pew Forum on Religion and Public Life, however, foreshadowed a much more important role for attitudes about Muslims in 2008.[4] The study asked respondents to evaluate both Muslims and a number of political figures. As can be seen in figure 7.1, the impact of Muslim favorability ratings on evaluations of Barack Obama was much larger than it was on assessments of Hillary Clinton, John Edwards, and George W. Bush. Even with party identification, ideology, and demographic factors controlled for, changing from a very unfavorable to a very favorable impression of Muslims increased respondents' appraisal of Obama by nearly 30 percent of our favorability scale's range—an effect twice as large as the impact these ratings of Muslims had on evaluations of his two main Democratic rivals for the party's presidential nomination, Hillary Clinton and John Edwards.

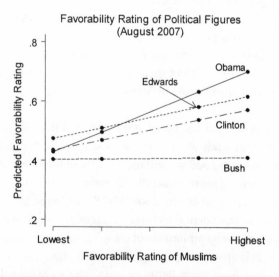

Figure 7.1. Politicians' favorability ratings as a function of Muslim favorability (0=very unfavorable, 1=very favorable). Favorability ratings were based on the OLS coefficients in table A7.1 of the online appendix (http://www.press.uchicago.edu/books/tesler/). Predicted ratings were calculated by setting all other variables to their sample means. Source: August 2007 Pew Forum on Religion and Public Life.

This large impact of Muslim favorability on support for Barack Obama could have disappeared in the midst of the general election campaign, however (Tesler 2008). Citizens may have relied on their attitudes toward Muslims more when evaluating Obama in mid-2007 as a relatively unknown, long-shot primary candidate, with an odd and vaguely Muslim name, four months before the first primary votes were ever cast. Maybe Muslim favorability would take a back seat to other factors when Americans evaluated the well-known, highly scrutinized, partisan frontrunner for the White House one month prior to the election. After all, Barack Obama became the de facto head of the Democratic Party after securing the nomination. So the early influence of attitudes about Muslims documented in figure 7.1 might have been swamped by partisan and ideological predispositions during the general election campaign. Moreover, the unusually large impact of Muslim favorability in August 2007 may have been the product of a substantial proportion of public thinking that Obama himself was an adherent of Islam, and should have receded if it was an artifact of such mistaken identity. The electorate undoubtedly had much more information about Obama and his Christian faith on Election Day than they had in the summer of 2007. If nothing else, the great publicity given to Reverend Wright certainly emphasized Obama's rootedness in Christianity.

Surprisingly enough, though, this chapter will show that the impact of attitudes about Muslims on support for Obama did *not* decline in 2008. Both Muslim affect, as operationalized by the ANES's 0–100 thermometer rating, and by favorability ratings of Muslims in the CCAP were important determinants of general election vote choice. There are several plausible explanations for why these attitudes about Muslims continued to matter throughout Obama's 2008 campaigns for the nomination and presidency. This chapter evaluates the following four testable hypotheses about the large impact of attitudes about Muslims on vote choices in 2008:

H1, *The partisan-ideological hypothesis*: The impact of attitudes toward Muslims may have stemmed from post-9/11 differences between Democrats and Republicans in their policies and rhetoric toward both the Islamic world and the civil liberties of Muslim Americans.

H2, *The confounded prejudices hypothesis*: It may have simply been an artifact of conflating antiblack and anti-Muslim attitudes.

H3, *The mistaken identity hypothesis*: It may have resulted from a sizable minority of the population thinking that Obama was himself a believer in Islam.

H4, *The Obama as "other" hypothesis*: More ominously, it may have resulted
from Obama's not being evaluated by the public just as an African
American but more fundamentally as someone who exemplifies "other"
status.

The evidence presented in this chapter is highly consistent with these
last expectations—the Obama as "other" hypothesis—and offers the least
support for the partisan-ideological explanation.

Method

We once again employ data from the CCAP and the ANES. Our focal explanatory variable in the CCAP is a five-category favorability rating of Muslims
asked in the October 2008 wave of the study. Attitudes toward Muslims are
operationalized in the 2004 and 2008 ANES with 0–100 thermometer ratings provided by respondents in the postelection wave of both survey years.

These self-reported evaluations of racial and ethnic groups are often
problematic in discerning true attitudes. Americans have become sensi-
tive to the unacceptability of expressing naked racial prejudice (Schuman
et al. 1997). As a result, a "norm of evenhandedness" in surveys has been
developed whereby American respondents are reluctant to deviate in their
evaluations from one racial or ethnic group to another. That norm results in
substantial proportions of respondents providing equal ratings for different
races and ethnicities (Sears and Savalei 2009).

Pressure from societal norms to default to consistent group ratings in-
troduces considerable error into these attitudinal measures. Such errors in
variable measurements are known to attenuate relationships with political
evaluations (see Ansolabehere, Rodden, and Snyder 2008 for a review). That
is one important reason for operationalizing attitudes toward African Americans with racial resentment rather than respondents' global evaluations of
blacks on the feeling thermometers.

Self-reported evaluations of Muslims, however, are less prone to this
source of measurement error because the norm of evenhandedness has apparently not yet been extended to them. The average thermometer ratings
of Muslims in the 2004 and 2008 ANES, for instance, were about 15 to
20 degrees lower than the ratings of whites, blacks, Hispanics, Asians, Cath-
olics, and Jews. There were also more respondents who rated Muslims unfa-
vorably than favorably in both the CCAP and the above-referenced August
2007 Pew Poll. From a methodological standpoint, the willingness of Amer-

icans to openly express negative feelings about Muslims alleviates some of the concern about using such evaluations as measures of affect toward this group (Sears and Savalei 2009; Iyengar et al. 2009). The open expression of anti-Muslim attitudes also has important substantive implications. Politicians have long been inhibited in how directly they can appeal to racial prejudice because of the strong societal norm of racial equality (Mendelberg 2001). Judging by the public's much lower evaluations of Muslims, however, the same normative considerations may not constrain appeals to anti-Muslim attitudes.

The Partisan-Ideological Hypothesis

The background and expectations from the partisan-ideological hypothesis share much in common with explanations put forth for how racial attitudes came to shape American politics in the post–civil rights era. Partisan polarization of racial liberals and conservatives into the two parties is well documented, beginning at the elite level and then becoming reflected in mass opinion (Carmines and Stimson 1989; Laymen and Carsey 2002; Valentino and Sears 2005). Similarly, the partisan-ideological explanation for the impact of individuals' attitudes toward Muslims in the 2008 general election begins with elite-level differences between Democrats and Republicans in their policies and rhetoric toward both Muslim Americans and the Muslim world in the aftermath of 9/11.

The Bush administration delivered many repeated admonitions that Islam is a religion of peace and that anger over the September 11 attacks should not be transferred to Muslim Americans. Nevertheless, the White House's rhetoric and policies were often viewed as antagonistic to both Muslim Americans and the Islamic world. The former president's September 2001 comments regarding a "crusade" against terror, along with his administration's policies toward Afghanistan, Iraq, Iran, Palestine, and the 2006 Israeli-Lebanese conflict were considered hostile to Muslims by commentators both at home and abroad (Cooper 2009). There were also concerns about transgressions against Muslim Americans' civil liberties. President Bush's attorney general, John Ashcroft, and his FBI director, Robert Mueller, were sued by over 700 Muslim Americans for false arrests following the 9/11 attacks.

These concerns over cultural insensitivity and civil liberties violations were often cited as the primary reason for the increase in Democratic presidential vote share by an estimated 50 percentage points among Muslim

Americans from 2000 to 2004 (Skerry and Fernandes 2004). With the Bush administration's actions presumably provoking such a profound backlash on Muslim Americans' partisan preferences, attitudes about Muslims might be expected to factor prominently in the partisan evaluations of Americans more generally in the post-9/11 era.

The partisan-ideological hypothesis, therefore, posits that the effects of Muslim affect on Obama evaluations in 2008 were party-specific rather than Obama-specific. These expectations are inconsistent, however, with the results already presented in figure 7.1. If the effects of Muslim affect were primarily partisan and ideological then they should have roughly the same sizable impact on evaluations of all ideologically comparable Democratic rivals for the nomination, not just on Obama evaluations. Yet that display showed Muslim favorability had a considerably bigger impact on Obama favorability than it did on Clinton's and Edwards's ratings in August 2007. Likewise, we would not expect a significant impact of attitudes about Muslims in the Democratic primaries because the two favorites for the party's presidential nomination, Hillary Clinton and Barack Obama, shared the same party and nearly identical ideological positioning.

Contrary to this expectation, figure 7.2 shows that attitudes toward Muslims were, in fact, an important determinant of vote choice between Obama and his rivals in the primaries. This display graphs the effect of Muslim favorability in the March CCAP and Muslim affect in the ANES on support for Obama against the field of Democratic challengers, with ideology, party identification, and demographic factors held constant. We should acknowledge, though, that neither data source is quite ideal for assessing the impact of attitudes about Muslims. The ANES's assessment of primary vote choice was taken several months after the contest, during the fall preelection survey. The CCAP did not ask about Muslims until its October wave, so those results somewhat unorthodoxly test the effect of panel respondents' favorability ratings of Muslims in October on March vote choice seven months earlier.

Despite these limitations, the results are quite suggestive. All else being equal, changing from the lowest appraisal to the most positive assessment of Muslims increased Obama's primary vote share by 40 points in the CCAP and over 30 points in the ANES. More important, this effect is specific to Obama himself. The partisan/ideological hypothesis would not expect attitudes toward Muslims to produce such a large polarization in the primary vote, because Hillary Clinton and Barack Obama shared the same party and ideological voting record (Carroll et al. 2008).

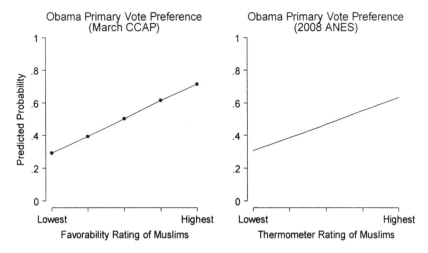

Figure 7.2. Vote preference for Obama in the primaries as a function of evaluations of Muslims (1=Obama, 0=other Democrat). Probabilities were based on the logistic coefficients in table A7.2 of the online appendix (http://www.press.uchicago.edu/books/tesler/). Predicted probabilities were calculated by setting all other variables to the mean respondent included in each separate analysis. *Source*: 2008 ANES; March 2008 CCAP.

There is also little reason to expect from the partisan-ideological explanation that attitudes about Muslims would have significantly smaller effects in McCain vs. Clinton trial heats than in McCain matchups against Obama. If the influence of attitudes about Muslims were a byproduct of partisan and ideological differences, their effects should be similar on support for either potential Democratic challenger against the probable Republican nominee. Finally, the impact of Muslim affect should be similar in both 2004 and 2008 because the Democratic and Republican candidates had similar policy positions in both election years.[5]

The results in figure 7.3 strongly contradict these expectations from the partisan-ideological hypothesis. It graphs the impact of Muslim favorability on separate McCain-Clinton and McCain-Obama March trial heats. As can be seen, the effect of Muslim favorability is markedly stronger on support for Obama over McCain than its impact on Clinton vs. McCain vote intentions. All else being equal, changing from a very unfavorable to a very favorable impression of Muslims increased Obama's predicted vote share against McCain by roughly 60 points. That effect is three times greater than the 20-point increase in Clinton's vote share associated with the same movement in feelings about Muslims.

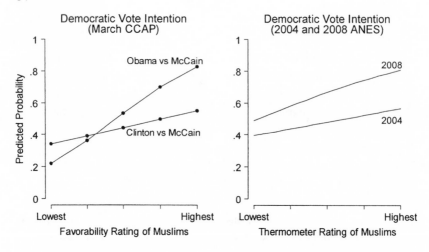

Figure 7.3. Democratic vote intention as a function of evaluation of Muslims. Probabilities were based on the logistic coefficients in table A7.3 of the online appendix (http://www .press.uchicago.edu/books/tesler/). Predicted probabilities were calculated by setting all other variables to their respective sample means. *Source*: March 2008 CCAP; 2004 and 2008 ANES.

The results from the second panel of figure 7.3 are also inconsistent with the partisan-ideological hypothesis. That display graphs the impact of Muslim thermometer ratings on Democratic vote intentions in the 2004 and 2008 general elections, while holding our familiar control variables constant. The impact of Muslim affect is shown in the figure to be twice as big in 2008 as it was in 2004. Moving from coldest to warmest on the Muslim thermometer scale increased Barack Obama's predicted vote share by 32 points in 2008 against John McCain, but by only 16 points in support for John Kerry against George W. Bush in 2004.[6]

Taken together, then, these results contradict the partisan-ideological hypothesis. Public reactions to Barack Obama himself, rather than simply to a generic white liberal Democrat, were responsible for the significant effects of attitudes about Muslims on 2008 voting behavior. That conclusion is based on the larger impact of Muslim favorability ratings on evaluations of Obama than of his ideologically similar Democratic rivals in August 2007, the large effects of attitudes about Muslims in the nonpartisan primary, and the greater role of these feelings in the 2008 general election than on 2004 vote intention or Clinton vs. McCain trial heats.

The Confounded Prejudices Hypothesis

In contrast, the confounded prejudices hypothesis would expect that attitudes about Muslims played a substantial role in the 2008 primaries and would be a much larger determinant of voting behavior in the 2008 general election than 2004. In other words, this hypothesis suggests that the impact of Muslim affect in 2008 is Obama-specific rather than party-specific. Yet it also would contend that these effects have little to do with attitudes about Muslims per se. Rather, it suggests that negative feelings about African Americans and Muslims have become conflated because of general ethnocentrism (Adorno et al. 1950; Duckitt 1992; Kinder and Kam 2009). Chapter 6 showed that the positive relationship between modern sexism and primary votes for Hillary Clinton against Barack Obama was an artifact of the correlation between racial and gender conservatism. In analogous fashion, the confounded prejudices hypothesis argues that the strong effects of attitudes about Muslims on support for Barack Obama in 2008 could have resulted from the conflation of racial resentment with anti-Muslim affect.

One would certainly expect that such attitudes about African Americans and Muslims might be constrained by an overarching ethnocentric belief system. We also know quite well by now that the effect of racial resentment was much larger in the 2008 campaign than it was in the all-white general election contests of the past. So the increased impact of attitudes about Muslims in 2008 could simply be a byproduct of the relationship between these feelings and symbolic racism. If the effects of attitudes about Muslims were, in fact, merely an artifact of the confounded prejudices hypothesis, we would expect them to have little impact after controlling for racial resentment. To be sure, controlling for racial resentment will likely reduce the impact of attitudes about Muslims. Anti-Muslim affect, as the confounded prejudices hypothesis would suspect, is significantly correlated with racial resentment in the 2008 ANES ($r = .31$), and this relationship between antiblack and anti-Muslim attitudes is even greater in the October CCAP ($r = .47$).

To test the confounded prejudices hypothesis, figure 7.4 graphs the effects of these attitudes on primary and general election vote choice in both the ANES and the CCAP with and without racial resentment controlled in the regression model. As expected, the display provides some support for the confounded prejudices explanation. Including racial resentment in the vote models noticeably reduced the impact of anti-Muslim attitudes in all four panels.[7]

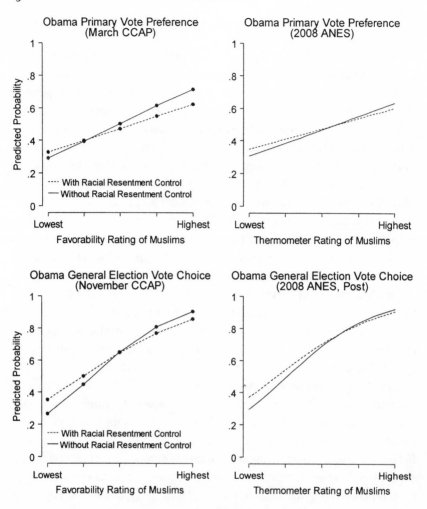

Figure 7.4. Obama vote preference as a function of evaluation of Muslims. Probabilities were based on the logistic coefficients in table A7.4 of the online appendix (http://www .press.uchicago.edu/books/tesler/). Predicted probabilities were calculated by setting all other variables to their respective sample means. *Source*: March and November 2008 CCAP; 2008 ANES.

More important, though, and contrary to the confounded prejudices hypothesis, the dashed lines in figure 7.4 show that attitudes about Muslims continue to strongly influence both 2008 primary and general voting behavior even after controlling for racial resentment. In other words, there are important effects of attitudes about Muslims that were *independent* of attitudes about blacks. With racial resentment along with our familiar control variables held constant, moving from having the lowest to the highest appraisal of Muslims still increased Obama's primary vote share by 30 points in the CCAP and 25 points in the ANES. Moreover, the same changes in opinions about Muslims were associated with roughly 50-point increases in both Obama's CCAP and ANES vote shares against John McCain. Also contrary to the confounded prejudices hypothesis is that the results presented in chapters 2 and 3 between opposition to Obama and racial resentment were hardly weakened at all by including attitudes about Muslims in the model.[8]

Unlike the spurious relationships between measures of gender conservatism and support for Hillary Clinton in the primaries, then, the relationship between attitudes about Muslims and voting for Obama in his 2008 campaigns cannot merely be attributed to confounded antiblack and anti-Muslim prejudices. Nor can the negative relationship of racial resentment to Obama votes.

The Mistaken Identity Hypothesis

McCain Supporter: *"I can't trust Obama. I have read about him, and he's . . . a . . . he's an Arab."*

John McCain: *"No Ma'am. He's a decent family man citizen that I just happen to have some disagreements with on fundamental issues, and that's what this campaign is all about. He's not. Thank you."*

This memorable exchange between Senator McCain and one of his supporters at a town hall meeting in Minnesota exemplifies the expectations of the mistaken identity hypothesis.[9] Between 10 and 20 percent of the American public consistently answered that Obama was a practicing Muslim from the first media polling on his religion in March 2008 up until Election Day.[10] Over a quarter of registered voters also believed that he was raised a Muslim.[11] Perhaps because of the concerted effort by some Republicans to refer to the Democratic nominee only by his full name, Barack *Hussein* Obama,[12] 41 percent of registered voters with an unfavorable opinion of Obama in September 2008 publicly cited the Democratic candidate's Islamic faith as a reason for their negative assessments.[13]

The mistaken identity hypothesis holds that the large impact of attitudes toward Muslims on vote choice in both the primaries and general election was predominantly caused by the significant minority who believed Obama is, or was at one time, a Muslim. If so, anti-Muslim attitudes should not have significantly affected the vote choices of the majority who did not believe

Obama was an adherent of Islam. Or if they did, then Muslim favorability ratings should at least have a substantially greater impact for those who mistakenly thought Obama subscribed to the Islamic faith than those who did not.

Fortunately, we can test this expectation because the October CCAP asked respondents about both Muslims and the two presidential candidates' religions. As expected from the mistaken identity hypothesis, regressing general election vote choice on Muslim favorability, racial resentment, partisanship, ideology, and demographic variables does yield a somewhat larger logistic regression coefficient for the 17 percent of October respondents who thought Obama was a Muslim in that survey than for the 83 percent who did not. But contrary to the hypothesis, the difference between the two groups is not very large (2.22 and 1.83, respectively).

The predicted probabilities based on these coefficients tell a much more important story. Those probabilities are graphically displayed in figure 7.5. While the coefficient may be larger for the minority who thought Obama was a Muslim, the display shows that the substantive impact of Muslim favorability ratings was considerably greater for the majority who did *not* think Obama was a believer in Islam. All else being equal, 40 percentage points separated the most pro- and anti-Muslim respondents who did not

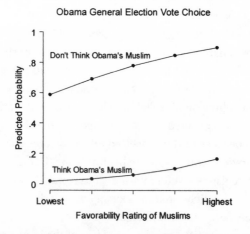

Figure 7.5. Obama general election vote choice as a function of Muslim favorability and knowledge of his religion. Probabilities were based on the logistic coefficients in table A7.5 of the online appendix (http://www.press.uchicago.edu/books/tesler/). Predicted probabilities were calculated by setting all other variables to the mean respondent in each separate analysis. *Source*: November 2008 CCAP.

say Obama was a practicing Muslim. This same change from least to most favorable, however, was associated with only about a 15 percentage point increase in support for John McCain among those who mistakenly thought Obama was a Muslim.

The other underlying symbolic predispositions of respondents who mistakenly thought Obama was a Muslim help explain why attitudes about Muslims did not substantially affect this group's 2008 voting behavior. Individuals who thought Obama was a Muslim, for instance, were considerably more racially resentful, ideologically conservative, and Republican than their counterparts (nearly 80 percent of whom also had an unfavorable opinion of Muslims, by the way).[14] And because the racial and political predispositions of the mistaken-identity folks were overwhelmingly conservative, they were very unlikely to vote for Obama, no matter what their feelings about Muslims.

Moreover, we know from the CCAP's panel design that this greater political and racial conservatism among respondents who thought Obama was Muslim in October 2008 was apparent long before Obama won the nomination.[15] Given their ardently conservative predispositions back in 2007 and early 2008, it is much more probable that these individuals thought Obama was a Muslim because they were predisposed not to like him in the first place, rather than disliking him because they thought he actually was a Muslim. That is, the McCain supporter quoted at the beginning of this section, who mistakenly told the Republican presidential nominee that she could not trust Obama because he was an Arab, probably thought he was an Arab precisely because her racial, ideological, and partisan proclivities had predisposed her to distrust Barack Obama in the first place.

In sum, we started out with the puzzle of why antipathy toward Muslims had a substantial impact on opposition to Obama in 2008. It turns out not to have been just a case of mistaken identity. Nor, as we saw above, were these effects primarily caused by partisan-ideological considerations or spurious relationships produced by the conflation of antiblack and anti-Muslim affect.

Concluding Remarks: Obama as "Other"

Contrary to these first three hypotheses, all of the expectations from the Obama as "other" hypothesis have been borne out. Attitudes about Muslims were much more important in evaluating Obama than other partisan

figures, and such effects were not merely artifacts of the correlation of antiblack and anti-Muslim attitudes, nor of mistaken identity. The "other" hypothesis is based in large part on previous work showing that evaluations
of Muslims are defined principally by affect toward ethnic, religious, racial, and especially cultural out-groups; these groups are described by the
researchers as "a band of others" because they fall outside the "mainstream"
of American society (Kalkan et al. 2009). Kalkan et al., in fact, show that
far and away the most important determinant of attitudes about Muslims is
affect for cultural groups often thought to violate cultural norms or traditional values, such as homosexuals, atheists, illegal immigrants, feminists,
and welfare recipients.

With attitudes about Muslims so heavily shaped by feelings about non-
mainstream cultural out-groups, it becomes easier to understand why
Muslim affect would influence evaluations of Obama more than those of
other politicians. We began the chapter, for instance, with a Clinton campaign strategy memo from Mark Penn, discussing how she should highlight
Obama's "lack of American roots." As Evan Thomas (2009, 63) surmised
from this March 2007 memo, "The idea seemed to be to subtly emphasize
Obama's 'otherness.'" Similarly, David K. Shipler noted the following in an
April 2008 editorial for the *Los Angeles Times*: "Despite [Obama's] ability to
articulate the frustration and yearning of broad segments of Americans, his
'otherness' has been highlighted effectively by right-wingers who harp on his
Kenyan father and spread false rumors that he's a clandestine Muslim."

The McCain campaign in general, and Sarah Palin in particular, appeared to have pursued this strategy to an even greater extent in the general
election than the Clinton campaign did in the primaries. McCain, in fact,
regularly asked his supporters, "Who is the real Barack Obama?" The answer, according to Sarah Palin at least, "is someone who sees America, it
seems, as being so imperfect, imperfect enough, that he's palling around
with terrorists who would target their own country. This is not a man who
sees America as you see America and as I see America."[16] These comments
were straight out of the Mark Penn playbook of attacking Obama as a person
who is not "fundamentally American in his thinking and values." That is,
they were clearly trying to make Obama the "other."

Such appeals echo a long line of social science research that treats attitudes about African Americans as a subset of the larger human suspicion
of peoples defined as "other" (Kinder and Kam 2009). Several facets of
Barack Obama's background made him uniquely qualified to activate such
attitudes—attitudes that extend beyond mere feelings about African Ameri-

cans to encompass affect toward alien cultural, racial, and ethnic groups outside the mainstream of American society. Barack Obama is not just black or biracial, he is distinctly "other." His Kenyan father, his foreign upbringing, and being named Barack *Hussein* Obama all transcend the black-white American binary. With Kalkan et al. (2009) showing that evaluations of Muslim are a summary measure of out-group affect, it is expected that such attitudes would have a substantial impact on support for Barack Obama even after controlling for racial resentment and accounting for those who thought the Democratic nominee was in fact a believer in Islam.

We would conclude, then, that the large independent association of negative feelings about Muslims and opposition to Barack Obama in both the primaries and general election reflected his evaluation not just as an African American but also as someone who exemplified "other" status.

There could be important implications for American politics if, as this chapter contends, Obama's candidacy actually made attitudes about Muslims a more central component of political decision making. We may, for instance, witness a greater utilization of anti-Muslim and other antialien appeals during the Obama presidency. As mentioned before, politicians are now limited in their ability to make direct appeals to antiblack antipathy because of the norm of racial equality (Mendelberg 2001). The American public's lower evaluations of Muslims and other alien cultural groups, however, suggest that they could be easier targets of political attack. Candidates at risk of such attacks, and their advisors, will need to devise strategies aimed at dampening these potential appeals to antipathy toward the "other," such as highlighting their patriotism.

There should also be a sustained focus by scholars on how attitudes about Muslims and other groups out of the mainstream will shape public opinion and voting behavior during the Obama presidency. Our central focus has been on how our first African American president may polarize partisan politics by racial attitudes even more than they ever did in the past. But we urge, too, examining the potential for attitudes about more alien groups in general, and Muslims in particular, to divide Americans' partisan evaluations in the age of Obama.

8

Is the Obama Presidency Post-Racial?

Evidence from His First Year in Office

This president has exposed himself, I think, as a guy, over and over and over again,
who has a deep-seated hatred for white people, or white culture.

GLENN BECK, *Fox and Friends*, July 28, 2009

"You put your kids on a school bus you expect safety but in Obama's America the
white kids now get beat up with the black kids cheering 'yeah, right on, right on,
right on.' Of course everybody said the white kid deserved it—he was born a racist,
he's white."

RUSH LIMBAUGH, *The Rush Limbaugh Show*, September 15, 2009

Our results from the campaign could have profound implications for American partisan politics in the age of Obama. The most important potential repercussion is that political decision making could become increasingly organized by racial attitudes in the years ahead. A number of findings suggest that this might occur. First, the two sides of racialization are inherently polarizing. If racial liberals are more supportive of President Obama than they would be of an ideologically similar white Democratic president, and racial conservatives are more opposed to him than they would be absent his race, then public opinion should naturally be more divided by racial attitudes than ever.

We also know from chapter 4 that opinions of the president are not the only political evaluations that could become more racialized in the future. That chapter showed that people or policies strongly situated in opposition or harmony with Barack Obama also evoked strong racial predispositions because of the spillover of racialization. One might expect, then, that public opinion about policies on which President Obama takes a public stance, such as health care reform, would also sharply split the electorate by their levels of racial resentment. Given the visceral and divisive history of American race relations, that polarization would likely make it especially difficult for Obama to find common ground on his legislative agenda.

Whether the election of Barack Obama was, in fact, the watershed to such a hyperracialized era in partisan politics is dependent on whether *President* Obama continues to evoke racial predispositions as strongly as Candidate Obama did throughout 2008. It might seem hard to believe that he would not. After all, we showed that racial resentment was readily accessible in evaluations of Barack Obama in 2007 even when he was widely depicted as the racially transcendent candidate. Similarly, despite substantial changes in both the political landscape and the racialized campaign context from March 2008 to October 2008, the relationship between racial resentment and McCain-Obama vote preferences was remarkably stable throughout the election year. That same stability was also evident in racial resentment's link to Obama's favorability ratings among CCAP panelists and to his thermometer ratings among ANES respondents interviewed in both pre- and post-election surveys.[1]

These results all seem to suggest that the accessibility of racial attitudes in Obama-related evaluations is difficult to deactivate. It is a bit humbling to recall, however, that we came to a similar conclusion when looking at the evidence about Tom Bradley's Los Angeles mayoral campaigns of 1969 and 1973. Indeed, symbolic racism was the prime determinant of opposition to Bradley in these two contests (Kinder and Sears 1981; Sears and Kinder 1971). Yet after Bradley became mayor, he was not predominantly evaluated on the basis of prejudice. Racial predispositions, in fact, did not dominate either his successful bids for reelection as mayor or his unsuccessful gubernatorial campaign in 1982 (Hajnal 2007; Citrin et al. 1990).

It turns out that Bradley is not the only black mayor who succeeded in his efforts to have white voters judge him by his record rather than his skin color. Hajnal (2007), for instance, convincingly shows that many black mayors, though not all, became less racialized public figures as incumbents than they had been as candidates. He argues that the mechanism underlying this change is *credible* information provided by such black incumbents against charges of black radicalism. "Black challengers," according to Hajnal (2007, 16) "can and usually do try to counter the uncertainty surrounding their candidacies by running 'deracialized' or pro-white campaigns, but white voters tend to ignore these candidates' campaign statements, which they perceive as having little credibility." After African American mayors have gained office, white voters could see that their earlier fears of black radicalism were largely exaggerated. Voters then may begin to evaluate these politicians more on the basis of nonracial political factors such as their track records in office and their party affiliations and less on the basis of race.

By this account, Obama's concerted effort to deactivate "racial aversion" may have been unsuccessful in 2008 because Americans viewed his efforts as merely the cheap talk of campaign platitudes. By analogy to the black mayors, such fears might have been alleviated once Obama got into the White House and voters saw that he did not use his extensive presidential powers to favor blacks' interests over whites'. But the analogy may or may not hold. As Hajnal (2007, 11) states, "A black president . . . would surely be seen as much more powerful than a black mayor and would therefore present an interesting and important test case of the information model."

Despite Obama's mainstream Democratic agenda, he did not fully succeed in alleviating white fears of racial favoritism during his first year in office. If anything, he seemed to exacerbate them. An August 2009 poll by the *Economist*/YouGov, for example, revealed that 37 percent of whites and 65 percent of Republicans thought Obama's policies favored blacks over whites.[2] That is a three-fold *increase* from responses to similarly worded questions in October 2008 by both CBS/*New York Times* and NBC/*Wall Street Journal* about which racial group Obama's policies would favor if he became president.[3] These results seem to be more consistent with Moskowitz and Stoh's (1994) finding that many whites effectively "alter reality" in order to render a black candidate's message consistent with their prior expectations and racial beliefs than with the unbiased information processing in Hajnal's model. Despite not broaching any race-specific policies during his first year in office, the majority of Republicans thought Obama favored African Americans.

Perhaps more Americans believed President Obama favored African Americans in August 2009 than in October 2008 because the informational environment became more racialized once he took office. Two examples from the summer of 2009 clearly illustrated President Obama's potential for elevating the salience of race in popular political discourse, even if inadvertently. In July, the prominent black scholar, Henry Louis Gates, a distinguished professor at Harvard, was arrested for disorderly conduct following an investigation by the Cambridge, Massachusetts, police of a possible break-in at his home. The arrest created a storm of protest. The president was asked at a routine press conference what the controversial arrest said about American race relations. Obama's answer linked Gates's arrest to the long history of racial profiling by the police and accused the arresting officer, James Crowley, of acting "stupidly." This response, which Obama would later say was not well "calibrated," was widely condemned in the media and strongly disapproved of by white Americans—the large majority of whom thought that Gates had behaved inappropriately but that Crowley had not.[4]

The racial controversy touched off by Obama's comments was a great source of journalistic fodder. Gates's arrest, for instance, was the most heavily covered news story from July 23 to July 26 and was still prominently featured in American news reports throughout the following week.[5] As a result of that attention, 46 percent of Americans said that they heard "a lot" about Barack Obama's comments on the arrest.[6] The story eventually died down after Obama had Gates and Crowley over to the White House for a "Beer Summit." Yet the incident said much about the strong racial overtones that continue to surround Obama's presidency.

That politically divisive summer also saw the rise of the "birther movement" that claimed Obama was not born in the United States. It also saw the rise of the "tea party movement" with its angry protests of Obama's health care reform proposals. A South Carolina Congressman even shouted out "You lie" during the President's speech on health care reform before a joint session of Congress. Some liberal commentators believed that this fervent opposition to the president was rooted in racial animus.[7] President Jimmy Carter powerfully voiced such sentiments in September 2009 when he stated, "I think an overwhelming portion of the intensely demonstrated animosity toward President Barack Obama is based on the fact that he is a black man, that he's African American."[8]

Like the Gates incident, Carter's controversial racial comments generated considerable media attention. Claims of race-based opposition to Obama, in fact, received more attention than any other topic in the blogosphere from September 14 to September 25.[9] Not surprisingly, 40 percent of respondents interviewed during this time period recalled hearing "a lot" about "charges that racism is a factor in criticisms of President Obama and his politics."[10] The president once again immediately attempted to dampen this racially based media firestorm by telling four Sunday morning talks shows airing the week of Carter's comments that the vitriolic opposition facing his administration stemmed primarily from his policy positions, not his race.[11] Whether or not these accusations of racially motivated opposition were actually true, the fact that they garnered so much press interest suggests that the Obama White House was operating in a more racialized atmosphere in its early months than were previous presidents.

These events from the summer of 2009 could be interpreted as suggesting that race and racial attitudes were as important in evaluations of Obama early in his presidency as they had been in the campaign. If so, why would Obama not be following the same deracialized trajectory that Hajnal (2007) has shown most black mayors had in the past? Perhaps the profound racial hopes and fears embodied by our first African American president have made racial attitudes simply more accessible than they were for local black politicians who did not symbolize such sweeping racial changes. That chronic accessibility might make it more difficult for President Obama to deactivate racial attitudes than it had been for black mayors.

Fortunately we have considerable survey data on both racial attitudes and public responses to the first year of the Obama presidency. We can use them to test whether or not Obama conveyed enough credible information about his nonracial approach to the presidency to put him on the same path to deracializing white voters' evaluations as that experienced by most black mayors. The data come from both a long time series of cross-sectional surveys and from panel surveys initiated before 2009. As a result, we can determine if Americans were using their racial attitudes more in evaluating Obama than previous presidents and if racial resentment's impact on Obama-related assessments changed after he became president.

Our brief exposition of this evidence below shows that (1) Obama's early presidential job approval ratings were influenced considerably more by racial attitudes than was the case for previous presidents, (2) support for Obama from white racial liberals had much to do with those highly racialized presidential approval ratings, (3) the effect of racial resentment on evaluations of Obama remained remarkably stable from early 2008 to November 2009, (4) President Obama continued to be evaluated not just as an African American but as someone who was distinctly "other," and (5) Obama-induced racialization spilled over into issues on which the White House took visible positions, such as health care.

President Obama and the Two Sides of Racialization

We saw in chapter 3 that racial attitudes had a greater impact on presidential voting in 2008 than they had in any other general election contest on record. We also saw that this larger role of racial resentment on McCain-Obama vote intention was brought about by the two sides of racialization. Racial conservatives were more opposed to Obama than they probably would have been to a white Democratic candidate who was ideologically similar to him, such as Hillary Clinton. Racial liberals, of course, were more supportive of Obama than they were of previous Democratic candidates for president.

Our cross-sectional time-series data also allow us to assess whether racial attitudes have a similarly larger impact on President Obama's approval than previous presidents. Since 1987, the Pew Research Center and its predecessor Times Mirror, in their series of surveys on American values, have regularly asked a battery of four race-related questions that approximates the content of symbolic racism.[12] These questions gauge the extent of discrimination against African Americans, the group's societal advancement, whether we should do everything we can to help blacks and other minorities even if it means giving them special preferences, and whether the country has gone too far in pushing for equal rights (see appendix for question wording). The items do not form quite as reliable a scale as the Kinder and Sanders (1996) racial resentment battery does (α = .54 across survey years compared to about .75 for the racial resentment scale). They are also especially unreliable for African Americans (α = .29 across survey years), who as a result are excluded from our Pew analyses. Nevertheless, Pew's April 2009 update of their values time series provides substantial insights into how racial attitudes affected job performance evaluations of President Obama compared to those of his immediate White House predecessors.

Figure 8.1 shows how these racial predispositions influenced the presidential approval ratings of all five presidents going back to Ronald Reagan. The results tell a now-familiar story. It shows that the effects of racial attitudes on President Obama's job approval are noticeably larger than was the case for his predecessors. All else being equal, strong racial liberals and strong racial conservatives were separated by about 70 percentage points in their Obama approval ratings—a difference at least twice as large as the polarization of public opinion by racial attitudes produced by Presidents Ronald Reagan, George H. W. Bush, Bill Clinton, and George W. Bush. These effects of Pew's racial predisposition scale on presidential approval/ disapproval ratings since 1987 look strikingly similar to the considerably greater impact of racial resentment on GOP presidential vote intention in 2008 than in any other election since 1988, as shown earlier in figure 3.1.

Also paralleling the racialized voting patterns in 2008, much of President Obama's polarization of the electorate by racial attitudes in April 2009 was driven by his staunch support from racial liberals. All else being equal, we estimate that nearly all of the most racially liberal Americans approved of Obama's job performance in April 2009. Figure 8.1 indicates that President Obama continued to have the same special appeal among white racial liberals in the early months of his presidency that he did while running for president.

Obama's particular support among white racial liberals was again on display in an informative comparison that varied race but held partisanship constant. Respondents were asked in the April 2009 Pew Values Survey how much confidence they had in President Obama, Democratic leaders in

Predicted Probability of Presidential Approval/Disapproval

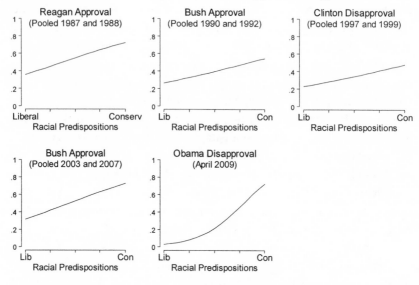

Figure 8.1. Approval of Republican presidents and disapproval of Democratic presidents as a function of racial predispositions. Probabilities were based on the logistic regression coefficients in table A8.1 of the online appendix (http://www.press.uchicago.edu/books/tesler/). Predicted probabilities were calculated by setting all other variables to their respective sample means. African Americans were excluded from the analysis. *Source*: Pew Values Survey Merged File.

Congress, and Republican leaders in Congress to do the right thing when it came to fixing the economy. Like our ubiquitous McCain-Obama and McCain-Clinton trial heats, comparing the effects of racial conservatism on confidence in Obama to its effects on confidence in congressional Democrats presumably isolates the effects of race by holding ideology and partisanship approximately constant across the two comparisons. The analogy with the March 2008 McCain trial heats is not exact, however. Both Obama and Clinton polled almost identically against John McCain, but Congress usually has much lower approval ratings than the president. In fact, about two-thirds of Pew's respondents had "a great deal" or "a fair amount" of confidence in Obama, but only 50 percent were similarly confident in Democratic leaders in Congress.

This greater confidence in Obama than in congressional Democrats in April 2009 came especially from white racial liberals; it was not spread evenly across the racial predispositions spectrum. Figure 8.2 shows that all else being equal, nearly all racial liberals had at least a "fair amount" of con-

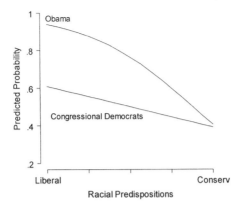

Figure 8.2. Confidence in politicians to fix the economy as a function of racial predispositions. Probabilities were based on the logistic regression coefficients in table A8.2 of the online appendix (http://www.press.uchicago.edu/books/tesler/). Predicted probabilities were calculated by setting all other variables to their sample means. African Americans were excluded from the analysis. *Source*: April 2009 Pew Values Survey.

fidence in Obama to fix the economy, compared to just 60 percent who had confidence in congressional Democrats. Racial conservatives, by contrast, had equivalent levels of confidence in Obama and congressional Democrats. In other words, the much larger effect of racial attitudes on assessments of Barack Obama than Democratic leaders in Congress stemmed largely from Obama's greater support from white racial liberals.

Assessments of Obama were almost certainly more racialized in the first year of his presidency than they would have been for a white Democratic president, therefore, as shown in figures 8.1 and 8.2. President Obama resembled Candidate Obama in drawing highly racialized evaluations. Yet, just as in the campaign, the sharp polarization in evaluations of President Obama by racial attitudes was not necessarily politically damaging because of his strong support from white racial liberals. Indeed, despite the outsized effects of racial attitudes on his approval ratings, only 26 percent of Pew's respondents disapproved of Obama's job performance in this April 2009 survey.

Chronic Accessibility of Racial Attitudes?

Figure 8.1 indicates that racial attitudes had a much stronger impact on assessments of President Obama's job performance shortly after he assumed office than they generally had during other recent presidents' incumbencies. This display, however, does not tell us how those effects might have changed later in his presidency. We can carry the story forward to the end of his first year in office, though, because we reinterviewed over 3,000 panelists in November 2009 who completed the March 2008 CCAP survey. These reinterviews allow us to determine how the impact of racial resentment on evaluations of Candidate Obama early in 2008 compared to its effects on assessments of President Obama late in 2009.

Recall from chapter 3 that racial resentment's impact on Obama-McCain vote intention was remarkably stable among the CCAP panel respondents interviewed four times from March to November 2008, despite the vastly different national conditions and campaign contexts across that period. We argued that the effect of racial resentment was likely to be constant because racial attitudes were chronically accessible in evaluations of Obama. In other words, the associative link between racial attitudes and Obama evaluations may be so strong that these predispositions were spontaneously activated even in the absence of situational cues like a racialized campaign appeal from John McCain. Such spontaneous activation would, therefore, make it difficult for new information to either deactivate *or* enhance the impact of racial resentment on assessments of Obama.

If racial attitudes are indeed readily accessible in evaluations of Barack Obama, we should find this same stability in racial resentment's effects on assessments of Obama across the three interviews of CCAP panel respondents in March 2008, November 2008, and November 2009. Figure 8.3 shows that this expectation is clearly borne out. The first panel in the display graphs the effects of racial resentment, as measured in March 2008, on Obama favorability at each of these three junctures. Like presidents before him (Brody 1991), Obama experienced widespread popularity after his election. The first panel of the display, for instance, shows that this "honeymoon period" made Obama more popular in November 2008 than he was either in March of that year or in November 2009. However, regardless of whether Obama's favorability was assessed shortly after the racially charged Reverend Wright incident of March 2008, or during the period of goodwill exhibited toward Obama after his victory in November 2008, or in the midst of a long and contentious debate over health care reform in the fall of 2009, figure 8.3 shows that the effects of racial resentment on these evaluations of Obama are nearly identical.

That same constancy of effects over time was produced when we asked our panel respondents whether they wanted President Obama to be re-

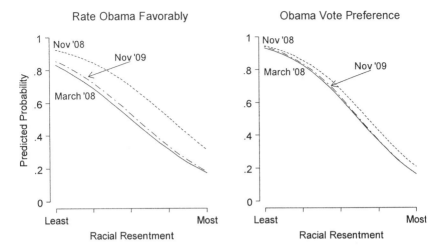

Figure 8.3. Support for Obama as a function of racial resentment. Probabilities were based on the logistic regression coefficients in table A8.3 of the online appendix (http://www .press.uchicago.edu/books/tesler/). Predicted probabilities were calculated by setting all other variables to their sample means. *Source*: March and November 2008 and November 2009 CCAP panelists.

elected in 2012 or if they preferred that a Republican win. The second panel of figure 8.3 shows that the impact of racial resentment on vote intention for Obama in this November 2009 generic reelection matchup is indistinguishable from either its effect on the Obama-McCain trial heat in March 2008 or reported general election vote decision in November 2008.

Such stability in the effects of racial resentment should, according to our reasoning, be limited to Obama himself. Being so well known as an African American and a historic racial figure makes his race highly cognitively accessible. That stability stands in stark contrast to the evidence in chapter 4 of the volatility over the exact same time period in the impact of racial resentment on evaluations of attitude objects that were not African American: Hillary Clinton, John McCain, and tax policy. Race is not as accessible in these latter political evaluations as it is in assessments of Obama. As a result, the impact of racial attitudes on an issue like tax policy would depend on how closely tax issues were associated with Barack Obama at the time of the survey. Figure 8.3 suggests that the effect of racial resentment on Obama-based evaluations is less susceptible to such contextual changes because racial predispositions are more likely to be spontaneously activated when the respondent is thinking about Obama.

President Obama as "Other"

We argued in chapter 7 that the large, independent effects of attitudes about Muslims on Obama vote intention stemmed from the fact that he is not simply evaluated as an African American but as someone who exemplifies the "other"—someone whose background is foreign and alien to many white Americans. Despite holding the presidency, the most uniquely American position imaginable, the "otherization" of Barack Obama by his political opponents seems to have only intensified since he took office. The most visible manifestation of such "other"-based opposition to the president is the emergence of the so-called birther movement, which claims that he was not actually born in the United States. In the first year of his presidency, this mistaken belief gained even more traction than the equally erroneous contention that Obama is an adherent of Islam. As indicated earlier, about 15 percent of Americans believed he was a Muslim during the 2008 campaign. A national poll of registered voters in September 2009 revealed that 23 percent of the public thought Obama was born outside the United States (the exact same percentage yielded in our November 2009 CCAP reinterviews), with 42 percent of Republicans saying the president was not American born.[13]

With this ongoing attempt to paint Obama as alien, we expected attitudes about Muslims—which Kalkan et al. (2009) show are primarily a function of feelings about cultural out-groups—still to be strong, independent predictors of Obama evaluations a year into his presidency. Figure 8.4 shows that positive attitudes toward Muslims did, in fact, powerfully predict both favorable opinions of Obama in November 2009 and support for his reelection, even with racial resentment and our base-model variables held constant. Although the effects of these attitudes on Obama favorability and his reelection seem to have diminished somewhat since November 2008, the continuing sizable impact of Muslim favorability on opinions about Obama suggests that the president is still not just viewed as an African American but as someone who is inherently "other."

Because opinions of Muslims are so strongly related to feelings about cultural out-groups more generally (Kalkan et al. 2009), we also wanted to assess their relationship with the belief that Obama was not born in the United States. One might suspect a priori that those most antagonistic to out-groups were also the ones most likely to embrace the "birther" belief that highlighted Obama's position as "other." To test this, figure 8.5 shows the effects of racial resentment, Muslim favorability, and partisanship on

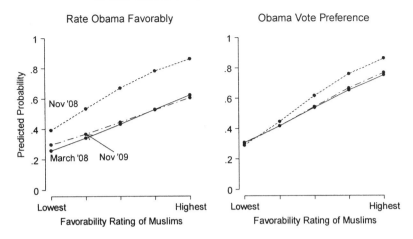

Figure 8.4. Support for Obama as a function of Muslim favorability. Probabilities were based on the logistic regression coefficients in table A8.4 of the online appendix (http://www.press.uchicago.edu/books/tesler/). Predicted probabilities were calculated by setting all other variables to their sample means. *Source*: March and November 2008 and November 2009 CCAP panelists.

answering the birther question correctly. Partisan and racial attitudes had a considerably stronger influence on support for Obama's reelection than impressions of Muslims for our CCAP panelists.[14] Yet the display shows that a change from having a very unfavorable impression of Muslims to rating them very favorably had just as strong an impact on rates of saying Obama was American-born as changes from most liberal to most conservative in racial resentment and partisanship. Even with racial resentment and our base-model variables held constant, individuals with the most favorable impressions of Muslims were 45 percentage points more likely to say Obama was American-born than were those with very unfavorable feelings about Muslims. It looks as if much of the driving force behind the dogged unwillingness of so many to acknowledge that Obama was born in the United States is not just simple partisan opposition to a Democratic president but a general ethnocentric suspicion of an African American president who is also perceived as distinctly "other."

Several liberal commentators have contended that media personalities like Glenn Beck and Rush Limbaugh in particular, and the Fox News Channel in general, have catered to these ethnocentric Americans since Obama became president.[15] With this in mind, we asked one-quarter of our panelists where they got most of their televised news about national and international affairs. Roughly 25 percent of respondents got most of their tele-

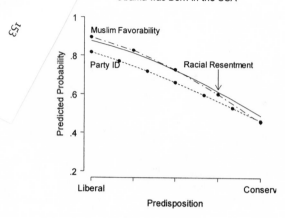

162

Figure 8.5. Beliefs about Obama's country of origin as functions of partisanship, racial resentment, and Muslim favorability. Probabilities were based on the logistic regression coefficients in table A8.5 of the online appendix (http://www.press.uchicago.edu/books/tesler/). Predicted probabilities were calculated by setting all other variables to their sample means. *Source*: November 2009 CCAP reinterviews.

vised information from Fox News, both in our CCAP reinterviews and in a July 2009 Pew Poll whose question wording we replicated.[16] We expected most respondents to say Obama was born in the United States, even those who relied most heavily on Fox News. We were surprised, however, to find that only 21 percent of Fox viewers said that Obama was American-born. To be sure, this widespread disbelief among Fox News viewers stemmed from the fact that they are most likely to hold the same conservative predispositions shown in figure 8.5 that underlie such mistaken beliefs about Obama. Yet, even after controlling for Muslim favorability, racial resentment, and our base-model variables, we estimated that Fox News watchers were more than 20 percentage points less likely to say Obama was American-born in November 2009 than those who got most of their news from other television sources.

Unfortunately, there is simply no way of knowing from these data whether the Fox News Channel plays an active role in casting doubt about Obama's citizenship, or whether Americans most inclined to think the worst of the president simply seek out Fox to reinforce their opinions. Either way, the reinforcing and/or persuasive role of oppositional media outlets like Fox News and conservative talk radio could make it increasingly difficult to disabuse the sizable minority of individuals disposed to accepting invalid assertions designed to paint Obama as the "other."

The Spillover of Racialization into the Obama Administration's Policies

As we mentioned in chapter 4, our results from the campaign on the spillover of racialization are likely to have the most important implications for American politics in the age of Obama. If the racialized evaluations associated with President Obama spill over to people and policies strongly situated in opposition or harmony with him, as they had during the campaign, then partisan politics might become increasingly polarized by race and racial attitudes in the years ahead.

The natural extension of our discussion of Obama-induced racialization in chapter 4 is that racial attitudes should have developed a greater impact on opinions about health care after the 2008 election because of its strong association with President Obama. Indeed, the spillover of racialization into public opinion on health care reform was a common media frame in the summer and fall of 2009. Some commentators regularly contended during that time that at least some of the uproar provoked by Obama's health care proposals was a product of race-related opposition to a black president's agenda (Krugman 2009; Dowd 2009; Hetherington and Weiler 2009; Hanania 2009; Robinson 2009).

A thorough treatment of the mechanisms underlying this suspected racialization of health care is well beyond the scope of this final chapter. Nevertheless, we have some preliminary evidence from our CCAP reinterviews suggesting that the policy's association with Barack Obama increasingly polarized Americans' health care opinions along the lines of their racial attitudes. The first panel of figure 8.6, for instance, shows the effects of racial resentment on saying health insurance should be voluntarily left up to individuals, among CCAP respondents interviewed in both December 2007 and November 2009. As was the case with tax policy preferences in December 2007, opinions about governmental versus individual responsibility for health care were already quite a bit racialized in 2007. That is not surprising given the connection many Americans make between African Americans and governmental services that provide a social safety net (Sears and Citrin 1985; Gilens 1999; Winter 2008).

Despite the large baseline effect of racial resentment in December 2007,

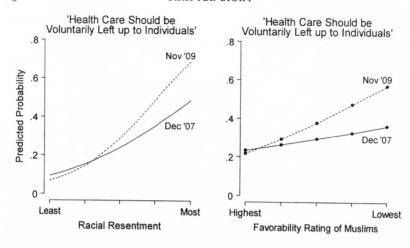

Figure 8.6. Health care opinions as functions of racial resentment and Muslim favorability. Probabilities were based on the logistic regression coefficients in table A8.6 of the online appendix (http://www.press.uchicago.edu/books/tesler/). Predicted probabilities were calculated by setting all other variables to their sample means. *Source*: December 2007, March 2008 and November 2009 CCAP panelists.

attitudes about health care did become considerably more racialized after Obama became the loudest spokesperson for health care reform. All else being equal, moving from least to most racially resentful increased the proportion of Americans saying that health care should be voluntary by nearly 40 percentage points in December 2007. This same change in racial resentment levels, however, increased support for private health insurance by over 60 percentage points in November 2009.

Aside from this spillover of racialization into health care opinions, the second panel of figure 8.6 suggests that the Obama presidency also caused what might be described as a spillover of "otherization." This display shows the effects of Muslim favorability on support for private health insurance in both December 2007 and November 2009. Consistent with the evidence from chapter 7 showing opinions about Muslims did not have much influence on partisan political decision making before Obama, the display shows only a modest impact of these attitudes on health care opinions in December 2007. This effect, however, more than doubled for these exact same respondents in November 2009. As can be seen, those possessing the most unfavorable impressions of Muslims were now more than 30 percentage points more likely to say health care should be voluntary than those rating Muslims very favorably. Like the spillover of racialization, this result suggests that

President Obama may also make opinions about out-groups a more important factor of partisan political decision making in the years ahead.

Much more work is needed to clarify the role of association with Obama in racializing health care. It could simply be, for instance, that racial resentment's impact increased because of its closer association with the more racially liberal political party rather than its central place in a black president's legislative agenda. Interestingly enough, though, the effects of partisanship and ideological self-placement on health care opinions hardly changed at all from December 2007 to November 2009.[17] This suggests that the increased effects of racial resentment during that time period were not simply the result of traditional partisan conflict over public policy.

We also witnessed a sharp increase in the effects of racial attitudes without a corresponding enhanced influence of partisanship in a fortuitous question wording experiment embedded within an August 2009 opinion poll for CNN.[18] The survey randomly assigned respondents to two different versions of a question on whether Sonia Sotomayor's nomination to the Supreme Court should be confirmed by the Senate. One version stated that Sotomayor had been nominated by President Obama. The other version did not provide any information about who had nominated her.[19] We would expect from the results previously presented on the spillover of racialization that racial attitudes would more powerfully affect support for Sotomayor among respondents who were told she was Obama's nominee.

We can test this racial-spillover hypothesis because the same survey also asked how common police discrimination against African Americans is. Denial of discrimination against African Americans is, of course, a key tenet of the symbolic racism belief system and is assessed in Kinder and Sander's (1996) racial resentment battery. As expected, figure 8.7 shows that the effect of this discrimination perception variable was nearly three times larger on support for Sotomayor's confirmation among respondents randomly assigned to the Obama-framed question. Among respondents not told Obama nominated her, a change from thinking discrimination against blacks by the police is "very common" to thinking it is "very rare" decreased support for Sotomayor by about 10 percentage points. Among respondents who were told she was appointed by President Obama, however, this same change in perceptions of discrimination decreased support for Sotomayor by roughly 30 percentage points. No such increase, however, occurred in the effects of partisanship[20]—again suggesting that Obama-induced racialization is not simply an artifact of an issue's increased association with a president from the more racially liberal political party.

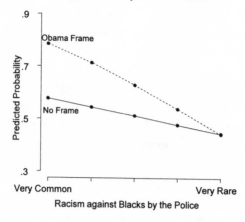

Figure 8.7. Support for Sotomayor's confirmation as a function of perceptions of discrimination and question frame. Probabilities were based on the logistic regression coefficients in table A8.7 of the online appendix (http://www.press.uchicago.edu/books/tesler/). Predicted probabilities were calculated by setting all other variables to their sample means. African Americans were excluded from the analysis. *Source*: July 31–August 3, 2009, CNN/ORC.

Concluding Remarks

Although these results from the first year of Obama's presidency are quite telling, the full story of racial attitudes' impact on evaluations of President Obama and partisan politics during his tenure in the White House is obviously yet to be told. A strong job performance and a race-neutral, moderate, political agenda could potentially reverse Obama's strong polarization of the electorate by racial attitudes in 2009 and put him on the same path to deracialized evaluations that Hajnal (2007) shows often occurs for black mayors. One could envision, for example, that pursuing policies more popular with racial conservatives than racial liberals, such as President Obama's escalation of the war in Afghanistan in 2009, might increase his popularity with high-resentment Americans and/or diminish his unprecedented support among individuals with low racial resentment scores. The upshot of such racially liberal movement away from the president combined with added support from racial conservatives would be the deracialization of Obama-based assessments.

The results presented in this chapter, however, do not augur well for such a post-racial atmosphere. Despite all that was learned about Barack Obama, first as a long-shot primary challenger, then as the Democratic nominee for president, and finally as President of the United States, the effects of racial resentment on his evaluations were virtually unchanged throughout all of 2008 and 2009. The symbolism of Barack Obama's position as the first black president, at least one year into his tenure in the White House, still appeared to make racial attitudes one of the most important determinants of how the American public responded to him. Whether or not this novelty eventually fades away and President Obama becomes primarily evaluated on the same partisan and performance factors that served as the principal basis for past presidential assessments remains to be seen. However, there is nothing in our most recent evidence, amassed one year after Obama's victory, to suggest that this would happen before the midterm elections in 2010.

Regardless of what the future holds, we can say with a great deal of confidence that the election of our first black president was not a post-racial moment. Rather, racial attitudes were heavily implicated in every aspect of Barack Obama's quest for the White House. From Americans' earliest evaluations of Candidate Obama to their primary voting to their general election vote choice, Obama was heavily judged in terms of his racial background. Racial attitudes were strongly associated with both support for and opposition to Obama throughout the election year. With these positive and negative effects largely canceling themselves out in Obama's aggregate vote tallies, many mistakenly took his victory as a sign that race no longer mattered in American politics. Behind such success in the primaries and general election, however, lay perhaps the most racialized presidential voting patterns in American history.

APPENDIX

Surveys

Cooperative Campaign Analysis Project

The following information on sampling methodology is taken directly from the Cooperative Campaign Analysis Project's codebook, and it explains how the sample of 18,250 total respondents was constructed.

1. SAMPLING FRAME AND TARGET SAMPLE. YouGov Polimetrix constructed a sampling frame from the 2007 American Community Study (ACS), including data on age, race, gender, education, marital status, number of children under 18, family income, employment status, citizenship, state, and metropolitan area. The frame was constructed by stratified sampling from the full 2007 ACS sample with selection within strata by weighted sampling with replacements (using the person weights on the public use file). Data on reported 2004 voter registration and turnout from the November 2004 Current Population Survey were matched to this frame using a weighted Euclidean distance metric. Data on religion, church attendance, born-again or evangelical status, news interest, party identification, and ideology were matched from the 2008 Pew Religious Life Survey. The target sample was selected by stratification by age, race, gender, education, and state (with battleground states double sampled) by simple random sampling within strata, excluding all nonregistered persons.

2. WITHIN PANEL SELECTION. Respondents were chosen from the YouGov Polimetrix PollingPoint Panel and the MyPoints Panel using a five-way cross-classification ($age \times gender \times race \times education \times state$). At each wave, additional cases were added to deficient cells to achieve approximately 30,000 interviews. All respondents who had completed any prior wave were reinvited to subsequent waves. The final set of completed interviews (numbering approximately 48,000, after quality controls were applied) was then matched to the target frame using a weighted Euclidean distances metric.

3. WEIGHTING. The matched cases were then weighted to the sampling frame using propensity scores. The matched cases and the frame were combined and a logistic regression was estimated for inclusion in the frame. The propensity score function included age, years of education, gender, black and Hispanic race indicators, news interest, party identification, and interactions of age and gender and race and education. The propensity scores were grouped into deciles of the estimated propensity score in the frame and poststratified according to these deciles. The final weights were then poststratified by state, gender, race, and turnout. Weights larger than seven were trimmed and the final weights normalized to equal the sample size.

American National Election Studies (ANES)

Information about the ANES can be found at its Web page: http://electionstudies.org. All ANES data sets are also directly downloadable from that site.

Pew Values Study Merged File

Information about the Pew Values Studies can be found at Pew's Web page: http://people-press.org. The Values Study Merged File is also downloadable from that site. However, the Merged File does not contain presidential approval. We appended presidential approval ratings to the Merged File from all individual Values surveys that were both publicly downloadable from the Roper Center's data archive and contained all four questions from their racial predispositions scale (1987, 1988, 1990, 1992, 1997, 1999, 2003, 2007, and 2009).

Other Surveys

The other surveys used are described in the endnotes upon presentation. Please contact Michael Tesler (mtesler2@ucla.edu) for replication files on all surveys used in the analysis.

Variable Measures

Base-Model Variables

AGE. Respondents' actual ages.

BLACK. An indicator variable taking on a value of 1 (African American) or 0 (nonblack).

EDUCATION. A five-category variable ranging from 0 (no high school diploma) to 1 (postgraduate).

IDEOLOGICAL SELF-PLACEMENT (ANES). A five-category variable ranging from 0 (extremely liberal) to 1 (extremely conservative).

IDEOLOGICAL SELF-PLACEMENT (CCAP). A five-category variable ranging from 0 (very liberal) to 1 (very conservative).

MALE. An indicator variable taking on a value of 0 (female) or 1 (male).

PARTISANSHIP (ANES and CCAP). A seven-category variable ranging from 0 (strong Democrat) to 1 (strong Republican).

SOUTH. An indicator variable taking on a value of 0 (non-South) or 1 (Southern residence).

RACIAL RESENTMENT. An additive index ranging from 0 (least resentful) to 1 (most resentful). Information on scale construction is presented in chapter 1.

Other Explanatory Variables

AUTHORITARIANISM (ANES). An additive index ranging from 0 (least authoritarian) to 1 (most authoritarian). The scale was constructed from respondents' preferences for the following childrearing traits: (1) independence or respect for elders, (2) curiosity or good manners, (3) self-reliance or obedience, and (4) being considerate or well behaved.

BLACK AFFECT (ANES). An additive index ranging from 0 (lowest) to 1 (highest). The scale was constructed from the following items: (1) The standard 0–100 ANES thermometer rating of blacks, (2) How often have you felt sympathy for blacks, very often, fairly often, not too often, or never? and (3) How often have you felt admiration for blacks, very often, fairly often, not too often, or never?

BLACK-WHITE COMPETITION (NPS). An additive index ranging from 0 (least intergroup competition) to 1 (most intergroup competition). The scale was constructed from responses to the following items: (1) More good jobs for whites means fewer good jobs for people like me, (2) The more influence whites have in politics, the less influence people like me will have in politics, (3) On the whole, do you think that most white people want to see blacks get a better break, do they want to keep blacks down, or don't they care one way or the other?

BLACKS WORK HARDER (NPS). A thirteen-point scale constructed by subtracting respondents' ratings of whites from their ratings of blacks on the 1–7 lazy to hardworking stereotype scale.

CLOSER TO BLACKS (NPS). A nine-point scale constructed by subtracting how close respondents felt toward whites (ranging from "very close" to "not at all close") from how close they felt toward blacks.

ECONOMIC EVALUATIONS (March CCAP). A five-category variable ranging
from 0 (the national economy is "much worse" than last year) to 1 (the
economy is "much better").

ECONOMIC ISSUES (March CCAP). An additive index ranging from 0
(most liberal) to 1 (most conservative). The scale was constructed from
the following items: (1) Which comes closest to your view about providing health care in the United States? (a) The government should provide
everyone with health care and pay for it with tax dollars, (b) Companies
should be required to provide health insurance for their employees and
the government should provide subsidies for those who are not working
or retired, (c) Health insurance should be voluntary. Individuals should
either buy insurance or obtain it through their employers as they do currently. The elderly and the very poor should be covered by Medicare and
Medicaid as they are currently; and (2) Do you favor raising federal taxes
on families earning more than $200,000 per year?

ENVIRONMENT (March CCAP). A 101-category variable ranging from 0
(the federal government should take action to slow climate change) to 1
(maintaining jobs and standards of living should be given priority).

EXPECTED GENERAL ELECTION MATCHUP (January CCAP). An indicator
variable taking on a value of 1 (expected both John McCain and Barack
Obama to win their parties' nominations) or 0 (all other responses).

EXPECTED GENERAL ELECTION MATCHUP (March CCAP). An indicator variable taking on a value of 1 (expected Barack Obama to win the
Democratic nomination) or 0 (all other responses).

GENDER TRADITIONALISM (March 2008 Pew). A four-category variable
ranging from 0 (completely disagree that women should return to their
traditional roles) to 1 (completely agree).

GENDER TRADITIONALISM (September CCAP). A four-category variable
ranging from 0 (strongly disagree that traditional marital roles are best)
to 1 (strongly agree).

IMMIGRATION (March CCAP). A three-category variable ranging from
0 (path to citizenship for illegal immigrants) to 1 (illegal immigrants
should be arrested and deported).

IRAQ SUPPORT SCALE (February 2008 Gallup). An additive index ranging from 0 (least supportive) to 1 (most supportive). The scale was constructed from the following responses: (1) In view of the developments
since we first sent our troops to Iraq, do you think the United States
made a mistake in sending troops to Iraq, or not? (2) Based on what you
have heard or read about the surge of U.S. troops in Iraq that began last

year, do you think the increase in the number of U.S. troops in Iraq is—
making the situation there better, not making much difference, or is it
making the situation there worse? (3) Do you think the United States
should withdraw all of its troops from Iraq as rapidly as possible, start-
ing now, or should the United States set a timetable that calls for a more
gradual withdrawal of troops from Iraq? (4) In the long run, how do you
think history will judge the U.S. invasion and subsequent involvement in
Iraq? and (5) In your opinion, in the long run, will Iraq be better or worse
off than before the United States and British invasion?

IRAQ WITHDRAWAL   (March CCAP). A three-category variable ranging
from 0 (leave within a year) to 1 (stay as long as it takes)

LINKED FATE (NPS). A four-category variable ranging from 0 (What happens to black people in this country does not affect my life) to 1 (it affects
my life a lot).

MODERN SEXISM   (ANES). An additive index ranging from 0 (least sexist)
to 1 (most sexist). The scale is constructed from how strongly respondents agreed or disagreed with the following assertions: (1) When women
demand equality these days, they are actually seeking special favors,
(2) Women often miss out on good jobs because of discrimination, and
(3) Women who complain about harassment cause more problems than
they solve.

MORAL ISSUES   (March CCAP). An additive index ranging from 0 (most
liberal) to 1 (most conservative). The scale was constructed from the following items: (1) Under what circumstances should abortion be legal?
and (2) Do you favor allowing civil unions for gay and lesbian couples?

MORAL TRADITIONALISM   (ANES). An additive index ranging from 0 (least
traditional) to 1 (most traditional). The scale was constructed from how
strongly respondents agreed or disagreed with the following assertions:
(1) We should be more tolerant of people who choose to live according
to their own moral standards, even if they are very different from our
own, (2) This country would have many fewer problems if there were
more emphasis on traditional family ties, (3) The world is always changing and we should adjust our view of moral behavior to those changes,
and (4) The newer lifestyles are contributing to the breakdown of our
society.

MUSLIM AFFECT   (ANES). A 101-category thermometer rating scale ranging from 0 (coldest) to 1 (warmest).

MUSLIM FAVORABILITY   (August 2007 Pew). A four-category variable ranging from 0 (very unfavorable) to 1 (very favorable).

MUSLIM FAVORABILITY (October CCAP). A five-category variable ranging from 0 (very unfavorable) to 1 (very favorable).

NEGATIVE BLACK STEREOTYPES (ANES). An additive index ranging from 0 (lowest stereotype endorsement) to 1 (highest stereotype endorsement). The scale is constructed from respondents' ratings of blacks on the following seven-point items: (1) Hardworking to lazy and (2) Intelligent to unintelligent.

NEGATIVE WHITE STEREOTYPES (ANES). An additive index ranging from 0 (lowest stereotype endorsement) to 1 (highest stereotype endorsement). The scale is constructed from respondents' ratings of whites on the following seven-point items: (1) Hardworking to lazy and (2) Intelligent to unintelligent.

OBAMA'S RELIGION (October CCAP). An indicator variable taking on a value of 1 (Obama is Muslim) or 0 (all other responses).

OBAMA'S TAX POSITION (October CCAP). An indicator variable taking on a value of 1 (Obama "strongly favors" or "somewhat favors" a tax increase on families making over $200,000) or 0 (all other responses).

POLICE DISCRIMINATION (August 2009 CNN). A five-category variable ranging from 0 (discrimination against blacks by the police is "very common") to 1 (discrimination is "very rare").

PRESIDENTIAL JOB APPROVAL (March CCAP). A five-category variable ranging from 0 ("strongly disapprove" of Bush) to 1 ("strongly approve" of Bush).

RACIAL PREDISPOSITIONS (Pew Values Studies). An additive index ranging from 0 (most liberal) to 1 (most conservative): The scale was constructed from how strongly respondents agreed or disagreed with the following statements: (1) We should make every possible effort to improve the position of blacks and other minorities, even if it means giving them preferential treatment, (2) Discrimination against blacks is rare today, (3) In the past few years there hasn't been much real improvement in the position of black people in this country, and (4) We have gone too far in pushing equal rights in this country.

WHITE AFFECT (ANES). A 101-category thermometer rating scale ranging from 0 (coldest) to 1 (warmest).

Dependent Variables

CONFIDENCE IN POLITICIANS TO FIX THE ECONOMY (April 2009 Pew). Variable is coded as a dummy taking on a value of 1 (a great deal or a fair amount of confidence) or 0 (all other responses). How much confidence do you have in [(1) President Obama or (2) Democratic leaders in Congress] to do the right thing when it comes to fixing the economy—a great deal of confidence, a fair amount of confidence, not too much confidence, or no confidence at all?

FAVORABILITY RATINGS (CCAP). A five-category scale ranging from 0 (very unfavorable) to 1 (very favorable).

FAVORABILITY RATINGS (August 2007 Pew). A four-category scale ranging from 0 (very unfavorable) to 1 (very favorable).

HEALTH CARE OPINIONS (CCAP). Variable is coded as a dummy taking on a value of 1 (Health care should be voluntarily left up to individuals) or 0 (all other responses). Which comes closest to your view about providing health care in the United States? (1) The government should provide everyone with health care and pay for it with tax dollars, (2) Companies should be required to provide health insurance for their employees and the government should provide subsidies for those who are not working or retired, (3) Health insurance should be voluntary. Individuals should either buy insurance or obtain it through their employers as they do currently. The elderly and the very poor should be covered by Medicare and Medicaid as they are currently, and (4) I'm not sure, I haven't thought much about this.

OBAMA'S COUNTRY OF ORIGIN (November 2009 CCAP reinterviews). Variable is coded as a dummy taking on a value of 1 (Obama was born in the United States) or 0 (all other responses). Do you believe that President Obama was born in the United States of America?

PRESIDENTIAL JOB APPROVAL OF REPUBLICAN PRESIDENTS (Pew Values Studies). Variable is coded as a dummy taking on a value of 1 (approve) or 0 (disapprove).

PRESIDENTIAL JOB DISAPPROVAL OF DEMOCRATIC PRESIDENTS (Pew Values Studies). Variable is coded as a dummy taking on a value of 1 (disapprove) or 0 (approve).

RATE OBAMA FAVORABLY (CCAP). Variable is coded as a dummy taking on a value of 1 (rate Obama "very favorable" or "somewhat favorable") or 0 (rate Obama, "very unfavorable," "somewhat unfavorable," or "neutral").

SOTOMAYOR'S CONFIRMATION (August 2009 CNN). Variable is coded as a dummy taking on a value of 1 (favor) or 0 (all other responses). Form A: As you may know, Sonia Sotomayor is the federal judge nominated to serve on the Supreme Court. Would you like to see the Senate vote in favor of Sotomayor serving on the Supreme Court, or not? Form B: As you may know, Sonia Sotomayor is the federal judge who Barack Obama nominated to serve on the Supreme Court. Would you like to see the Senate vote in favor of Sotomayor serving on the Supreme Court, or not?

SYMBOLIC RACISM (NPS). An additive index ranging from 0 (lowest) to 1 (highest): The scale was constructed from the following responses: (1) Irish, Italians, Jewish, and many other minorities overcame prejudice and worked their way up. Blacks should do the same without any special favors. Do you strongly agree, somewhat agree, somewhat disagree, or strongly disagree? (2) Over the past few years, blacks have gotten less than they deserve. Do you strongly agree, somewhat agree, somewhat disagree, or strongly disagree? (3) If racial and ethnic minorities don't do well in life, they have no one to blame but themselves. Do you strongly agree, somewhat agree, somewhat disagree, or strongly disagree? and (4) Do you think the following groups face a lot of discrimination, some, a little, or no discrimination at all: African Americans?

TAXES (2004 ANES). Variable is coded as a dummy taking on a value of 1 (favor increases) or 0 (all other responses). Do you favor increases in the taxes paid by ordinary Americans in order to cut the federal budget deficit?

TAXES (2008 ANES). Variable is coded as a dummy taking on a value of 1 (favor raising taxes) or 0 (all other responses). Would you favor, oppose, or neither favor nor oppose lowering the budget deficit by raising taxes?

TAXES (CCAP). Variable is coded as a dummy taking on a value of 1 (strongly favor or somewhat favor) or 0 (all other responses).Do you favor raising federal taxes on families earning more than $200,000 per year?

THERMOMETER RATINGS (ANES). A 101-category scale ranging from 0 (coldest) to 1 (warmest).

VOTE PREFERENCE. Variable is coded as a dummy taking on a value of 1 (vote preference) or 0 (prefer another candidate). The candidate who is coded as 1 and the candidate/candidates coded as 0 are indicated in text.

NOTES

1. MSNBC political commentator Chris Matthews, for instance, said immediately after the speech: "I have seen the first black president there. And the reason I say that is because I think the immigrant experience combined with the African background, combined with the incredible education, combined with his beautiful speech, not every politician gets help with the speech, but that speech was a piece of work."

2. For a detailed discussion of Obama's racially unifying actions in the wake of Hurricane Katrina, see Mendell 2007.

3. According to a September 6–7, 2005, Pew Poll, 66 percent of African Americans thought the federal government's response to Hurricane Katrina would have been faster if most of the victims had been white. Only 17 percent of white Americans, however, provided this answer.

4. The *Chicago Tribune*'s self-described "traditionally conservative" editorial page compared and contrasted Jackson and Obama's comments, praising Obama and criticizing Jackson in "Katrina's Racial Storm," September 8, 2005.

5. Obama, in fact, reiterated that he was "rooted in the black community but not defined by it" in an interview with CBS's Steve Kroft soon after announcing his intention to seek the presidency.

6. The title of the article was later changed online to "Destiny's Child."

7. Senate Majority Leader Harry Reid similarly came under fire in 2010 for saying before the primaries that Barack Obama's chances of winning the presidency were enhanced by his light skin color and lack of "Negro dialect" (quoted in Heilemann and Halperin 2010),

8. For more on Obama's 2007 support from African Americans, see: Krissah Williams, "A Shift Toward Obama is Seen among Blacks," *Washington Post*, January 21, 2008.

9. This assertion is based upon Evan Thomas's (2009) interviews with Obama staffers.

1. Useful sources for this history include Black and Black (1987, 1992, 2002); Carmines and Stimson (1989); Carter (1995); Gerstle (2002); Green et al. (2002); Martin (1996); Mayer (2002); McMahon (2005); O'Reilly (1995); Phillips (1969); Scammon and Wattenberg (1970); Schaller (2006); and Sundquist (1983).

2. Some have argued that symbolic racism is not fundamentally different from old-fashioned racism. Empirically, the two are indeed correlated, but they are distinctive in several important ways. First, the aggregate level of white support for symbolic racism is far greater than it is for old-fashioned racism. A majority of the white public usually

falls on the racially conservative side of the scale's midpoint, but the key elements of old-fashioned racism today generally attract the support of fewer than 10 percent of the white public (Henry and Sears 2002; Kinder and Sanders 1996; Kluegel 1990; Schuman et al. 1997). Second, factor analyses including only old-fashioned and symbolic racism items yield two separate factors that cleanly separate the two dimensions (Sears and Henry 2005). Third, symbolic racism has much greater influence in today's racial politics than does old-fashioned racism. The most comprehensive comparison, using four surveys and whites' opposition to three different racial policies (Sears, Van Laar, Carillo, and Kosterman 1997), yielded an average standardized regression coefficient for symbolic racism of .41, with all being statistically significant, and an average coefficient for old-fashioned racism of –.01, with only one significant.

3. Originally symbolic racism was said to reflect a "blend" of antiblack affect and conservative values, especially individualism (Kinder and Sears 1981; Sears and McConahay 1973). However, it was somewhat vague about what that "blend" involves (Kinder 1986; Sniderman and Tetlock 1986a; Wood 1994). Yet symbolic racism does prove to have strong components of both racial and nonracial attitudes. As mentioned above, factor analyses including racial and nonracial attitudes yielded separate racial and nonracial factors, with only symbolic racism loading substantially (and about equally) on both factors. It is the glue linking antagonism toward blacks with conventional conservative values and politics. In another study, a direct measure fusing individualism with antiblack affect proved to have a significant effect on symbolic racism above and beyond both measured separately and combined either additively or interactively. That is, the "blend" had some emergent properties those separate elements did not (Sears and Henry 2003).

4. Other similar concepts include "subtle prejudice" (Pettigrew and Meertens 1995), "laissez-faire racism" (Bobo, Kluegel, and Smith 1997), "aversive racism" (Gaertner and Dovidio 1986), and "ambivalent racism" (Katz and Hass 1988).

5. We might mention one methodological alternative we rejected as outdated. Early empirical research on race and politics after World War II (Key 1949) demonstrated that the most racially conservative candidates in the Jim Crow South received their greatest white support in areas of heavy black population concentrations. Presumably such whites felt the most threatened by blacks, and so were most motivated to maintain a strict system of white supremacy. More recent versions of this approach (Giles and Buckner 1996; Shafer and Johnston 2006) have correlated the percent black in various geographic areas with white support for racially conservative candidates or policy positions. However the best current evidence is that racial context, thus measured, has been displaced as a political force by "white flight," of racially conservative whites fleeing to homogeneously white communities from which they engage in racially conservative voting (Voss 1996), and by low neighborhood educational levels, which produce conservative racial policy attitudes more powerfully than does racial context (Oliver and Mendelberg, 2000).

6. More sophisticated scaling was employed in past research, but these produce only negligible increases in scale reliability (Kinder and Sanders 1996, 322n50). Simon Jackman also rescaled the 2008 racial resentment items using his item response model, IDEAL. No substantive differences, however, were produced between results from this scale and the simple additive average traditionally used in racial resentment research (Jackman and Vavreck 2008).

7. The .50 midpoint is, indeed, a rather arbitrary dividing line between racial liber-

als and racial conservatives. For example, if we just utilized the "blacks should work their way up with no special favors" racial resentment item, then nearly 70 percent of Americans would be classified as racial conservatives because they agree with this statement. On the other hand, if we just employed the "past discrimination has made it difficult for blacks" racial resentment item, then only about 40 percent of the public would be classified as racially resentful. As such, our references to the .50 midpoint are an interpretative tool, not an authoritative demarcation line between racial liberals and racial conservatives.

8. Tests of the internal consistency of symbolic racism yield two highly correlated subcomponents focusing on structural and individual attributions for blacks' disadvantages (Tarman and Sears 2005).The two subsets have almost exactly the same correlations with opposition to liberal racial policies (Sears and Henry 2005). By both standards, then, they seem best interpreted as quite similar variants of a single logically and psychologically consistent symbolic racism belief system.

9. A standard design has been to include all such variables in a regression equation predicting whites' racial policy attitudes. The standardized regression coefficients for symbolic racism are far higher than those for either political conservatism or traditional racial attitudes.

10. Symbolic racism is correlated with ideological conservatism (Hughes 1997; Sears, Van Laar, Carillo, and Kosterman 1997; Sidanius et al. 1992), but it has both strong racial *and* nonracial components. In one extensive study using eight surveys, factor analyses including traditional racial attitudes, nonracial political predispositions, and symbolic racism yielded both a racial and a nonracial factor. Only symbolic racism loaded strongly on both (Sears and Henry 2005). Second, the best-fitting statistical models simultaneously incorporating symbolic racism, old-fashioned racism, conservatism, and nonracial individualism represent each as separate and independent factors. Models allowing symbolic racism items to be distributed among other constructs did not fit the data nearly as well (Tarman and Sears 2005). Symbolic racism is an independent construct (though correlated with the others, of course). Moreover, symbolic racism provides the most powerful explanation of whites' contemporary political attitudes when race is involved. It has far greater explanatory value over white opposition to liberal racial policies than does ostensibly race-neutral conservatism (Henry and Sears 2002; Sears, Van Laar, Carillo, and Kosterman 1997; Tarman and Sears 2005). Moreover its effects in such analyses are not diminished by controlling ideology (Sears, Van Laar, Carillo, and Kosterman 1997; Sears and Henry 2005; Tarman and Sears 2005).

11. In the March 2008 CCAP, 63.4 percent of respondents viewed Hillary Clinton as a liberal, compared to 68.2 percent who said Obama was liberal.

12. This regression model included racial resentment, partisanship, ideological self-placement, education, age, and indicator variables for being black, male, and Southern.

13. Because most of our analyses involve the effects of racial resentment on dichotomous vote choices rather than continuous evaluations like the thermometer scale, we use a slightly more complicated technique called logistic regression to estimate the probability that an individual voted for Obama given his or her level of racial resentment. However, our ability to hold other factors constant and then graphically display these relationships between racial resentment and vote choice is analogous to the thermometer example in which we used linear regression.

14. We measure partisanship with the ANES seven-category party identification scale, ranging from "strong Democrat" to "strong Republican." Ideological self-placement is measured with a five-category item, ranging from very/extremely liberal to very/extremely conservative. For comparability purposes, we changed the ANES's seven-category ideological measure to comport with the CCAP's five-category item by collapsing "liberal and slightly liberal" into the same category. We did the same for "conservative" and "slightly conservative." Following Zaller (1992), we also coded respondents who could not place themselves ideologically as moderates.

15. Education is measured here as a five-category variable ranging from high-school dropout to postgraduate studies.

16. Cooperative Campaign Analysis Project (CCAP), 2007–2008 Panel Study, Simon Jackman and Lynn Vavreck, principal investigators. Common content advanced release 1.0, February 1, 2009.

17. The exact dates that these surveys were conducted were December 17, 2007–January 3, 2008; January 24–February 4; March 21–April 14; September 17–September 29; October 22–November 3; November 5–December 1.

18. Since these large sample sizes greatly enhance the efficiency of parameter estimates, they oftentimes make substantively uninteresting effects statistically significant at the .05 level. Most of our effects, therefore, are discussed in terms of magnitude and substantive importance rather than statistical significance.

19. Not all of our results can be weighted, though. Survey weights are not included in the 1986 and 1988 ANES, and we cannot weight the oversamples of African Americans and Latinos in the 2004 National Politics Study (NPS) and the 2008 ANES because doing so would shrink their size down to their numbers in the general population.

20. The one major difference between the two surveys seems to arise when we break down our analyses into ethnic and racial subpopulations. For example, there was a 15-point difference in Obama's vote share between Latinos interviewed in the CCAP and those in the ANES's Latino oversample (although the CCAP understates the Latino vote share in the national exit polls by a smaller margin than the ANES overstates it). Similarly, chapter 5 shows that black voters in the CCAP were considerably better educated and scored significantly lower in racial resentment than African Americans in the 2008 ANES. To be sure, subpopulation analyses will always be more variable than full-sample comparisons because their smaller sample sizes produce noisier estimates. We still proceed with more caution, though, in interpreting the results in chapter 5 by race and ethnicity than we do in the other chapters.

CHAPTER TWO

1. For more on this quotation see: Associated Press, "Obama: Values not Race or Beliefs Key to Voters", February 11, 2007.

2. For New Hampshire polling averages over time, see: http://www.realclearpolitics.com/epolls/2008/president/nh/new_hampshire_democratic_primary-194.html.

3. The Democratic primary in Michigan occurred before the January 26 South Carolina primary, but this contest was not officially sanctioned by the party because it violated their rules stipulating New Hampshire and South Carolina would be the first two primary contests.

4. According to ABC News/*Washington Post* polling, Obama increased his primary support among African Americans from 35 percent in late 2007 to 60 percent on the eve

of the South Carolina primary. For more on Obama's increased support from African Americans during this time period see Krissah Williams, "A Shift Toward Obama is Seen among Blacks," *Washington Post*, January 21, 2008.

5. Clinton's remarks came during a January 7, 2008, interview with Fox News' Major Garrett.

6. Heilemann and Halperin (2010, 214), for instance, report: "For many in the Democratic Party, the answer was all too clear. Clinton was comparing Obama to Jackson to diminish the former's victory, and to accomplish the blackening that Obama's advisers suspected was his objective all along."

7. Clinton only beat Obama 36 to 24 percent among the state's white voters.

8. Our discussion of race's role in the process by which Senator Kennedy came to endorse Barack Obama's candidacy is based mostly on Balz and Johnson's (2009) thorough documentation of the Kennedy endorsement.

9. Hillary Clinton reportedly told her fundraisers in December 2007 that the race "is all going to be over by February 5."

10. The Obama campaign, in fact, used the demographic composition of these states to successfully predict their post–Super Tuesday February victories. A campaign memo with these predictions was accidently sent to *Bloomberg News*, projecting that Obama "will do the best in cities and areas with large black populations and lose areas with high percentages of Hispanic voters." For more on the Obama campaign's demographic-based predictions see Catherine Dodge and Alex Tanzi, "Obama Advisors Foresee Delegate Draw with Clinton," *Bloomberg News*, February 7, 2008.

11. See: Jay Tolson, "Does Obama's Winning Streak Prove that Race Does Not Matter?" *U.S. News and World Report*, February 15, 2008.

12. Reverend Wright made this statement at a sermon before the congregation at Trinity United Church of Christ on September 16, 2001.

13. Reverend Wright made this statement at a sermon before the congregation at Trinity United Church of Christ on January 13, 2008.

14. This favorability variable is coded 0–1 in intervals of .25, with 0 representing very unfavorable and 1 being very favorable. The mean favorability ratings for the three candidates on this scale were .51 for Obama, .50 for Edwards, and .43 for Clinton.

15. Survey by *USA Today*. Methodology: Conducted by Gallup Organization, February 21–February 24, 2008, and based on telephone interviews with a national adult sample of 2,021. Data set accessed from the Roper Center's data archive.

16. Of the 2008 ANES respondents with racial resentment scores below .5, 24.5 and 26.3 percent said that they felt sympathy and admiration for blacks "very often"; only 6 and 7.6 percent of respondents with resentment scores above .50 reported such feelings of sympathy and admiration. Similarly, roughly 70 percent of the 2008 ANES respondents who scored on the racially liberal side of the scale reported that they at least "often" felt admiration and/or sympathy toward blacks; only 30 and 46 percent of respondents with resentment scores above the midpoint, however, reported such positive feelings of sympathy and admiration.

17. The parallelism here between the ANES and CCAP results also help mitigate concerns about the CCAP's Internet-based sampling methodology.

18. It is important to note that this gap among racial liberals was not produced by more African Americans in the 2008 analysis. In fact, African Americans made up 22 percent of Democratic primary voters in the 1988 ANES and 18 percent in the 2008 ANES.

19. For a comparison of McCain vs. Clinton and McCain vs. Obama trial heats in the early months of 2008 see both http://www.realclearpolitics.com/epolls/2008/president/us/general_election_mccain_vs_clinton-224.html and http://www.realclear politics.com/epolls/2008/president/us/general_election_mccain_vs_obama-225.html.

20. Obama and Clinton were found to be essentially ideologically identical based upon DW Nominate scores estimated from their roll call votes in the Senate (Carroll et al. 2008).

21. Several polls taken throughout 2008, in fact, consistently showed that less than 20 percent of Americans thought Obama's policies as president would favor blacks over whites.

CHAPTER THREE

1. This retrospective national economic evaluations question has been asked in the ANES since 1980. The years before 2008, which registered the highest percentages of respondents saying the national economy had gotten much worse over the last year were 1980 (43.4 percent), 1992 (38.5 percent), and 1982 (37.3 percent).

2. The economy as an issue accounted for 43 percent of campaign related news coverage the week of September 15–21 (Project for the Excellence in Journalism 2008a). Taken together, the economy as an issue, the financial crisis, and McCain's campaign suspension in response to it accounted for over 50 percent of campaign news the following week too (Project for the Excellence in Journalism 2008b). Moreover, Holbrook's (2009) content analysis revealed that there were 135 front-page stories in the *New York Times* about the economy during the final three months of the campaign compared to 13 in 2004 and 31 in 2000.

3. McCain, for instance, publicly condemned the North Carolina Republican Party's use of Wright in an April 2008 ad and asked them to take down the spot. The campaign similarly prohibited Sarah Palin from raising the Reverend Wright issue. Palin (2009), in fact, later wrote, "I will forever question the campaign for prohibiting discussion of such association [between Obama and Wright]."

4. Barack Obama made these comments during a campaign rally in Rola, Missouri, on July 30, 2008.

5. Palin later partially apologized for a campaign comment she made during an October 2008 campaign rally in North Carolina where she referred to small towns as "the real America" and the "pro-America areas of this great nation." For more on Palin's remarks and her subsequent apology see Lyndsay Layton, "Palin Apologizes for 'Real America' Comments," *Washington Post*, October 22, 2008.

6. The two statements listed by Ambinder (2009), which Belcher used to measure racial aversion were: "I often feel that African Americans aren't as proud and patriotic about this country as I am" and "As the result of racial preferences, less qualified minorities often get hired and promoted."

7. Like Obama's NAACP speech on July 14, 2008, he made a similar appeal to black responsibility on Father's Day, one month earlier.

8. Jackson made this comment to another guest during a break in an interview with Fox News on July 6, 2008.

9. Of the respondents interviewed by Pew Research Center between July 11 and July 14, 2008, 48 percent said that they had heard a lot about "Jesse Jackson being overheard making a crude comment about Barack Obama," 29 percent said they heard a little about this story, and 22 percent reported hearing nothing at all.

10. This tally excludes three of the published forecast models in *PS: Political Science and Politics* that included early trial heats between McCain and Obama as predictors (Wlezien and Erikson 2008; Campbell 2008b; Klarner 2008), because McCain-Obama matchups would already have reflected the effects of the candidates' races.

11. As just indicated, Lewis-Beck and Tien's (2008) preferred forecast included a 6.5 percent penalty for Obama's race. Our average, however, includes their 56.6 percent forecast based on nonracial indicators rather than the 50.1 percent that reflects their estimate of the adverse effect his race was expected to have on his vote share.

12. There are no results from 1996 in this table because the racial resentment items were not included in that year's ANES. The 1994–1996 ANES panel study, however, strongly suggests that racial resentment had only a modest impact on vote intention in that election. We can use racial resentment, as measured in 1994, to predict political variables, as measured in 1996, because of racial resentment's high individual-level stability and the fact that three-quarters of the respondents in the 1996 ANES were previously interviewed in 1994. Using 1994 measures of our base-model variables to predict 1996 vote intention yields a nonsignificant logistic regression coefficient on racial resentment. This resentment coefficient of .740 in 1996 is slightly smaller than the average resentment coefficient of 1.10 in the other presidential years from 1988 to 2004.

13. The logistic regression coefficients yielded from our base model of ANES vote intention and vote choice are as follows: 1988 vote intention = 1.09, vote choice = 1.78; 1992 vote intention = 1.16, vote choice = 1.52; 2000 vote intention = .646, vote choice = .447; 2004 vote intention = 1.52, vote choice = 2.77; and 2008 vote choice = 2.99, vote choice = 3.54.

14. The large increase in racial resentment's effect from a logistic regression coefficient of 1.52 on vote intention to a coefficient of 2.77 on vote choice seemed quite anomalous given the similarities between racial resentment's effect on vote intention and vote choice in both the preceding and proceeding elections. As such, we searched for additional evidence to determine whether racial resentment's impact on 2004 vote preferences was right in line with the previous elections, as the vote intention results indicate, or whether it had a significantly larger impact on preferences for Bush and Kerry than earlier elections, as suggested by the vote choice results.

First, we examined the relationship between racial resentment and vote choice in the 2004 ANES panel study. Along with their standard preelection and postelection surveys, the ANES reinterviewed a completely different set of respondents (n = 840) after the 2004 election who had previously been interviewed in their 2000 and 2002 surveys. Our base model yielded a racial resentment coefficient of 1.41 on *vote choice* in that survey—a figure right in line with the effects of racial resentment on vote choice from 1988 to 2000.

Next, we turned to the 2004 National Politics Study, which we draw on heavily in chapter 5. This survey carried two of the racial resentment items—"without any special favors" and "blacks have gotten less than they deserve." Using this two-item racial resentment scale, our base model yielded a resentment coefficient of .752 on vote preference in that survey. In comparison, the coefficients for this two-item racial resentment scale on vote choice in the 1988, 1992, and 2000 ANES were 1.40, 1.26, and .081, respectively. These results again suggest that racial resentment did not have an atypically large effect on vote preference in 2004. Moreover, roughly half of the NPS's 3,339 respondents were interviewed before the election, with the remaining half giving postelection interviews.

Unlike the 2004 ANES, this survey actually yielded a larger resentment effect on vote intention than vote choice (.866 to .338, respectively).

After that we looked at racial resentment's impact on vote choice in multiple General Social Surveys (GSS). Following Kinder and Kam (2009, 243), we used three items asked in every GSS since 1994 to create a racial resentment scale. These included the standard "without any special favors" question and two additional items asking whether racial inequality stems from discrimination or a lack of black motivation. The GSS also asks respondents whom they voted for in the last presidential election. We, therefore, used the 1994, 1998, 2002, and 2006 GSSs to assess racial resentment's impact on vote choice in 1992, 1996, 2000, and 2004. Using this three-item racial resentment scale, our base model of vote choice yielded the following resentment coefficients: .405 for 1992 vote choice; .461 for 1996 vote choice; .643 for 2000 vote choice; and .523 for 2004 vote choice. Once again, these results suggest that racial resentment did not have the outsized influence on the 2004 election that the vote choice results from the 2004 ANES yielded.

Finally, each ANES asks respondents whom they voted for in the previous election. We, therefore, looked at how racial resentment affected 2004 vote choice using the 2008 ANES. We expected that this measure might be more racialized if respondents misreported their 2004 votes to make them congruent with the 2008 contest that included Barack Obama. However, our base model yielded a logistic regression coefficient of 1.57 on racial resentment—a figure that is again right in line with both vote intention in the 2004 ANES and the results from previous ANES surveys. To ensure that using the 2008 ANES to estimate the impact of racial resentment in 2004 did not systematically underestimate its effect, we compared the effects of racial resentment on 1988 and 2000 vote choice, measured four years later, to the results yielded from the 1988 and 2000 ANES. The later measures produced almost identical racial resentment effects to those yielded four years earlier.

Taken together, then, the results from these four surveys make us quite confident in our use of 2004 vote intention, which was not unusually impacted by racial resentment.

15. Willie Horton was a convicted murderer who was released from a Massachusetts prison as part of a weekend furlough during Michael Dukakis's tenure as governor. While on furlough, Horton, who is black, twice raped a white woman after brutally assaulting her white fiancé. Mendelberg (2001) and Kinder and Sanders (1996) persuasively argue that Republicans intentionally used the Horton issue to appeal to racial anxieties. Both of their findings suggest that this strategy succeeded in priming white racial resentment.

16. The Pollster.com trend analyses also show McCain in the lead immediately after the Republican Convention but that lead was less than one-half of a percentage point and only lasted a few days (http://www.pollster.com/polls/us/08-us-pres-ge-mvo .php).

17. And a lead of 47.3 to 42.3 percent among panel respondents interviewed in all four survey waves from March to November.

18. The analysis actually includes panelists interviewed in all four waves from March to November. The effects of racial resentment on reported vote choice in the November postelection, however, were dropped from the display because the pattern of support is identical to the October relationship. See table A3.1 in the online appendix for November results (http://www.press.uchicago.edu/books/tesler/).

19. These are "retrospective" evaluations that compare the current state of the economy to the recent past.

20. Using economic assessments from the September or October CCAP opens up the ambiguity of whether economic evaluations caused vote choice or vice versa (i.e., that vote intention caused economic evaluations). Americans are especially likely to rationalize their votes by altering their positions on economic issues (Sears and Lau 1983).

21. Our national economic evaluation variable codes responses from 0 to 1 by .25, with 0 representing much worse and 1 being much better. The mean for our panel respondents on this scale was just .19 in March, as less than 3 percent of respondents combined said things were either better or much better. In comparison, the mean for our panelists in September was .14.

22. The logistic regression coefficients for economic evaluations in the vote intention models that included presidential approval were .058 for March and .253 for October. Removing presidential approval from the model, however, increases the size of these coefficients to .848 and 1.64, respectively, but still controlling for all other factors.

23. CCAP panel respondents who supported Clinton in March preferred Obama to McCain by a margin of 52.5 to 32.1. This gap had expanded to 70.6 to 20.4 in October. Clinton primary voters accounted for the majority of Obama's 7.4-point gain among CCAP panelists interviewed in all waves from March to October, as the remainder of the sample netted him only 3 points.

CHAPTER FOUR

1. Aside from our analysis of racialized voting patterns in the 2008 primaries and general election, Obama's ANES thermometer ratings were also highly racialized. As we saw in figure 1.1, even with partisan, ideological, and demographic controls in place, moving from least to most resentful, decreased Obama's thermometer ratings by 30 degrees. This effect with the same control variables in place was only 12 degrees for John Kerry's 2004 ratings.

2. Hillary Clinton's favorability was only asked in the first four CCAPs from December 2007 to September 2008.

3. Correct general election predictions are operationalized here by respondents who thought both McCain and Obama would become their party's respective nominees in the January CCAP. With McCain already the presumptive Republican nominee by the March CCAP, a correct prediction is operationalized by those respondents who thought Obama would beat out Hillary Clinton for the Democratic nomination.

4. Only 4.2 percent of CCAP panel respondents thought both John McCain and Barack Obama were their two respective parties' most expected presidential candidates in December 2007.

5. By October, the once large differences in McCain-Obama favorability correlations for these two groups had shrunk to r = –.76 and r = –.74.

6. Since the racial resentment battery was not asked in 1996, we use only 1994–1996 panel respondents in the Dole analyses. All variables for that analysis were measured in 1994. Also, the 1998 ANES only includes the "no special favors," and "less than they deserve" racial resentment items. The 2000 resentment scale is, therefore, also trimmed down to these two items to make the results comparable for George W. Bush.

7. See table A4.4 of the online appendix for the coefficients on partisanship (http://www.press.uchicago.edu/books/tesler/).

8. The ANES did not have a regular time-series survey in 2006, so we have to use a four-year comparison for McCain rather than the two-year comparisons employed for the other candidates.

9. According to Pew's Project for Excellence in Journalism, 8 percent of all campaign news coverage was devoted solely to Joe the Plumber between October 13 and October 19. As a result, an October 17–20 survey by Pew reported that 64 percent of the public had heard "a lot" about Joe the Plumber (Pew Research Center 2008).

10. This question was asked as a two-category question in 2004 and a three-category question, with a neither favor nor oppose option, in 2008. Answers are coded 1 for favor and 0 for all other answers in both years. See the appendix for exact question wordings.

11. CNN/ORC asked in all of their "insta-polls" taken immediately after the debate, which candidate seemed like a stronger leader. Obama bested McCain 49 to 43 in the September 26 debate, 54 to 43 in the October 7 debate, and 56 to 39 in the October 15 debate.

12. With our base-model variables controlled for, moving from least to most resentful decreased Obama's favorability in December by .386 or 38.6 percent of the favorability scale's range and .381 in October for the same respondents.

13. For transition approval see http://www.pollster.com/polls/us/jobapproval-obama .php.

14. With our base-model variables controlled for, moving from least to most resentful decreased Obama's ANES thermometer ratings by 29 degrees, or 29 percent of the scale's range in the preelection interview and 30 degrees for the same respondents in the postelection survey. Similarly, the effect for the CCAP panel respondents was .38 in October and .37 in the postelection survey.

CHAPTER FIVE

1. For more on this quotation see Blake Fleetwood, "Obama's Problem, He Happens to be Black," *Huffington Post*, February 28, 2008 (http://www.huffingtonpost.com/ blake-fleetwood/obamas-problem-he-happens_b_89078.html).

2. This moniker was coined by the famed African American author Toni Morrison.

3. The National Politics Study (NPS) was a project undertaken by the Program for Research on Black Americans (PRBA) and the Center for Political Studies (CPS) at the University of Michigan's Institute for Social Research, in cooperation with DataStat Inc., a survey research organization located in Ann Arbor, Michigan. The NPS was developed under the sponsorship of the National Science Foundation, the University of Michigan, and the Carnegie Corporation. From September 2004 to February 2005, a total of 3,339 telephone interviews were conducted throughout the United States. The sample consisted of 756 African Americans, 919 non-Hispanic Whites, 404 Caribbean Blacks, 757 Hispanic Americans, and 503 Asian Americans.

4. Of the Latinos sampled in the NPS, 54.4 percent were foreign born. Of this group, 39.5 have become citizens; that means 33.3 percent of Latinos in the NPS were noncitizens. In contrast, only 25.9 percent of Latinos in the 2008 ANES and 20.9 percent of Latinos in the September CCAP were born outside of the United States.

5. Of course, the exit polls are not free from error either in their Latino numbers (i.e., language and interviewing complications), so it's difficult to know precisely how this group voted.

6. The double-digit difference in mean resentment scores for African Americans

in the ANES and CCAP is likely a product of different sample composition in the two surveys. The CCAP's Internet-based registered voter sample produced a much better educated black sample than did the ANES. These educational differences are especially important because higher education is one of the strongest predictors of both lower resentment scores and group consciousness among African Americans.

7. This finding is consistent with Kinder and Kam's (2009) work, which shows that out-group hostility is an important predictor of black support for race-targeted policies.

8. Dawson's (1994) research also shows that education has a significant negative relationship with African Americans' beliefs that blacks are better off than whites and a sizable positive impact on saying that the black rights movement affected one's life.

9. The two omitted resentment items in the 2004 NPS are "blacks could be just as well off as whites if they only tried harder" and "generations of slavery and discrimination have created conditions that make it difficult for blacks to work their way out of the lower class." These items were replaced in our symbolic racism scale from the NPS with, "If racial and ethnic minorities don't do well in life they have no one to blame but themselves" and "Do you think the following groups face a lot of discrimination, some, a little, or no discrimination at all: African Americans?"

10. Consistent with previous research showing that white symbolic racism is not strongly influenced by either objective or subjective measures of white racial group consciousness (Kinder and Sears 1981; Oliver and Mendelberg 2000; Sears and Henry 2005), beliefs that more jobs and political influence for blacks means less for them is a much weaker predictor of symbolic racism for white Americans than zero-sum competition with whites is for African Americans. Regressing racial resentment on the same variables in table 6.3 for whites yields a standardized coefficient for competition with blacks of only .073.

11. The one exception was Arizona where, according to the exit polls, Obama received 41 percent of the Latino vote and 38 percent of the white vote. The other states with large Hispanic populations included Nevada, California, Illinois, New Jersey, New Mexico, and Texas (Barreto et al. 2008).

12. Obama received 68.5 percent of the two-party vote share from Latinos who supported Clinton compared to just 56 percent from whites. If we include undecided respondents, 54.6 percent of Latinos who supported Clinton said they would vote for Obama compared to 46.6 percent of whites.

13. For more information on these surveys see Pew Hispanic Research Center, "2008 National Survey of Latinos: Hispanic Voter Attitudes," July 24, 2008, and Pew Research Center, "McCain's Enthusiasm Gap, Obama's Unity Gap," July 10, 2008.

14. We regrettably cannot expand our analysis to Asian Americans because there are simply too few cases in the ANES and CCAP to make valid inferences about the effects of racial resentment on this group's voting behavior.

15. The difference between the 65-point effect reported on Latino vote intention here and the 70-point effect reported in the trial heat comparison is that the trial heat comparison included all Latinos interviewed in the March CCAP, whereas the March to October comparisons only include panel respondents who completed both survey waves.

16. The logistic regression coefficients for racial resentment in our base vote intention model are 3.02 and 2.79 for Latinos and whites, respectively (see table A5.4 of the online appendix, http://www.press.uchicago.edu/books/tesler/).

17. The two items used in these abbreviated scales are "blacks should work their

way up without special favors" and "blacks have gotten less than they deserve" (reverse coded). The mean resentment scores on these two-item scales among Latinos who reported a vote intention were very similar in the two surveys (.61 in the NPS and .63 in the ANES) consistent with our general finding that racial resentment is highly stable at both the aggregate and individual levels.

18. The predicted vote shares in 2004, for instance, are barely outside of the upper 95 percent confidence band surrounding our predicted probabilities in 2008 on the liberal side of the spectrum. As such, the lower bound of the confidence interval for our 2004 predicted probabilities and the upper bound for our 2008 predicted probabilities overlap. In other words, we cannot be fully confident that Obama's predicted support on the left-hand side of the spectrum was different than it was for Kerry in 2004.

CHAPTER SIX

1. The quotation is from an interview with Gwen Ifill (2009, 61).

2. All else being equal, moving from highest to lowest in modern sexism decreased Hillary Clinton's thermometer ratings by 15 degrees and increased Cheney's by 16 degrees. The other ten political figures evaluated in the survey were George W. Bush, John Kerry, Ralph Nader, John Edwards, Laura Bush, John McCain, Colin Powell, John Ashcroft, Bill Clinton, and Ronald Reagan.

3. For polling trends in the New Hampshire primary see http://www.realclearpolitics .com/epolls/2008/president/nh/new_hampshire_democratic_primary-194.html.

4. The Begala quote comes from Rich 2008.

5. Barack Obama won 35 percent of women in the Iowa entrance polls, compared to 30 percent for Hillary Clinton. Clinton outperformed Obama 46 percent to 34 percent among New Hampshire women in the exit polls, with the vast majority of undecided women breaking for Hillary Clinton in the final days (Thomas 2009). In fact, Obama's pollsters told him "every undecided woman swung to Hillary that last three days" (Balz and Johnson 2009, 142).

6. Suzanne Goldenberg, International Section, "Hill's Angels: How Angry Women of New Hampshire Saved Clinton," *Guardian*, January 13, 2008 (http://www.guardian .co.uk/world/2008/jan/12/hillaryclinton.uselections2008).

7. These data on modern sexism and the 2008 Democratic primary are not ideal in that both were taken months after the contest was over. Similarly, analyses of gender traditionalism in the CCAP must use respondents' recollection of their primary votes in the September wave because these predispositions were not assessed during the primaries. As mentioned in chapter 3, though, the retrospectively assessed vote shares in the ANES comport quite well with the actual results.

8. Survey by Pew Research Center for the People and the Press. Methodology: Conducted by Princeton Survey Research Associates International, March 19–March 22, 2008, and based on telephone interviews with a national adult sample of 1,503. This data set was accessed from the Roper Center's data archives.

9. Methodology: Conducted by CBS News, March 15–March 18, 2008, and based on telephone interviews with a national adult sample of 1,067. This data set was accessed from the Roper Center's data archives.

10. There were 165 white female Clinton voters in the national sample.

11. See Katznelson (2005) for an overview of the role past discrimination has played in creating these large racial disparities in contemporary economic conditions.

12. Katharine Q. Seelye, and Julie Bosman, "Media Charged with Sexism in Clinton Coverage," *New York Times*, June 13, 2008.

13. An ABC/*Washington Post* Poll taken shortly before the February 5 Super Tuesday primaries showed that 58 percent of Democrats thought that Clinton was the stronger leader of the two, compared to only 31 percent who picked Obama (Survey by ABC/*Washington Post*, January 30–February 1, 2008. Retrieved from the iPOLL Databank, Roper Center for Public Opinion Research, University of Connecticut). Obama, however, had double-digit favorability leads over Clinton throughout the primaries.

14. Morris made these comments on the January 7, 2008, episode of *Hannity and Colmes*, which aired the night of the New Hampshire incident.

15. This December 2006 memo from Mark Penn can be read in full at http://www.theatlantic.com/a/green-penn-12–21-06.mhtml.

16. Ibid.

CHAPTER SEVEN

1. For the full memo from Mark Penn to Hillary Clinton see http://www.theatlantic.com/a/green-penn-3–19-07.mhtml.

2. Studies of priming show that sustained information flows about a particular subject can make that factor a more important ingredient of subsequent political evaluations (Iyengar and Kinder 1987). Yet favorability ratings of Muslim Americans failed to produce a significant independent relationship with presidential approval even in the July 2005 poll taken by the Pew Forum on Religion in Public Life immediately following the highly publicized 7/7 attacks in London by Islamic terrorists.

3. Though Sides and Gross (2007) show that stereotypes about Muslims significantly influenced opinions about war on terror policies.

4. Survey by Pew Forum on Religion and Public Life, Pew Research Center for the People and the Press. Methodology: Conducted by Schulman, Ronca, and Bucuvalas, August 1–August 18, 2007, and based on telephone interviews with a national adult sample of 3,002—half of whom were asked to evaluate Muslims. This data set was accessed from the Roper Center's data archive.

5. The effect, if anything, should be bigger in 2004 because Bush himself had become a particular lightening rod for criticism in the Islamic world.

6. As we show later on in the chapter, the impact of Muslim affect was considerably greater on reported vote choice in the ANES postelection wave than it was for vote intention in the preelection wave. Vote intention is presented here, though, for a closer comparison to the vote intention measure used in the March CCAP trial heats. However the impact of Muslim affect is not bigger on reported vote choice than vote intention in the 2004 ANES. The differences between 2004 and 2008, therefore, are more pronounced for vote choice than for vote intention.

7. Specifically, the impact of moving from the most negative to the most positive evaluation of Muslims on support for Obama in the primaries is reduced by 8 points in the ANES and 12 points in the CCAP. Controlling for racial resentment also diminishes the effect of Muslim affect on general election vote choice (rather than the vote intention measure used in fig. 7.3) by 10 points in the ANES and 14 points in the CCAP.

8. The regression coefficients for this model can be found in table A8.4 of the online appendix (http://www.press.uchicago.edu/books/tesler/).

9. There are obviously many Arabs who are not Muslims, but it is unlikely that this woman was making such a distinction at this October 10, 2008, town hall meeting.

10. The first poll on Obama's religion documented in Roper's iPOLL revealed that 12 percent of the public thought Obama was Muslim, with 37 percent saying they did not know. Survey by Pew Research Center for the People and the Press. Methodology: Conducted by Princeton Survey Research Associates International, March 19–March 22, 2008, and based on telephone interviews with a national adult sample of 1,503. Retrieved from the iPOLL Databank, Roper Center for Public Opinion Research, University of Connecticut.

11. Of registered voters, 26 percent answered that Obama was raised a Muslim in the following poll: Survey by *Newsweek*. Survey by Princeton Survey Research Associates International, July 9–July 10, 2008, and based on telephone interviews with a national adult sample of 1,209. Retrieved from the iPOLL Databank, Roper Center for Public Opinion Research, University of Connecticut.

12. Bill Cunningham, Ann Coulter, the Tennessee Republican Party, and multiple introductory speakers at McCain-Palin events were among the many conservatives and Republicans who pursued this strategy.

13. Survey by *Time* and Abt SRBI, September 26–September 29, 2008. Retrieved from the iPOLL Databank, Roper Center for Public Opinion Research, University of Connecticut.

14. This minority, in fact, scored .20, .17, and .25 higher on our respective 0–1 racial resentment, ideology, and partisanship scales than the remainder of the CCAP respondents.

15. The differences in December 2007 party identification and ideological self-placement (both coded 0–1) between CCAP panel respondents who did and did not think Obama was Muslim in October 2008 were.69 to .44, respectively, for party identification and .69 to .52 for ideological self-placement. Racial resentment was first measured in the March CCAP, which produced resentment scores of .80 and .60 for those who did and did not think Obama believed in Islam, respectively.

16. Palin made this statement at a campaign rally in Englewood, Colorado, on October 4, 2008.

CHAPTER EIGHT

1. All else being equal, moving from least to most resentful decreased Obama's ANES thermometer ratings by 29 degrees, or 29 percent of the scale's range in the pre-election interview and 30 degrees for the same respondents in the postelection survey. Similarly, the effect for the CCAP panel respondents was .381 in October and .371 in the postelection survey.

2. For full poll results and crosstabs see http://media.economist.com/media/pdf/Tabs20090819.pdf.

3. Of registered voters interviewed from October 19–22, 2008, for the CBS/*New York Times* poll, 11 percent believed that the policies of the Obama administration would favor blacks over whites. For full results from the CBS/NYT poll see http://graphics8.nytimes.com/packages/pdf/politics/octo8d.trn.pdf. Of Americans interviewed from October 17–20, 2008, for the NBC/*Wall Street Journal* poll, 13 percent believed that if elected, President Obama's policies would favor blacks over whites. For full results from the NBC/*WSJ* poll see http://s.wsj.net/public/resources/documents/WSJ_NBCPoll_102108.pdf.

4. Only 22 percent of white respondents interviewed on July 27, 2009, for the Pew Research Center approved of Obama's handling of the Gates situation. Similarly 58 percent of white respondents interviewed from July 31–August 3, 2009, for CNN/ORC said that Gates "acted stupidly" compared to only 29 percent of whites who said the arresting officer, James Crowley, "acted stupidly."

5. These statements about the prevalence of stories about the Gates incident in the news media are based upon weekly content analyses conducted by Pew's Project for Excellence in Journalism. See Project for Excellence in Journalism, "From Health Care to 'Skip' Gates, Obama Makes Big News." *PEJ News Coverage Index*, July 20–26, 2009, and "High-Stakes Health Care Fight Drives the News." *PEJ News Coverage Index*, July 27–August 2, 2009.

6. Survey by Pew Research Center for the People and the Press. Methodology: Conducted by Princeton Survey Research Associates International on July 27, 2009, and based on telephone interviews with a national adult sample of 480. Respondents were originally interviewed July 22–26, 2009, as part of a national adult sample of 1,506. Retrieved from the iPOLL Databank, Roper Center for Public Opinion Research, University of Connecticut.

7. Paul Krugman, for instance, wrote the following in an August 2009 op-ed for the *New York Times* about Obama's opposition: "But they're probably reacting less to what Mr. Obama is doing, or even to what they've heard about what he's doing, than to who he is. That is, the driving force behind the town hall mobs is probably the same cultural and racial anxiety that's behind the 'birther' movement, which denies Mr. Obama's citizenship." See Paul Krugman, "Town Hall Mob," *New York Times*, August 6, 2009.

8. Carter made these comments in an interview with Brian Williams for NBC *Nightly News* on September 15, 2009.

9. These statements about the prevalence of stories regarding race-based opposition to Obama are based upon weekly content analyses conducted by Pew's Project for Excellence in Journalism. See Project for Excellence in Journalism, "Bloggers Focus on Obama's Opposition." *PEJ New Media Index*, September 14–18, 2009, and "Afghanistan and a Charge of Racism Lead the Blogs." *PEJ New Media Index*, September 21–25, 2009.:

10. Survey by Pew Research Center for the People and the Press. Methodology: Conducted by Opinion Research Corporation, September 18–September 21, 2009, and based on telephone interviews with a national adult sample of 1,001. Retrieved from the iPOLL Databank, Roper Center for Public Opinion Research, University of Connecticut.

11. Obama made similar comments about how his fervent opposition primarily stemmed from feelings about the role of government, not racism, on *Meet the Press*, *This Week*, *State of the Union*, and *Face the Nation*, all of which aired on September 18, 2008. For more on these interviews, see Mark Silva, "In Media Blitz, Obama Says Vitriol Isn't Racism-Based," *LA Times*, September 19, 2009.

12. The Values Study by the Pew Research Center for the People and Press began in 1987, and has been updated thirteen times since then. The study asks respondents whether they agree or disagree with a series of approximately 80 statements covering core beliefs about government, businesses, religion, race, and several other topics. Not every one of these thirteen surveys included all four statements used in our racial predispositions scale. As such, we restrict our analyses to the surveys that contain both all four of these statements and presidential approval (1987, 1988, 1990, 1992, 1997, 1999,

2003, 2007, and 2009). These data sets were accessed from the Roper Center's data archive.

13. Of respondents interviewed on September 21, 2009, by Public Policy Polling, 59 percent said Obama was born in the United States, with 23 percent saying he was not and 18 percent unsure. For full poll results and crosstabs see http://www.publicpolicypolling .com/pdf/surveys/2009_Archives/PPP_Release_National_9231210.pdf. Of our CCAP panelists reinterviewed in November 2009, 57 percent said Obama was born in the United States, with 23 percent saying he was not and 20 percent unsure.

14. See table A8.4 of the online appendix (http://www.press.uchicago.edu/books/ tesler/).

15. MSNBC's Keith Olbermann and the liberal organization Media Matters, for instance, regularly call attention to racially insensitive comments appearing on conservative talk radio and the Fox News Channel.

16. The Pew question was only asked of respondents who get most of their news from TV. Of this group, 27 percent said they get most of their information about national and international affairs from Fox News. Survey by Pew Research Center for the People and the Press. Methodology: Conducted by Princeton Survey Research Associates International, July 22–July 26, 2009, and based on telephone interviews with a national adult sample of 1,506. Of these, 1,129 respondents were interviewed on a landline telephone and 377 were interviewed on a cell phone, including 114 who had no landline telephone. Percentages accessed from iPOLL. We asked what televised source respondents get most of their news from, and 26 percent of these respondents said they get most of their information about national and international affairs from Fox News.

17. The coefficients on partisanship and ideology in December 2007 were 2.3 and 2.44, respectively. In November 2009, these respective coefficients were 2.32 and 2.36. See table A8.6 of the online appendix for full results (http://www.press.uchicago .edu/books/tesler/).

18. Survey by CNN. Methodology: Conducted by Opinion Research Corporation, July 31–August 3, 2009, and based on telephone interviews with a national adult sample, including an oversample of blacks, of 1,136. Data set accessed from the Roper Center's data archive.

19. The exact wording of these questions is as follows:

No Frame, Form A (half of respondents): As you may know, Sonia Sotomayor is the federal judge nominated to serve on the Supreme Court. Would you like to see the Senate vote in favor of Sotomayor serving on the Supreme Court, or not?
Obama Frame, Form B (half of respondents): As you may know, Sonia Sotomayor is the federal judge who Barack Obama nominated to serve on the Supreme Court. Would you like to see the Senate vote in favor of Sotomayor serving on the Supreme Court, or not?

20. The coefficient on partisanship, in fact, actually decreased in absolute magnitude from –1.68 in the no-frame version down to –1.27 in the Obama-framed condition. See table A8.7 of the online appendix for full results (http://www.press.uchicago .edu/books/tesler/).

REFERENCES

AAPOR. 2009. *An Evaluation of the Methodology of the 2008 Pre-Election Primary Polls: A Report of the Ad Hoc Committee on the 2008 Presidential Primary Polling.* Lenexa, KS: American Association for Public Opinion Research.

Abramowitz, Alan I. 1989. "Viability, Electability, and Candidate Choice in a Presidential Primary Election: A Test of Competing Models." *Journal of Politics* 51 (4):977–92.

———. 2008. "Forecasting the 2008 Presidential Election with the Time-for-Change Model." *PS: Political Science and Politics* 41(4): 691–95.

Adams, Greg D. 1997. "Abortion: Evidence of an Issue Evolution." *American Journal of Political Science* 41:718–37.

Adorno, Theodor W., Else Frenkel-Brunswik, Daniel J. Levinson, and R. Nevitt Sanford. 1950. *The Authoritarian Personality.* New York: Harper and Row.

Ambinder, Marc. 2009. "Race Over?" *Atlantic*, January/February.

Ansolabehere, Stephen, Jonathan Rodden, and James M. Snyder. 2008. "The Strength of Issues: Using Multiple Measures to Gauge Preference Stability, Ideological Constraint, and Issue Voting." *American Political Science Review* 102 (3): 215–32.

Arrillaga, Pauline. 2008. "Can Black Candidate Woo Hispanics?" *Associated Press*, February 10.

Balz, Dan, and Haynes Johnson. 2009. *The Battle for America 2008: The Story of an Extraordinary Election.* New York: Viking.

Barreto, Matt A., Luis R. Fraga, Sylvia Manzano, Valerie Martinez-Ebers, and Gary M. Segura. 2008. "'Should They Dance with the One Who Brung 'Em?' Latinos and the 2008 Presidential Election." *PS: Political Science and Politics* 61 (4): 753–61.

Bartels, Larry M. 1988. *Presidential Primaries and the Dynamics of Public Choice.* Princeton: Princeton University Press.

———. 2000. "Partisanship and Voting Behavior, 1952–1996." *American Journal of Political Science* 44 (1): 35–50.

———. 2006a. Three Virtues of Panel Data for the Analysis of Campaign Effects. In *Capturing Campaign Effects*, ed. Henry E. Brady and Richard Johnston, 134–63. Ann Arbor: University of Michigan Press.

———. 2006b. Priming and Persuasion in Presidential Campaigns. In *Capturing Campaign Effects*, ed. Henry E. Brady and Richard Johnston, 78–112. Ann Arbor: University of Michigan Press.

———. 2008. *Unequal Democracy: The Political Economy of the New Gilded Age.* New York: Russell Sage Foundation.

Berelson, Bernard R., Paul F. Lazarsfeld, and William N. McPhee. 1954. *Voting: A Study of Opinion Formation in a Presidential Campaign.* Chicago: University of Chicago Press.

Berinsky, Adam J. 2009. *In Time of War: Understanding American Public Opinion from World War II to Iraq.* Chicago: University of Chicago Press.

Black, Earl, and Merle Black. 1987. *Politics and Society in the South.* Cambridge, MA: Harvard University Press.

———. 1992. *The Vital South: How Presidents Are Elected.* Cambridge, MA: Harvard University Press.

———. 2002. *The Rise of Southern Republicans.* Cambridge, MA: Harvard University Press.

Blinder, Scott B. 2007. "Dissonance Persists: Reproduction of Racial Attitudes among Post–Civil Rights Cohorts of White Americans." *American Politics Research* 35 (3): 299–335.

Bobo, Lawrence. 2000. Race and Beliefs about Affirmative Action: Assessing the Effects of Interests, Group Threat, Ideology, and Racism. In *Racialized Politics: The Debate about Racism in America,* ed. David O. Sears, James Sidanius, and Lawrence Bobo, 137–64. Chicago: University of Chicago Press.

Bobo, Lawrence, and James R. Kluegel. 1997. Status, Ideology, and Dimensions of Whites' Racial Beliefs and Attitudes: Progress and Stagnation. In *Racial Attitudes in the 1990s: Continuity and Change,* ed. Steven A. Tuch and Jack K. Martin, 93–120. Westport, CT: Praeger.

Bobo, Lawrence, James R. Kluegel, and Ryan A. Smith. 1997. Laissez-Faire Racism: The Crystallization of a Kinder, Gentler Antiblack Ideology. In *Racial Attitudes in the 1990s: Continuity and Change,* ed. Steven A. Tuch and Jack K. Martin, 93–120. Westport, CT: Praeger.

Brewer, Mark D., and Jeffrey. M. Stonecash. 2007. Class Divides in the American Public. In *Split: Class and Cultural Divides in American Politics,* 67–86. Washington, DC: CQ Press.

Brody, Richard A. 1991. *Assessing the President: The Media, Elite Opinion, and Public Support.* Stanford, CA: Stanford University Press.

Campbell, Angus, Philip E. Converse, Warren E. Miller, and Donald E. Stokes. 1960. *The American Voter.* Chicago: University of Chicago Press.

Campbell, James E. 2008a. "Editor's Introduction: Forecasting the 2008 National Elections." *PS: Political Science and Politics* 61 (4): 679–83.

———. 2008b. "The Trial-Heat Forecast of the 2008 Presidential Vote: Performance and Value Considerations in an Open-Seat Election." *PS: Political Science and Politics* 41 (4): 697–701.

Carmines, Edward G., and James A. Stimson. 1989. *Issue Evolution: Race and the Transformation of American Politics.* Princeton, NJ: Princeton University Press.

Carroll, Royce, Jeff Lewis, James Lo, Nolan McCarty, Keith Poole, and Howard Rosenthal. 2008. "Who Is More Liberal, Senator Obama or Senator Clinton?" Working Paper Voteview Web site, Department of Political Science at the University of California, San Diego.

Carroll, Susan J. 2009. "Reflections on Gender and Hillary Clinton's Presidential Campaign: The Good, the Bad, and the Misogynic." *Politics and Gender* 5:1–20.

Carter, Dan T. 1995. *The Politics of Rage*. Baton Rouge: Louisiana State University Press.

Citrin, Jack, Donald Phillip Green, and David O. Sears. 1990. "White Reactions to Black Candidates: When Does Race Matter?" *Public Opinion Quarterly* 54 (1): 74–96.

Converse, Philip E. 1964. The Nature of Belief Systems in Mass Publics. In *Ideology and Discontent*, ed. David E. Apter, 206–61. New York: Free Press.

Cooper, Helene. 2009. "Muslims Will Judge Obama by Actions More than Words." *New York Times*, June 4.

Dawson, Michael. 1994. *Behind the Mule: Race and Class in African American Politics*. Princeton, NJ: Princeton University Press.

———. 2001. *Black Visions: The Roots of Contemporary African-American Political Ideologies*. Chicago: University of Chicago Press.

Dowd, Maureen. 2009. "Boy, Oh, Boy." *New York Times*, September 12.

D'Souza, Dinesh. 1995. *The End of Racism*. New York: Free Press.

Duckitt, John. 1992. *The Social Psychology of Prejudice*. New York: Praeger.

Edsall, Thomas B. 2006. *Building Red America: The New Conservative Coalition and the Drive for Permanent Power*. New York: Basic Books.

Edsall, Thomas B., and Mary D. Edsall. 1992. *Chain Reaction: The Impact of Race Rights and Taxes on American Politics*. New York: Norton.

Entman, Robert M., and Andrew Rojecki. 2000. *The Black Image in the White Mind: Media and Race in America*. Chicago: University of Chicago Press.

Falk, Erika. 2008. *Women for President: Media Bias in Eight Campaigns*. Champaign: University of Illinois Press.

Finkel, Steven E., Thomas M. Guterbock, and Marian J. Borg. 1991. "Race-of-Interviewer Effects in a Preelection Poll." *Public Opinion Quarterly* 55:313–30.

Fiorina, Morris P. 1981. *Retrospective Voting in American National Elections*. New Haven, CT: Yale University Press.

———. 2006. *Culture War? The Myth of a Polarized America*. New York: Pearson Longman.

Frank, Thomas. 2004. *What's the Matter with Kansas? How Conservatives Won the Heart of America*. New York: Metropolitan Books.

Fredrickson, George M. 1971. *The Black Image in the White Mind: The Debate on Afro-American Character and Destiny, 1817–1914*. New York: Harper and Row.

Gaertner, Samuel L., and John F. Dovidio. 1986. The Aversive Form of Racism. In *Prejudice, Discrimination, and Racism: Theory and Research*, ed. John F. Dovidio and Samuel L. Gaertner, pp. 61–89. New York: Academic Press.

Gelman, Andrew. 2010. *Red State, Blue State, Rich State, Poor State: Why Americans Vote the Way They Do*. Princeton, NJ: Princeton University Press.

Gelman, Andrew, and Gary King. 1993. "Why Are American Presidential Election Campaign Polls so Variable when Votes Are so Predictable?" *British Journal of Political Science* 23:409–51.

Gerstle, Gary. 2002. *American Crucible: Race and Nation in the Twentieth Century.* Princeton, NJ: Princeton University Press.

Gilens, Martin. 1999. *Why Americans Hate Welfare: Race, Media, and the Politics of Antipoverty Policy.* Chicago: University of Chicago Press.

Giles, Michael W., and Melanie A. Buckner. 1996. "Racial Threat Redux." *Journal of Politics* 58 (4): 1171–80.

Green, John, and E. J. Dionne Jr. 2008. Religion and American Politics: More Secular, More Evangelical, or Both? In *Red, Blue, and Purple America: The Future of Election Demographics*, ed. Ruy Teixeira, 194–224. Washington: Brookings Institution.

Green, Donald, Bradley Palmquist, and Eric Schickler. 2002. *Partisan Hearts and Minds.* New Haven: Yale University Press.

Gurin, Patricia, Shirley Hatchett, and James Jackson. 1989. *Hope and Independence: Blacks' Response to Electoral and Party Politics.* New York: Russell Sage Foundation.

Hacker, Andrew. 1995. *Two Nations: Black and White, Separate, Hostile, Unequal.* New York: Ballantine Books.

Hajnal, Zoltan. L. 2007. *Changing White Attitudes Toward Black Political Leadership.* Cambridge: Cambridge University Press.

Hanania, Ray. 2009. "Opposition to Health Care Reform Driven by Racism Not Fear of Increasing Debt." *Huffington Post*, July 22.

Harris-Lacewell, Melissa. 2004. *Barbershops, Bibles, and BET: Everyday Talk and Black Political Thought.* Princeton, NJ: Princeton University Press.

Hayes, Christopher. 2007. "Obama's Media Maven." *Nation*, February 6.

Heilemann, John, and Mark Halperin. 2010. *Game Change: Obama and the Clintons, McCain and Palin, and the Race of a Lifetime.* New York: Harper Collins.

Hendon, Ricky. 2009. *Black Enough/White Enough: The Obama Dilemma.* Chicago: Third World Press.

Henry, P. J., and David O. Sears. 2002. "The Symbolic Racism 2000 Scale." *Political Psychology* 23 (2): 253–83.

Henry, P. J., and David O. Sears. 2009. "The Crystallization of Contemporary Racial Prejudice across the Lifespan." *Political Psychology* 30 (4): 569–90.

Hetherington, Marc J. 1996. "The Media's Role in Forming Voters' National Economic Evaluations in 1992." *American Journal of Political Science* 40 (3): 372–95.

Hetherington, Marc J., and Jonathan D. Weiler. 2009. "Health Care, Race, and Political Polarization." *Washington Post*, September 21. http://voices.washingtonpost .com/shortstack/2009/09/health_care_race_and_political.html (accessed March 2, 2010).

Hillygus, D. Sunshine, and Simon Jackman. 2003. "Voter Decision Making in Election 2000: Campaign Effects, Partisan Activation, and the Clinton Legacy." *American Journal of Political Science* 47: 583–96.

Hitlin, Paul, Mahvish Shahid Khan, and Tom Rosenstiel. 2008a. "Gaffe Coverage: Jackson Tops Graham." *Project for Excellence in Journalism*, July 15.

———. 2008b. "War Takes Center Stage as Obama (and Media) Move Overseas." *Project for Excellence in Journalism*, July 23.

Holbrook, Thomas M. 2008. "Economic Considerations and the 2008 Presidential Election." *PS: Political Science and Politics* 42 (3): 473–78.

———. 2009. "Incumbency, National Conditions, and the 2008 Presidential Election." *PS: Political Science and Politics* 41 (4): 709–12.

Hopkins, Daniel. 2009. "No More Wilder Effect, Never a Whitman Effect: When and Why Polls Mislead about Black and Female Candidates." *Journal of Politics* 71:769–81.

Howell, Susan E. 1994. "Racism, Cynicism, Economics, and David Duke." *American Politics Quarterly* 22:190–207.

Huber, Gregory A., and John Lapinski. 2006. "The 'Race Card' Revisited: Assessing Racial Priming in Policy Contests." *American Journal of Political Science* 50 (2): 421–40.

Hughes, Michael. 1997. Symbolic Racism, Old-Fashioned Racism, and Whites' Opposition to Affirmative Action. In *Racial Attitudes in the 1990s: Continuity and Change*, ed. Steven A. Tuch and Jack K. Martin, 45–75. Westport, CT: Praeger.

Hurwitz, Jon, and Mark Peffley. 1997. "Public Perceptions of Race and Crime: The Role of Racial Stereotypes." *American Journal of Political Science* 41 (2): 375–401.

———.1998. Introduction. In *Perception and Prejudice: Race and Politics in the United States*, 1–16. New Haven, CT: Yale University Press.

Hutchings, Vincent L., and Nicholas A. Valentino. 2004. "The Centrality of Race in American Politics." *Annual Review of Political Science* 7:383–408.

Ifill, Gwen. 2009. *The Breakthrough: Politics and Race in the Age of Obama*. New York: Doubleday.

Iyengar, Shanto, Kyu Hahn, Christopher Dial, and Mahzarin R. Banaji. 2009. "Explicit and Implicit Attitudes: Black-White and Obama-McCain Comparisons." Paper presented at the annual meeting of the International Society of Political Psychology, Dublin.

Iyengar, Shanto, and Donald Kinder. 1987. *News That Matters: Television and American Opinion*. Chicago: University of Chicago Press.

Jackman, Simon, and Lynn Vavreck. 2008. Data 2008: Survey Analyses in Real Time. Paper presented at "The American Electoral Process" conference at the Center for the Study of Democratic Politics, Princeton University.

———. 2009. "The Magic of the Battleground: Uncertainty, Learning, and Changing Information Environments in the 2008 Presidential Campaign." Paper presented at the annual meeting of the Midwest Political Science Association, Chicago.

Jacobs, Carly M., and Michael W. Gruszczynski. 2009. "America's Ultimate Tree House: Gender, Emotion, and Campaigning for the Presidency." Paper Presented at the annual meeting of the Midwest Political Science Association, Chicago.

Jacobson, Gary C. 2007. *A Divider, Not a Uniter: George W. Bush and the American People*. New York: Pearson Education.

Johnston, Richard, Michael G. Hagen, and Kathleen Hall Jamieson. 2004. *The 2000 Presidential Election and the Foundations of Party Politics*. New York: Cambridge University Press.

Kalkan, Kerem Ozan, Geoffrey C. Layman, and Eric M. Uslaner. 2009. "'Bands of Others?' Attitudes toward Muslims in Contemporary American Society." *Journal of Politics* 71:847–62.

Katz, Irwin, and R. Glen Hass. 1988. "Racial Ambivalence and American Value Conflict: Correlational and Priming Studies of Dual Cognitive Structures." *Journal of Personality and Social Psychology* 55:893–905.

Katznelson, Ira. 2005. *When Affirmative Action Was White: An Untold History of Racial Inequality in Twentieth-Century America.* New York: Norton.

Kaufmann, Karen M., and John R. Petrocik. 1999. "The Changing Politics of American Men: Understanding the Sources of the Gender Gap." *American Journal of Political Science* 43:864–87.

Kelley, Stanley, Jr. 1983. *Interpreting Elections.* Princeton, NJ: Princeton University Press.

Kenski, Kate. 2006. The Rolling Cross-Section Design. In *Capturing Campaign Dynamics, 2000 and 2004: The National Annenberg Election Survey,* ed. Daniel Romer, Kate Kenski, Kenneth Winneg, Christopher Adasiewicz, and Kathleen Hall Jamieson, 68–78. Philadelphia: University of Pennsylvania Press.

Kenski, Kate, and Daniel Romer. 2006. Analyses of Panel Data. In *Capturing Campaign Dynamics, 2000 and 2004: The National Annenberg Election Survey,* ed. Daniel Romer, Kate Kenski, Kenneth Winneg, Christopher Adasiewicz, and Kathleen Hall Jamieson, 150–64. Philadelphia: University of Pennsylvania Press.

Key, V. O., Jr. 1949. *Southern Politics in State and Nation.* New York: Vintage Books.

Kiewiet, D. Roderick. 1983. *Macroeconomics and Micropolitics: The Electoral Effects of Economic Issues.* Chicago: The University of Chicago Press.

Kinder, Donald R. 1986. "The Continuing American Dilemma: White Resistance to Racial Change Forty Years after Myrdal." *Journal of Social Issues* 42:151–71.

———. 1998. Opinion and Action in the Realm of Politics. In *Handbook of Social Psychology,* ed. Daniel T. Gilbert, Susan T. Fiske, and Gardner Lindzey, 778–867. Oxford: Oxford University Press.

———. 2003. Communication and Politics in the Age of Information. In *Oxford Handbook of Political Psychology,* ed. David O. Sears, Leonie Huddy, and Robert Jervis, 357–93. Oxford: Oxford University Press.

Kinder, Donald R., and Katherine W. Drake. 2009. "Myrdal's prediction." *Political Psychology* 30 (4): 539–68.

Kinder, Donald R., and Cindy D. Kam. 2009. *Us against Them: Ethnocentric Foundations of American Opinion.* Chicago: The University of Chicago Press.

Kinder, Donald R., and D. Roderick Kiewiet. 1979. "Economic Discontent and Political Behavior: The Role of Personal Grievances and Collective Economic Judgments in Congressional Voting." *American Journal of Political Science* 23 (3): 495–527.

———.1981. "Sociotropic Politics: The American Case." *British Journal of Political Science* 11 (2): 129–61.

Kinder, Donald R., and Lynn M. Sanders. 1996. *Divided by Color: Racial Politics and Democratic Ideals.* Chicago: University of Chicago Press.

Kinder, Donald R., and David O. Sears. 1981. "Prejudice and Politics: Symbolic Racism

Versus Racial Threats to the Good Life." *Journal of Personality and Social Psychology* 40 (3): 414–31.

Klarner, Carl. 2008. "Forecasting the 2008 U.S. House, Senate, and Presidential Elections at the District and State Level." *PS: Political Science and Politics* 61 (4): 723–8.

Klein, Joe. 2006. "The Fresh Face." *Time*, October 15.

Kluegel, James R. 1990. "Trends in Whites' Explanations of the Black-White Gap in Socioeconomic Status, 1977–1989." *American Sociological Review* 55:512–25.

Krugman, Paul. 2009. "Town Hall Mob." *New York Times*, August 6.

Layman, Geoffrey C., and Thomas M. Carsey. 2002. "Party Polarization and 'Conflict Extension' in the American Electorate." *American Journal of Political Science* 46 (4): 786–802.

Leege, David C., Kenneth D. Wald, Brian S. Krueger, and Paul D. Mueller. 2002. *The Politics of Cultural Differences: Social Change and Voter Mobilization Strategies in the Post-New Deal Period*. Princeton, NJ: Princeton University Press.

Lenz, Gabriel. S. 2009. "Learning and Opinion Change, Not Priming: Reconsidering the Evidence for the Priming Hypothesis." *American Journal of Political Science* 53 (4): 821–37.

Lewis-Beck, Michael S., and Charles Tien. 2008. "The Job of President and the Jobs Model Forecast: Obama for '08?" *PS: Political Science and Politics* 41 (4): 687–90.

Lipset, Seymour M. 1960. *Political Man*. Garden City, NY: Doubleday.

Lowery, Rich. 2008. "How Hillary Clinton Became a Social Conservative (Sort of)." *National Review*, May 5.

Martin, William. 1996. *With God on Our Side: The Rise of the Religious Right in America*. New York: Broadway Books.

Mayer, Jeremy D. 2002. *Running on Race: Racial Politics in Presidential Campaigns, 1960–2000*. New York: Random House.

McCarty, Nolan, Keith T. Poole, and Howard Rosenthal. 2006. *Polarized America: The Dance of Ideology and Unequal Riches*. Cambridge, MA: MIT Press.

McConahay, John B. 1986. Modern Racism, Ambivalence, and the Modern Racism Scale. In *Prejudice, Discrimination, and Racism*, ed. John F. Dovidio and Samuel L. Gaertner, 91–126. New York: Academic Press.

McConahay, John B., Betty B. Hardee, and Valerie Batts. 1981. "Has Racism Declined in America? It Depends Upon Who Is Asking and What Is Asked." *Journal of Conflict Resolution* 25:563–79.

McConahay, John B., and Joseph C. Hough Jr. 1976. "Symbolic Racism." *Journal of Social Issues* 32:23–45.

Mendelberg, Tali. 2001. *The Race Card: Campaign Strategy, Implicit Messages, and the Norm of Equality*. Princeton, NJ: Princeton University Press.

———. 2008. "Racial Priming Revived." *Perspectives on Politics* 6 (1): 109–23.

Mendell, David. 2007. *Obama: From Promise to Power*. New York: Harper Collins.

Miller, Warren E., and J. Merrill Shanks. 1996. *The New American Voter*. Cambridge, MA: Harvard University Press.

Moskowitz, David, and Patrick Stoh. 1994. "Psychological Sources of Electoral Racism." *Political Psychology* 15 (2): 307–29.

Myrdal, Gunnar. 1944. *An American Dilemma: The Negro Problem and Modern Democracy*. New York: Harper and Row.

Nadeau, Richard, and Michael S. Lewis-Beck. 2001. "National Economic Voting in U.S. Presidential Elections." *Journal of Politics* 63:159–81.

Nagourney, Adam, and Jennifer Steinhauer. 2008. "In Obama's Pursuit of Latinos, Race Plays Role." *New York Times*, January 15.

Obama, Barack. 2006. *The Audacity of Hope*. New York: Crown.

Oliver, J. Eric, and Tali Mendelberg. 2000. "Reconsidering the Environmental Determinants of White Racial Attitudes." *American Journal of Political Science* 44:574–89.

O'Reilly, Kenneth. 1995. *Nixon's Piano: Presidents and Racial Politics from Washington to Clinton*. New York: Free Press.

Palin, Sarah. 2009. *Going Rogue: An American Life*. New York: Harper Collins.

Petrocik, John R. 1987. "Realignment: New Party Coalitions and the Nationalization of the South." *Journal of Politics* 49:347–75.

Pettigrew, Thomas F., and R. W. Meertens. 1995. "Subtle and Blatant Prejudice in Western Europe." *European Journal of Social Psychology* 25:57–75.

Pew Research Center. 2008. "Most Voters Say News Media Wants Obama to Win: 'Joe the Plumber' a Top Campaign Story." October 22. http://pewresearch.org/pubs/1003/joe-the-plumber (accessed March 2, 2010).

Phillips, Kevin P. 1969. *The Emerging Republican Majority*. New Rochelle, NY: Arlington House.

Project for Excellence in Journalism. 2007. *The Portrait from Iraq: How the Press Has Covered Events on the Ground*. December 19. http://www.journalism.org/node/8996 (accessed March 2, 2010).

———. 2008a. "The Latest Campaign Narrative—'It's The Economy, Stupid.'" *PEJ Campaign Coverage Index*, September 15–21. http://www.journalism.org/node/12900 (accessed March 2, 2010).

———. 2008b. "Media Narrative Whipsaws Between Bailout, Debate." *PEJ Campaign Coverage Index*, September 22–28. http://www.journalism.org/node/13007 (accessed March 2, 2010).

Rahn, Wendy M., Jon A. Krosnick, and Marijke Breuning. 1994. "Rationalization and Derivation Processes in Survey Studies of Political Candidate Evaluation." *American Journal of Political Science* 38:582–600.

Reeves, Keith. 1997. *Voting Hopes or Fears? White Voters, Black Candidates, and Racial Politics in America*. Oxford: Oxford University Press.

Reno, Jaime. 2008. "Black-Brown Divide." *Newsweek*, January 26.

Rich, Frank. 2008. "Haven't We Heard This Voice Before?" *New York Times*, January 13.

Rivers, Douglas. 2006. "Sample Matching: Representative Sampling from Internet Panels." Polimetrix White Paper Series.

Robinson, Eugene. 2009. "The Favor Jimmy Carter Did Us All." *Washington Post*, September 18.

Scammon, Richard M., and Ben J. Wattenberg. 1970. *The Real Majority*. New York: Coward-McCann.

Schaller, Thomas F. 2006. *Whistling Past Dixie: How Democrats Can Win Without the South*. New York: Simon and Schuster.

Schuman, Howard, Charlotte Steeh, Lawrence Bobo, and Maria Krysan. 1997. *Racial Attitudes in America*. Rev. ed. Cambridge, MA: Harvard University Press.

Sears, David O. 1993. Symbolic Politics: A Socio-Psychological Theory. In *Explorations in Political Psychology*, ed. Shanto Iyengar and William J. McGuire, 113–49. Durham, NC: Duke University Press.

Sears, David O., and Jack Citrin. 1985. *Tax Revolt: Something for Nothing in California*. Enlarged Edition. Cambridge, MA: Harvard University Press.

Sears, David O., Jack Citrin, and Richard Kosterman. 1987. Jesse Jackson and the Southern White Electorate in 1984. In *Blacks in Southern Politics*, ed. Robert P. Steed, Laurence W. Moreland, and Tod A. Baker, 209–225. New York: Praeger.

Sears David O., Hillary Haley, and P. J. Henry. 2008. Cultural Diversity and Sociopolitical Attitudes at College Entry. In *The Diversity Challenge: Social Identity and Intergroup Relations on the College Campus*, ed. Jim Sidanius, Shana Levin, Colette van Laar, and David O. Sears, 65–99. New York: Russell Sage Foundation.

Sears, David O., and P. J. Henry. 2003. "The Origins of Symbolic Racism." *Journal of Personality and Social Psychology* 85 (3): 259–75.

———. 2005. Over Thirty Years Later: A Contemporary Look at Symbolic Racism. In *Advances in Experimental Social Psychology*, vol. 37, ed. Mark P. Zanna, 98–150. New York: Academic Press.

Sears, David O., Carl P. Hensler, and Leslie K. Speer. 1979. "Whites' Opposition to 'Busing': Self-Interest or Symbolic Politics?" *American Political Science Review* 73:369–84.

Sears, David O., and Donald R. Kinder. 1971. Racial Tensions and Voting in Los Angeles. In *Los Angeles: Viability and Prospects for Metropolitan Leadership*, ed. Werner Z. Hirsch, 51–88. New York: Praeger.

Sears, David O., and Richard R. Lau. 1983. "Inducing Apparently Self-Interested Political Preferences." *American Journal of Political Science* 27:222–52.

Sears, David O., and Sheri Levy. 2003. Childhood and Adult Development. In *Handbook of Political Psychology*, ed. David O. Sears, Leonie Huddy, and Robert L. Jervis, 60–109. New York: Oxford University Press.

Sears, David O., and John B. McConahay. 1973. *The Politics of Violence: The New Urban Blacks and the Watts Riot*. Boston: Houghton Mifflin.

Sears, David O., and Victoria Savalei. 2006. "The Political Color Line in America: Many Peoples of Color or Black Exceptionalism?" *Political Psychology* 27:895–924.

———. 2009. "Sharp or Blunt Instruments? Measuring Affect Toward Ethnic and Racial Groups in Contemporary America." Paper presented at the annual meeting of the International Society for Political Psychology, Dublin.

Sears, David O., Colette van Laar, Mary Carillo, and Richard Kosterman. 1997. "Is It Really Racism? The Origins of White Americans' Opposition to Race-Targeted Policies." *Public Opinion Quarterly* 61 (1): 16–53.

Shafer, Byron E., and Richard Johnston. 2006. *The End of Southern Exceptionalism:*

Class, Race, and Partisan Change in the Postwar South. Cambridge, MA: Harvard University Press.

Shaw, Daron R. 2007. *The Race to 270: The Electoral College and the Campaign Strategies of 2000 and 2004.* Chicago: University of Chicago Press.

Shields, Stephanie A. 2002. *Speaking from the Heart: Gender and the Social Meaning of Emotion.* Cambridge: Cambridge University Press.

Sidanius, Jim, Shana Levin, Joshua L. Rabinowitz, and Christopher M. Federico. 1999. Peering into the Jaws of the Beast: The Integrative Dynamics of Social Identity, Symbolic Racism, and Social Dominance. In *Cultural Divides: Understanding and Overcoming Group Conflict,* ed. D. A. Prentice and D. T. Miller, 80–132. New York: Russell Sage Foundation.

Sides, John, and Kimberley Gross. 2007. "Stereotypes of Muslims, Their Causes, and Their Consequences." Paper presented at the annual meeting of the Midwest Political Science Association, Chicago.

Sigelman, Carol K., Lee Sigelman, Barbara J. Walkosz, and Michael Nitz. 1995. "Black Candidates, White Voters: Understanding Racial Bias in Political Perceptions." *American Journal of Political Science* 39 (1): 243–65.

Skerry, Peter, and Devin Fernandes. 2004. "Interpreting the Muslim Vote." *Boston Globe,* November 24.

Sniderman, Paul M., and Edward G. Carmines. 1997. *Reaching Beyond Race.* Cambridge, MA: Harvard University Press.

Sniderman, Paul M., Gretchen C. Crosby, and William G. Howell. 2000. "The Politics of Race." In *Racialized Politics: The Debate About Racism in America,* ed. David O. Sears, James Sidanius and Lawrence Bobo, 236–79. Chicago: University of Chicago Press.

Sniderman, Paul M., and Thomas Piazza. 1993. *The Scar of Race.* Cambridge, MA: Harvard University Press.

———. 2002. *Black Pride and Black Prejudice.* Princeton, NJ: Princeton University Press.

Sniderman, Paul M., and Philip Tetlock. 1986a. "Symbolic Racism: Problems of Motive Attribution in Political Debate." *Journal of Social Issues* 42 (2): 129–50.

———. 1986b. "Reflections on American Racism." *Journal of Social Issues* 42 (2): 173–87.

Steele, Shelby. 2008. *A Bound Man: Why We are Excited About Obama and Why He Can't Win.* New York: Free Press.

Stein, Sam. 2008. "Hillary at Martha's Vineyard: On Clinton, Guns, Elitism and John Kerry." *Huffington Post,* April 14.

Sullivan, Andrew. 2008. "They Daren't Mention Race." *Daily Dish,* May 20. http://andrewsullivan.theatlantic.com/the_daily_dish/2008/05/they-darent-men.html (accessed March 2, 2010).

Sundquist, James L. 1983. *Dynamics of the Party System: Alignment and Realignment of Political Parties in the United States.* Washington, DC: Brookings Institution.

Swim, Janet K., Kathryn J. Aikin, Wayne S. Hall, and Barbara A. Hunter. 1995. "Sexism and Racism: Old-Fashioned and Modem Prejudices." *Journal of Personality and Social Psychology* 68:199–214.

Swim, Janet K., and Laurie Cohen. 1997. "Overt, Covert, and Subtle Sexism: A Comparison between the Attitude Toward Women and Modern Sexism Scales." *Psychology of Women Quarterly* 21:103–18.

Tarman, Christopher, and David O. Sears. 2005. "The Conceptualization and Measurement of Symbolic Racism." *Journal of Politics* 67:731–61.

Tate, Katherine. 1994. *From Protest to Politics: The New Black Voters in American Elections.* Cambridge, MA: Harvard University Press.

Tesler, Michael. 2008. "Muslim Favorability and Obama Support." *The Sprint: UCLA Professors Blog the Final Leg of the 2008 Race for President.* September 24. http://newsroom.ucla.edu/portal/ucla/election-blog-post.aspx?id=1236 (accessed March 2, 2010).

Thomas, Evan. 2008. "A Memo to Senator Obama." *Newsweek*, June 2.

Thomas, Evan, with the staff of *Newsweek.* 2009. *A Long Time Coming: The Inspiring Combative 2008 Campaign and the Historic Election of Barack Obama.* New York: Public Affairs.

Tocqueville, Alexis de. 1835/1969. *Democracy in America.* Ed. J. P. Mayer. A new translation by George Lawrence. Garden City, NY: Anchor Press.

Valentino, Nicholas A. 1999. "Crime News and the Priming of Racial Attitudes during Evaluations of the President." *Public Opinion Quarterly* 63:293–320.

Valentino, Nicholas A., Vincent L. Hutchings, and Ismail K. White. 2002. "Cues That Matter: How Political Ads Prime Racial Attitudes During Campaigns." *American Political Science Review* 96 (1): 75–90.

Valentino, Nicholas A., and David O. Sears. 2005. "Old Times There Are Not Forgotten: Race and Partisan Realignment in the Contemporary South." *American Journal of Political Science* 49 (3): 672–88.

———. 2008. "As the Twig Is Bent: Race and Partisan Realignment in the Contemporary South." Paper presented at the annual meeting of the Midwest Political Science Association, Chicago.

Vanneman, Reeve D., and Thomas F. Pettigrew. 1972. "Race and Relative Deprivation in the Urban United States." *Race.* 13:461–86.

Vavreck, Lynn. 2009. *The Message Matters: The Economy and Presidential Campaigns.* Princeton, NJ: Princeton University Press.

Vavreck, Lynn, and Douglas Rivers. 2008. "The 2006 Cooperative Congressional Election Study." *Journal of Elections, Public Opinion, and Parties* 18 (4): 355–66.

Voss, Stephen D. 1996. "Beyond Racial Threat: Failure of an Old Hypothesis in the New South." *The Journal of Politics*, 58 (4): 1156–70.

Walters, Ron. 2007. "Barack Obama and the Politics of Blackness" *Journal of Black Studies* 38 (1): 7–29.

Wlezien, Christopher, and Robert S. Erikson. 2008. "Leading Economic Indicators, the Polls, and the Presidential Vote." *PS: Political Science and Politics* 61 (4): 703–7.

Winter, Nicholas J.G. 2008. *Dangerous Frames: How Ideas About Race and Gender Shape Public Opinion*. Chicago: University of Chicago Press.

Wood, Jeremy. 1994. "Is 'Symbolic Racism' Racism? A Review Informed by Intergroup Behavior." *Political Psychology* 15 (4): 673–86.

Zaller, John R. 1992. *The Nature and Origins of Mass Opinion*. Cambridge: Cambridge University Press.

Zeleny, Jeff. 2005. "Judicious Obama Turns Up Volume." *Chicago Tribune*, September 12.

INDEX

ABC News, 31
abortion, 14, 165
affective prejudice, 98
affirmative action, 2, 5–6, 11, 17, 75–76
Afghanistan, war in, 158
African Americans: inclusion in vote models, 25–26, 162; proportion of the electorate, 33, 94; racial resentment and, 26, 96–101, 114, 170n20, 178n6; support for Barack Obama, 4–5, 8, 26, 35, 40, 94–95, 103–4, 106, 113–14, 169n8, 172n4; support for Hillary Clinton, 5, 95, 113, 120
age, 20, 120, 162
American Community Study, 28
American National Election Studies (ANES), 18, 22, 27–28, 162
ANES. *See* American National Election Studies
antiblack affect, 20, 26, 97–101, 163, 170n3
antiblack stereotypes, 20, 32, 96, 98–99, 166
antiwhite stereotypes, 98–99, 166
Ashcroft, John, 131
Audacity of Hope, The, 1
authoritarianism, 98–99, 163
Axelrod, David, 4, 51

Bartels, Larry, 14, 40, 67, 71
base vote choice model, 24–26
Beck, Glenn, 142, 153
Begala, Paul, 117
Belcher, Cornell, 55, 174n6
Bendixen, Sergio, 105
Berelson, Bernard, 70–71
Biden, Joe, 4
Bond, Julian, 1
Bradley, Tom, 30, 34, 143
Bradley Effect, 30
Bush, George H. W., 13–15, 53, 76, 85–86, 147
Bush, George W., 2, 21, 27–28, 53, 57–58, 67, 69–71, 73, 85–86, 89, 92, 127–28, 131–32, 134, 147, 175n14, 177n6, 180n2, 181n5
busing, 17

California primary, 8, 102, 105, 113, 179n11
Callejo, Adelfa, 94, 105
Carmines, Edward, 15
Carroll, Susan, 124–25
Carter, Jimmy, 13, 145, 183n8
CBS News/*New York Times* Poll, 144, 182n3
CBS News Poll, 123, 180n9
CCAP. *See* Cooperative Campaign Analysis Project
Cheney, Dick, 116
chronic accessibility, 6–8, 16, 35, 38, 51, 66, 93, 108, 114, 143, 146, 149–51
Citrin, Jack, 34
Civil Rights Act of 1964, 13, 30
Civil War, 12, 124
Clinton, Bill, 14, 30–31, 76, 80, 92, 95, 102, 113, 115, 147, 180n2
Clinton, Hillary, 5, 7–8, 21, 33, 38, 40–45, 47, 67, 75–77, 82, 124–26, 128, 132, 171n11, 173n5, 173n9, 173n14, 174n20, 181n13; and gender conservatism, 8, 115–16, 118–123, 135, 137, 180n7; New Hampshire primary victory, 29–30, 117–18, 180n5; primary voters of, 44, 52, 70–73, 177n23; and racial resentment, 7, 36–37, 48–50, 78–80, 84–88, 121–22, 146, 151; Senate voting record compared to Obama's, 21, 43, 132, 174n20; South Carolina primary campaign, 30–31, 173n7; support from African Americans, 5, 95, 113, 120; support from Latinos, 95, 102, 105–8, 179n12; trial heats against John McCain, 7–8, 47, 53, 59–61, 107–8, 110, 112, 133–34, 148, 174n19
CNN Poll, 157, 178n11, 183n4, 184n18
Compromise of 1877, 12
Cooperative Campaign Analysis Project (CCAP), 20, 28, 42, 161–62, 172nn16–17
Coulter, Ann, 182n12
cross-sectional time-series surveys, 26–28, 63, 146

197